ISLAM
AND
MODERNIZATION

ISLAM
AND
MODERNIZATION

A Comparative Analysis
of Pakistan, Egypt, and Turkey

Javaid Saeed

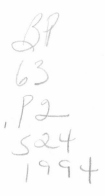

PRAEGER

Westport, Connecticut
London

Library of Congress Cataloging-in-Publication Data

Saeed, Javaid.
    Islam and modernization : a comparative analysis of Pakistan,
Egypt, and Turkey / Javaid Saeed.
       p. cm.
    Includes bibliographical references (p.) and index.
    ISBN 0–275–94566–9 (alk. paper)
    1. Islam—Pakistan. 2. Islam—Turkey. 3. Islam—Egypt.
4. Economic development—Religious aspects—Islam. 5. Islam—
Economic aspects—Pakistan. 6. Islam—Economic aspects—Turkey.
7. Islam—Economic aspects—Egypt. 8. Islam and state—Pakistan.
9. Islam and state—Turkey. 10. Islam and state—Egypt.
11. Pakistan—Politics and government. 12. Turkey—Politics and
government. 13. Egypt—Politics and government. I. Title.
BP63.P2S24   1994
306.6'97—dc20   93–5856

British Library Cataloguing in Publication Data is available.

Library of Congress Catalog Card Number: 93–5856
ISBN: 0–275–94566–9

First published in 1994

Praeger Publishers, 88 Post Road West, Westport, CT 06881
An imprint of Greenwood Publishing Group, Inc.

Printed in the United States of America

The paper used in this book complies with the
Permanent Paper Standard issued by the National
Information Standards Organization (Z39.48–1984).

10 9 8 7 6 5 4 3 2 1

CONTENTS

TABLES

PREFACE

This book examines the Middle East in a new light, and in doing so it illumines issues that are generally not touched or understood. Essentially, we learn why things are the way they are in the Middle East and other Islamic countries. In studying issues related to Islam and modernization in the context of three Muslim societies, Pakistan, Egypt, and Turkey, this study shows us the treatment of Islam at the hands of Muslim societies. In the process, the study tells us a good deal about matters related to Islam. The Middle East, indeed, the entire Muslim world, cannot really be analyzed, explained, and understood without knowing what Islam means. Several myths are in circulation in both the West and Muslim countries which form the basis of people's ideas about Islam, the Middle East, and other Muslim countries. The reader will find these myths shattered at several places in the book.

This study is based on years of critical reflective thought. It was undertaken solely in the pursuit of truth and knowledge. It is likely to surprise many in the West and in the Islamic world. In both cases such a reaction would be due essentially to the habituated and often ill-informed ways of thinking and looking at matters pertaining to the Middle East, or the Islamic world, and consequently Islam. How this is so will become apparent as the book unfolds.

Following the political upheaval in Iran in which the cruel and corrupt regime of the Shah was overthrown, developments in that country have greatly reinforced the prevalent ideas in the West about Islam and the Middle East. This has led to a further misunderstanding about Islam, the Middle East, and other Muslim societies. Muslim countries have further contributed to Western ideas about Islam and Islamic societies through the Iran-Iraq War, Saddam Hussein's adventure in Kuwait, and authoritarian regimes of different kinds in many parts of the Islamic world.

In the last several centuries, Muslim societies have themselves been the worst representatives of Islam, thereby contributing enormously to the negative ideas and opinions prevalent in the West about Islam and Muslims. Since a Western scholar's knowledge of Islam is not rooted in the Qur'an but is based primarily on the evidence provided by Muslim societies in different parts of the world, the ideas and explanations offered about Islam and the Muslim world are generally not well informed. Thus, Elie Kedourie, for instance, believed that Islam and industrialization were incompatible. A recent poll in the United States by the John Zogby Group International has shown that 36 percent of those polled had an unfavorable view of Islam, 41 percent had no opinion, and only 23 percent had a favorable view.

The depth of misunderstanding that exists in the West about Islam was illustrated further during the recent Algerian crisis. An American colleague was rather worried that the agitators in the Algerian crisis were raising slogans about the Qur'an. My response was that there was nothing to worry about on that score and that I hoped they would study it. I stated that the crises which erupt in the Middle East and other Islamic countries are due to the fact that in the last several centuries Muslim societies have not studied the Qur'an. Our studies of Pakistan, Egypt, and Turkey substantiate this conclusion. For the Middle East and other Muslim countries to stabilize and become progressive, the first condition is that the *study* of the Qur'an in a modern system of education becomes a mass phenomenon. The study also unmistakably shows that the Middle East, indeed, the entire Muslim world, is gripped by a crisis of thought that explains the stagnant and chaotic conditions existing in these countries.

This book is intended for advanced undergraduate and graduate students who study the Middle East and for those who are concerned with matters related to the Middle East. It is equally intended for the people in the Middle East and other Muslim societies. It will challenge the reader to think afresh matters related to the Middle East, Islam, and the Muslim world.

1

INTRODUCTION

Although a considerable literature exists on the Middle East and it has occupied center stage in world politics for the past two centuries, the Middle East has remained an enigma for those who study and formulate policies regarding the region. The ruling circles and the mass of the populations within these Muslim countries are themselves not fully aware of what is happening in their societies or why certain things are happening or not happening. Therefore, the functioning and state of the societies remain largely misunderstood by the societies themselves. The scores of books and articles written on the Middle East, though useful in some ways, generally lack explanatory value. Most works describe *how* things are, or have been, in the Middle East; they do not explain, in a real sense, the *"why."* It is for this reason that the enigma of the Middle East persists, both for the societies of the region and for analysts at large. In this book, by examining the role of Islam in the modernization efforts of Pakistan, Egypt, and Turkey, we analyze issues that have hitherto not been fully studied, nor are their implications generally understood.

The argument presented in this book is that the issue of development or modernization of Islamic countries cannot be analyzed, explained and addressed in terms of the existing paradigms in the discipline formulated to analyze and explain the issues involved in the development and modernization processes of developing countries as a whole. My argument is that a fundamental issue in Muslim countries—that of the prevalent ideas about Islam, and the so-called Islamic traditions which affect every aspect of life in a Muslim society—has been largely left out of the study. This is understandable for two reasons. First, the study of developing countries has been undertaken mainly by Western scholars, who approached the issue of development and modernization through their understanding of the structures and processes in the Western experience, and their emphasis tended to be on the more recent experience of the West. Of course, they have known that the Western process of modernization originated when the reformation of religious thought took place in the West. In their studies of the presently developing countries of the world, however, they have largely ignored the role of religion in the societies. Second, in order to analyze and explain Muslim societies in a meaningful way, the analyst must be well-versed in the Qur'an; it is impossible to evaluate, understand, and explain Muslim societies without a thorough knowledge of the Qur'an.

Another reason why Western scholars have not examined the religious dimension of the societies concerned appears to have been the result of adhering too strictly to the doctrine of secularism, which made religion a private affair. As a result, in their studies of the developing countries, they have generally ignored the religious dimension of the societies, which is actually of fundamental importance. Chapter 3 draws attention to this aspect of the modernization process. The major reason why Western scholars have not examined the religious issue in the modernization process of Muslim societies appears to have been that their understanding of Islam is based on the empirical evidence provided by the societies themselves—that is, on the conceptions and practices that the societies have themselves proclaimed to be Islamic.

Scholars from Muslim societies, barring some outstanding exceptions, have provided mainly an apologia of the existing religious conceptions and practices in Muslim societies, which further reinforced the ideas of Western scholars.[1] Its effect has been that Islam has been accepted as a given, and the critical appraisal of Muslim societies on this score has largely gone unattended.

It was this awareness which led me to undertake this study and to analyze the role of Islam in the modernization efforts of Muslim countries through a comparative historical perspective so that whatever the conclusions, they were substantiated by the different geographical and historical situations of Muslim countries. The choice of the three countries, Pakistan, Egypt, and Turkey was deliberate; all three are sizable and have predominantly Muslim populations, and all three are apparently engaged in modernizing their societies. Turkey's case made the study more interesting because it has followed the doctrine of secularism as a state policy; it provided an antithesis to the case of Pakistan which emerged in 1947 as an Islamic state. Pakistan's objective is to be a modern progressive country through Islam. Prior to that, Turkey, which had existed as a Muslim country for over six centuries, officially declared itself to be secular in 1928. Its goal was to modernize the country through secularization. When Egypt became independent in 1952 through a military coup, its aim was also to become a modern country.

This study, then, analyzes the effects of the existing conceptions of Islam on the modernization efforts of Pakistan, Egypt, and Turkey. The specific question examined in this study is whether Islam, as interpreted and advocated historically in these countries or the territories that eventually gave birth to these countries, has a positive, negative, or no impact on the modernization process.

As Donald Eugene Smith has said, "religion constitutes the core of the traditional cultures"[2] of the regions in which the countries to be examined are located. The study is thus an examination of how religion affects, and has affected in the past, the political culture of these countries, and consequently how this culture affects the modernization process.

In the countries under study, indeed, in all the developing countries that derive their values from religion, religion is a key variable in explaining the modernization process,[3] whatever direction it might take. For any meaningful analysis of Pakistan, Egypt, and Turkey, therefore an examination of what role religion plays in these societies is of vital importance. While all three are endeavoring to modernize, an analysis of the role of religion in the politics of their polities has largely remained unexamined. No systematic study has been carried out about developing Islamic countries to determine how the present religious ideas, practices, and traditions, which are deeply embedded in their cultures, might be affecting modernization efforts, or indeed how they might be affecting the societies generally. In examining the role of religion in the modernization efforts of Pakistan, Egypt, and Turkey, we are provided with an accurate picture of how the prevalent ideas and practices, which are passed off as Islamic, affect the societies in everyday life. These three countries provide a good representative sample of the Muslim world, for they are in several ways at the forefront of the modernizing efforts in the Muslim world. Therefore, the conclusions that we reach through this study are applicable to other Muslim countries as well.

By identifying religion as a crucial variable in the modernization efforts of Islamic countries, this study adds a new dimension to the theories of development in societies with predominantly Muslim populations. At the same time, it points to a new direction for the modernization efforts in Muslim countries.

One of the main conclusions of this study is that, unless major changes are made, the modernization efforts of the three countries will not amount to much. All the available evidence indicates that the same would hold true for other Muslim countries. Some incremental changes may occur, but the overall pattern and structure of the societies will remain unchanged. That is, they will remain less developed and will continue to trail behind the other developed countries of the world. These changes are directly related to the existing state of Islamic religious thought in Muslim countries. Nearly a thousand years ago Islamic thought began to be distorted and with the passage of time became more corrupted through a number of factors. At another level, because philosophy was banished in the Muslim world, this thought remained stagnant. This grossly distorted and stagnant religious thought is prevalent in the present-day Muslim countries. As a result, it has affected all thought, which has led to a crisis in the Muslim world.

The crises and dormancy witnessed in the Middle East and in other Muslim countries reflect the crisis of thought that has engulfed the entire Muslim world.

How and why this has happened will become apparent as we proceed with our analysis. For positive changes to occur in these societies which can lead to the advancement of these societies, it is in the realm of religious thought and practices that the answers will first have to be found. In other words, it is the reformation of Islamic religious thought on which depends the development of Muslim societies. This conclusion has powerful ramifications for domestic as well as international politics.

Since Islamic religious thought, practices, and traditions in vogue have had a paramount influence on the political culture of these countries, this book focuses on the dominant patterns of these cultures and on how these cultures have so far responded and reacted to the modernization efforts of the secular-modernizing regimes of the three countries.

The period covered by this study is as follows: (1) Pakistan, from its creation in 1947 to the present; (2) Egypt, from the time of Nasser's coup in 1952 to the present; and (3) Turkey, from 1923, when it became a republic, to the present. When the study got under way, however, I found it necessary to delve into the earlier history of each country, which provided a broader perspective to the present situation and developments in these countries.

This study is based on comparative historical analysis. As Theda Skocpol has stated, through this method "one tries to establish valid associations of potential causes with the given phenomenon one is trying to explain."[4] The phenomenon under examination in this study is the role of the existing conceptions of Islam in the modernization process in Pakistan, Egypt, and Turkey. There could, of course, be several factors which may have an impact on the modernization process. This study concentrates on one potentially crucial variable in this process, that is, religion (crucial, because of its apparent all-encompassing role in the societies under study), to determine if there is any causal link between Islamic religious thought, practices, and traditions in vogue in the three countries and modernization.

There are two main approaches to comparative historical analysis, the method of agreement and the method of difference, which can be applied individually or, for better effect, in combination. In the method of agreement one tries to "establish that several cases having in common the phenomenon one is trying to explain also have in common a set of causal factors, although they vary in other ways that might have seemed causally relevant."[5] In the method of difference one contrasts "the cases in which the phenomenon to be explained and the hypothesized causes are present to other cases in which the phenomenon and the causes are both absent, but which are otherwise as similar as possible to the positive cases."[6]

These two comparative logics are in operation in this book. I shall argue that in Pakistan, Egypt, and Turkey similar causal patterns are observable when the role of the existing ideas and practices mistakenly attributed to Islam are examined in the functioning of the societies. Turkey's example also serves as a contrast to the other two countries, for secular Turkey officially chose to approach life in a different way than the other two countries, mistakenly believing that by taking Islam out of its polity it could become a modern progressive country. Turkey's case illustrates, in fact, that secular or not, what is of paramount importance in a Muslim country is the state of the prevalent religious thought, for it affects all thought, and consequently all action. The same would, of course, hold for other societies. The Western example, discussed in Chapter 3, is also utilized to construct similarities and contrasts to the three Muslim countries examined in this book.

In the modernization process of developing countries, both internal and external factors are involved, which may have a direct impact on the process involved. And while the external factors may be relevant to a degree, this study focuses on the internal factors, that is, the religiopolitical systems of the three countries. It is in this context that the effects of the existing ideas and conceptions of Islam on the modernization efforts in Pakistan, Egypt, and Turkey are examined. These conceptions affect both the policymakers and implementers of what are considered to be modernization plans and efforts, and the mass of the population which is ostensibly engaged in executing the plans.

After the problem was initially conceptualized and a working hypothesis formulated, I created a framework of analysis for each country in which the following indices were included:

1. An assessment of the role of religion in culture. This was done by examining the stated goals, positions, and activities of Islamic religious groups, sects, organizations, leaders, and scholars.
2. Religious and cultural traditions and their impact on the modernization efforts of the regimes.
3. Modernization goals of the regimes; an assessment of the development plans (past and projected) of the regimes.
4. State position and policies vis-à-vis religion.
5. Institutional arrangements for critical evaluation of traditional religious-social practices and for carrying out reforms in religious-social traditions of different kinds.
6. Religious functionaries' and leaders' responses to modernist intellectuals' views or critiques of existing social-religious practices.
7. State responses to the modernist intellectuals' views or critiques of existing social-religious practices.
8. An assessment of reforms, if any, that have been carried out by the state in traditional religious-social practices.
9. Popular attitudes toward religious functionaries or ulema.
10. Power of religious functionaries or ulema vis-à-vis the state.
11. Religious educational system.

Later, however, when the analysis got under way, I found some of the indices to be interrelated; and to give greater coherence, integration, and unity to the study, instead of examining such indices independently, I reformulated the framework of analysis by blending such elements together. The reformulated framework of analysis consists of the following indices through which I have carried out the study:

1. State position and policies regarding Islam and religious leaders' responses.
2. Modernist intellectuals' views of religious matters and practices.
3. State responses to modernist intellectuals' views of religious matters and practices.
4. State responses to religious leaders' views and demands regarding Islam.
5. Religious educational system.
6. Assessment of the development plans and modernization goals of the state.

In each case I have adhered to this framework as far as possible; where I found that further readjustment of the indices was necessary, I have done so, keeping in view that the information relevant to the indices, which were readjusted, is brought into the body of the study.

After analyzing the role of the existing state of Islamic religious thought, practices, and traditions in the polities of each case, an assessment of the developmental plans and modernization goals of the state is made to show that there is a causal link between the former and the latter, and why modernization efforts have so far been far from satisfactory. My argument is that the modernization efforts are not successful or meaningful because of the existing state of Islamic religious thought and practices in these countries, which affects every aspect of life. Therefore, the first condition for the development and progress of these and other Muslim societies is the reformation of the existing religious thought. The elites who formulate and implement the developmental plans are products of these societies and are, therefore, themselves conditioned and affected by the prevalent religious conceptions and practices. The impact of the existing state of religious thought on them as well as on society as a whole is subtle but exceedingly powerful. Beyond the impact of the preceding several centuries in which grossly distorted Islamic religious ideas, customs, traditions, and practices have been in vogue in these societies, the reason for this is that religion affects the totality of a person "engaging intellect, emotion, and will,"[7] and also affects values, habits, and traditions. It follows that both the content of a particular religious doctrine and its interpretation, dissemination, and application are vitally important. It can even be argued that it affects the process of evolution itself, which Lloyd Morgan has described as emergent evolution:

Evolution, in the broad sense, is the name we give to comprehensive plan of sequences in all natural events. But the orderly sequence, historically viewed, appears to present from time to time something genuinely new. . . . Salient examples are afforded in the advent of life, in the advent of mind, and in the advent of reflective thought. If nothing new emerges, if there be only regrouping of pre-existing events and nothing more—then there is no emergent evolution.[8]

In Chapter 4 I discuss the question of Islam and modernization and bring out the real and deep-seated problem that exists in Muslim societies and that explains their present stagnant condition. At the same time, Chapter 4 explains how the problem can be overcome. The studies of Pakistan, Egypt, and Turkey should be viewed in the context of this chapter.

This study is theoretically anchored in the literatures of political culture and economic development; it provides an application of theory to concrete cases. In doing so, it shows serious flaws in the existing theories of development and modernization. Indeed, in light of this study, dependency theories lose their validity insofar as Islamic societies are concerned.

This book goes beyond the country studies or case studies done on the Middle East and other Islamic countries. While such studies provide useful information on particular countries, they lack both on the analytical and the explanatory levels. They do not tell us matters of real substance. This book examines the Middle East through a new approach and raises and addresses issues that are either generally ignored or their implications are not understood. The Middle East, indeed the entire Muslim world, is thus cast in a new explanatory light in this book. In examining the complex relationship between Islam and modernization of the Middle East, this study, in the process, dissects the politics of the Middle East to show how Islam is not only politicized in the region, but also how it is distorted.

2

EXPLAINING
MODERNIZATION

Development is a complex phenomenon, and the central issue of development is the question of modernity, or "what it is to be modern."[1] The fundamental goal of all developmental efforts in the developing countries is to modernize their societies, and the image of modernity, insofar as it relates to material goods, is that of the more developed countries of the West. Generally, development in the developing countries has been evaluated by making comparisons with the present state of the more developed Western countries. Instead, Harry Eckstein advocates a universal approach to development based on "abstract theories regardless of time, place, and circumstance—theory that spans the whole of history, from primal origins to modernity."[2] Considering the complexity of the development process, however, it is highly unlikely that a general, universal approach to development can be found. Much of what has happened since the primal origins of humans to the present time is not really known. Such an approach, therefore, cannot have much validity.

A better approach for both the more developed and the developing countries is to focus on the present and to plan for the future. With regard to the developing countries, the more fruitful approach is to analyze the development process in any given polity and to identify those aspects that appear to hinder developmental efforts. For this purpose, the more developed countries of the West provide empirical evidence. The West can therefore serve as a useful developmental model. So far, the developing countries have been content with merely imitating the Western countries as they exist at present, without paying due attention to the processes through which the West had to go through to arrive at its present state of development. The developing countries are, in a way, at an advantageous position, for they have a model to learn from, to evaluate, and to modify the model if it is found wanting. The more developed countries are, on this score, in a precarious situation, for having come a long way and having materially developed to the extent that they have, and there being no model to follow, some very serious questions remain unanswered.

Since modernization and development involve change, we will examine how change takes place or what are its necessary components. In our discussion of different aspects of modernization and development, we will approach modernization through the characteristics of a modern person, for a modern society is created by and composed of modern persons. It is the individuals of a society who determine its shape and direction. Once we know the characteristics of a modern person, we are in a good position to know what is required of a society to become modern. In this way we can meaningfully understand the concept of modernization as well as the process involved in modernizing a society.

Studies dealing with dependency theory have generally tended to be more of rationalizations of the conditions existing in developing countries rather than addressing the core issues, mostly existing in the structures and fabrics of the societies, which thwart attempts to develop or modernize. Their message amounts to encouraging passivity and apathy at all levels, particularly for the elites, who find in such studies a ready explanation for the conditions existing in their societies and the acceptance of the status quo.[3] The elites in any case benefit from maintaining the status quo. The biggest problem with the dependency theory is that with one stroke it rules out the possibility that substantial progress can occur in all the developing countries. Dependency theory argues, in effect, that as long as the current world economy is structured as it is, the developing countries will find it well-nigh impossible to change their economic conditions. Such a conclusion completely ignores the inner dynamics of developing societies—the way they are structured and run, and the kind of ideas that are prevalent and propagated—which seem far more directly related to the state of a society than any other outside factor.

While modernity and growth in the material sense are desirable and sought after the world over, there are limits to them. The growth and development of individuals is far more important, and for this only ultimate values can provide the answer. This does not mean however that material growth loses its relevance; material growth is necessary, for it frees people from the struggle to merely subsist and provides the time necessary for their spiritual needs; time to reflect upon life, and to confront and attempt to understand the larger issues of life, like death.

The literature on modernization and development emphasizes the idea that secularization is a necessary component of modernization. Daniel Lerner, for instance, in arguing that the Western model of modernization has global relevance, states that it was the secular process of social change which modernized Western countries. It has, therefore, he argues, relevance to the Middle East situation. The Western model, he explains, is the most developed model of societal attributes (i.e., power, wealth, skill, and rationality), which is also the goal of the Middle East spokesmen and policymakers.[4] Although the

Western model of modernization certainly has relevance for the Middle East and other developing countries, the argument presented in this book is that Muslim countries will have to approach modernization through a totally different method, as far as the question of secularization is concerned, if they are to succeed and move forward. At the same time, they will have to make a radical departure from the way the societies have so far been organized and run.

Great misunderstanding and myth surround the concept of secularization. Secularization, as commonly understood, and the politicization of religion in Islamic societies, operating individually or concurrently, are the two approaches that constantly eat at the roots of the societies and prevent them from becoming modern, progressive societies. This will become apparent, as well as how secularization and the politicization of religion can operate concurrently, when we examine the countries under study. Apart from the fact that secularization, in the Islamic context, is as pernicious in its effects as the politicization of Islam, secularization, as it has evolved in the West, inheres some very serious problems. Secularization eventually leads to a situation, both individual and societal, where all values other than narrow self-interest break down.[5] The serious social ills and problems observable in secularized cultures all over the world clearly indicate that the secularized way of life is beset with very serious problems.

Contrary to what scores of writers have proclaimed, secularization is not a necessary condition for development and modernization. In fact, it is fraught with grave danger. It is one thing to reject the power of any religious group or "class," but quite another to reject alongwith the first rejection what the revealed religions have to offer. As will be shown in Chapter 4, Islam is not opposed to development or modernization. There is, then, sound reason to reject the power of any religious group or class in the Islamic setting. In the first instance, there is no basis for it in Islam; second, the historical experience of both the Islamic countries and the West has shown that such a group or class has a proclivity to appropriate, so to say, life and death to itself. It does not follow from this, however, that the entire society should be secularized. In any case, the idea of secularization is contrary to what Islam is; that is, it has a direct relationship with the life processes.

Even the Western experience has shown how grossly flawed the idea of secularization is. Peter Sederberg, in an insightful analysis, has pointed out that the Western experience has shown that when value pluralization and relativization become the norm, the social fabric is rent apart. When everything is relative, tyranny has no less merit than anything else. Secularization and skepticism have corroded established religious belief systems in the West. Yet the suffering and death that traditional religions sought to explain continue. The secular West has demonstrated that "the frantic pursuit of material pleasures and the exaggerated pride in the accomplishments of the scientific mind are attempts to paper over the abyss with an ineffectual veneer of arrogance and escapism.

. . . modern man has lost God through secularization."[6]

SOCIAL CHANGE, PROGRESS, AND HUMAN RATIONALITY

A society's overall development is related to changes in the social system. Thus, political and economic development are directly related to changes in the social system. Indeed, social change is the key in the modernization process. For developing countries to become modern, the rate, direction, and quality of social change is the deciding factor; in social change, multiple and interconnected factors are involved.[7]

A major approach in the study of modernization and development has been to examine the differences between the developed and developing countries with a view to finding out how development can be brought about in the developing countries. This approach has provided valuable insights. In their eagerness, however, many writers thought they would soon see the fruits of their labor,[8] and in the process overlooked the fact that the modernization process is long and arduous.[9] They also forgot that development cannot be taken for granted and that development or progress has historically been the exception rather than the rule.[10] While this seems to be true, the analysis suggests that what is involved in the whole process of development is human creativity, perhaps a test of human creativity, and certainly the exercise of human rationality.

In Islamic societies what appears to have happened in the last several centuries is that the so-called religious leaders, in an environment of autocratic rule, which shunned criticism and open debate and discussion, mistook God's statements in the Qur'an to the effect that nothing happens in the world unless God wishes it, that He is all powerful and human beings very weak, to mean that humanity had no control over its environment and that things will happen naturally or on their own. The purpose of such statements, quite clearly, was only to warn human beings of their powerlessness vis-à-vis God, so that people do not start playing God or start thinking that they are not answerable for their actions. This was particularly so at the time the Qur'an was revealed, for people at that time still questioned the existence of God, as is apparent from the study of the Qur'an. Of course, even in the present world, some people still question the existence of God, but that is a separate issue altogether. The point which emerges from the foregoing is that, in the course of time, in the Islamic societies the erroneous belief grew which is present even today, based on partial or faulty understanding of some of the Qur'anic verses, that God will do things for humans. This seems to explain the lack of enterprise in Islamic societies, which recent history bears out. In the process, human creativity and rationality have been relegated to an obscure corner. And here is the rub, for as David Apter states, "reason as applied to human affairs is the foundation of modernity."[11] Moris Ginsberg explains it thus:

> . . . the fundamental assumptions underlying the belief in Providence and the belief in Progress are incongruous and . . . the latter, could not take a firm hold over men's minds while the former was indisputably in the ascendant. The idea of progress was hardly likely to obtain wide credence until attention was shifted from the kingdom to come to the kingdom of this world . . . . It was thus essentially linked with the growth of modern science, with the spread of the rationalist outlook and with the struggle for political and religious liberty.[12]

This does not mean, however, that belief in Providence is any fault. People have spiritual needs without which life would seem utterly meaningless, and the discovery of ultimate values has only been possible through revealed religions. The problem has only been with the religious functionaries, whether they be religious leaders or priests. Ginsberg, explaining the development of the idea of progress, states that Christian theologians apparently became interested in the idea of progress only after it acquired a dominant position in Western thought. On occasion, the Catholic church has explicitly repudiated the idea, and even the Protestant writers have had great difficulty accepting the idea. The concept of history as a forward movement, and not an endless repetition, exists in Judaism, Christianity, and Islam. The same idea also existed in Zoroastrianism but bore no fruit because the Zoroastrian idea did not come into contact with rationalist thought and was not stimulated by the idea that people could mold their own fate through applied science. Had this situation also continued in Christianity, it seems probable that the germs of the idea of progress in Christian thought would have remained undeveloped and would never have emerged from the state of resignation and otherworldliness in which they existed.

The belief in progress reached its high point in the West toward the end of the nineteenth century. "Its high priests and incense bearers were . . . all rationalists. It owed its wide prevalence to the optimism inspired by the triumphs of applied science."[13] In the Islamic world, in the past several centuries, the idea of progress has remained dormant essentially because rational approach to life was forsaken, a state of affairs that exists in the present age.

Inherent in the process of modernization or development is the idea of progress that was debated extensively by the eighteenth-century philosophers. To them progress meant human perfectibility. Condorcet stated this notion most clearly when he said that "the human species can be improved, firstly by new discoveries in the arts and sciences, and consequently in the means of well-being and common prosperity, secondly, by progress in the principles of conduct and moral practice and thirdly by the improvement of human faculty."[14] He acknowledged, however, that it was not inevitable that this would happen; it was possible only if "we know how to use the forces at our command."[15] The emphasis was, therefore, on human reason. Similarly, the writers of the French

Enlightenment stressed the importance of human reason in humanity's future development.[16]

The process of development involves advances in the economic, political, and technological spheres. Yet none of them can be separated, for each one of them directly impinges on the others. Neither can development be separated from moral questions, if human development in its true form is to be achieved. [17] In fact, moral questions are the bedrock on which human development stands and can prosper. Basic to the whole process of development is a normative question: "What are the requirements of the good life and of the good society in the modern world?"[18] Underlying the whole notion of development, it seems to me, is or ought to be, the idea of self-perfection. This entails psychological freedom as well as economic and social changes that "will permit the individual to become free in terms of the realization of self."[19] This alone makes the case for an open or democratic society, which is the best that humanity has thus far come up with—hence, the importance of what is generally termed as political development. Freedom, as Thomas Hill Green put it, is "essentially the opportunity to strive for self-perfection," and the state's main role is to provide this opportunity for all.[20] The civil institutions have value only when individuals can exercise their capacities of will and reason. The exercise of these capacities makes it possible for individuals to strive for perfection instead of being at the mercy of external forces. In exercising the capacity called will, an individual is given the opportunity to "realize his reason, i.e., his idea of self-perfection, by acting as a member of a social organization in which each contributes to the better-being of all the rest."[21]

THE NECESSITY OF MATERIAL PROGRESS

People need physical goods to discover themselves and their potentials, provided, of course, that material goods do not become an end in themselves. They need goods "to give material support to their actualizing and transcending activities," and while it may be possible for "exceptional mystics or poets to realize themselves through introspection, contemplation, or simple human communion," they are the exceptions. Most people require physical goods before they can pursue such activities.[22] In Denis Goulet's words:

Whatever may be the ultimate meaning of life, it is something more than simple existence. Beyond subsistence, survival, and all useful functions, man in society has an endless range of enhancement needs, the satisfaction of which perfects him, actualizes his potentialities, thrusts him beyond perceived limits and into new environment he himself creates.[23]

Within the realm of material goods, however, there is a paradox: "Men in want possess too little to become human, but satiated men, on the contrary, are prevented from becoming human because they possess too much."[24] Materialism by itself, however, is not at fault; it is the choices made which determine outcomes. There are two forms of materialism. The first is healthy and guards against escapism, which views material goods as unimportant and misery as an outcome of fate or the will of God. Healthy materialism accepts reasonable acquisitive desires and acknowledges that human virtue cannot exist when there is massive suffering. A second form of materialism, however, is deadly. It transforms an individual into a manipulator or an object of manipulation; an individual's value is measured in terms of possessions. This kind of materialism "feeds on a mindless and insensitive system which allows the quest for abundance to depersonalize life."[25]

Although the processes of development can be perceived and studied in economic, political, and cultural domains, "its ultimate goals are those of existence itself: to provide all [people] with the opportunity to live full human lives."[26] For this reason, normative values cannot be divorced from the pursuit of development or modernization. How these values are arrived at will depend on each society. "Which values ought to be preserved and which sacrificed for the sake of modernization? No answers exist except those which emerge from vital processes of critical reflection."[27] This is all the more necessary because "modernity and traditionalism are linked together in fundamental ways, even in the context of modernization. The synthesis between them serves as a primary moral focus."[28] This, of course, presupposes an open society where debate and discussion can take place unhesitatingly. In the synthesizing process, "tradition may be discarded, changed, stretched, or modified, but still a great use can be made of the traditional elements in a society's efforts to establish a consensual base to political authority and economic development."[29]

STRUCTURAL DIFFERENTIATION, MODERNIZATION, AND POLITICAL DEVELOPMENT

As a polity modernizes or develops, structural differentiation and specialization of roles occur. Structural differentiation is a process in which the social role or organization splits into two or more roles or organizations that function more effectively than was the case before.[30] Differentiation brings major changes in economic and family activities. In the economic realm, economic activity moves beyond the family-community setting, which is usually the case in the rural areas of the developing countries. As a consequence, old forms of integration change. The controls of old forms of family and village life begin to dissolve. Several related and important processes follow: (1) "Apprenticeship within the family declines"; (2) "Demands of economic rationality" take precedence; (3) control of elders and kinsmen weakens, which allows greater freedom of action; (4) change of status takes place for women, who now become less subordinated; and (5) ascriptive standards become more differentiated from economic, political, and other standards.[31] Yet, differentiation by itself is not sufficient for modernization. In the modernization process, an interplay occurs between differentiation (which is divisive of existing social role or organization) and integration (which unites newly differentiated structures). The process of integration itself, however, produces more differentiated structures like trade unions, associations, political groups, and state institutions.[32]

In the modernization process, structural differentiation gains importance because it is the undifferentiated structures that are often the primary social barriers to modernization.[33] The transition from a less differentiated to a more differentiated society is, however, a gradual process and influences the social structure selectively.[34]

Differentiation of societal structures provides an impetus for political institutions to develop, and it enables the populace to participate in the decision-making process. When social systems become more complex, political systems are modified, which leads to a growth in political institutions.[35] This whole process is of vital importance, as evidence has shown that there is a direct relationship between democratic political process and economic development (industrialization, urbanization, wealth, and education).[36] Economic growth and political-social change are mutually dependent.[37] Critics can argue, however, that economic development has also occurred in authoritarian political systems like the former Soviet Union. But in all authoritarian systems, whatever their form, the costs in human terms are astounding, for while these system may achieve a degree of economic development they dehumanize people. This effect militates against the core idea of development: the development of individual human beings.

Authoritarian structures, whether they are political or social, seem to hinder economic development. The authoritarian hierarchical traditional social structure is based on ascriptive rather than prescriptive values, and is generally found in a traditional agricultural society.[38] It is a common feature of such developing societies that individual status is determined largely by birth antecedents rather than by individual abilities. This has far-reaching consequences for the societies concerned. Individuals who gain privileged positions in life through accident of birth feel superior to the simple folk and develop a repugnance to the material details of life.[39] They also are not interested in changing the socioeconomic system that gives them and their families the hereditary status, power, and authority.

Such attitudes spread in the entire society, for the elites serve as role models. These attitudes undercut the human need for achievement that historically has undergirded the human capacity for development or advancement. The need for achievement has been found to be a major source of innovation and economic development in the economically prosperous societies.[40] Traditional social structures undermine the need for achievement and, at the same time, tend to prevent human creativity from coming into full play. Such a social structure also prevents the active participation of women in the economic field. Rapid long-term economic development requires the active participation of women in the workforce. It also leads to healthy psychological effects when women are freed from their traditional setting and roles, which in turn make the society buoyant and vibrant. The development of a society in all areas of life, and consequently the development of civilization itself, is neither adaptation nor sublimation but a creative enterprise of people made dynamic by a high level of the need for achievement.[41]

ATTITUDE AND VALUE CHANGES

Change in attitudes and values at both the individual and societal level, is of crucial importance in the modernization of developing countries. Alex Inkles and David Smith's study of six developing countries provides glaring evidence that "the attitude and value changes defining individual modernity are accompanied by changes in behavior precisely of the sort which . . . give meaning to, and support, those changes in political and economic institutions which lead to the modernization of nations."[42] We must therefore challenge the assumption that a "mere" change in attitudes and values cannot lead to the development of societies.[43] Although it is true that a host of factors, natural, human-made, international, prior history, and the like, may impede modernization, underdevelopment fundamentally "is a state of mind"; "mental barriers and psychic factors are key obstacles to more effective economic and social development in many countries."[44]

For societies to become modern, the foremost requirement is to develop "attitudinal modernization," or, to put it another way, the existence of "modern" individuals in a society. Modern individuals are those "who are better educated, more urbanized, more engaged in industry and related non-traditional occupations, and more exposed to the newer media of mass communications."[45] Among the most outstanding characteristics of modern individuals are their openness to new experiences and their willingness to change. A modern person is not parochial in his or her outlook but identifies with larger entities like state, region, or the world. He or she participates in societal issues and activities. A modern person is highly independent and autonomous, with a high sense of personal efficacy, and is markedly independent of traditional sources of influence in personal affairs. Such a person is not dependent on priests, religious leaders, or village elders in making decisions regarding private or public life. A modern person rejects passivity, resignation, and fatalism in the pursuits of life and, instead, takes control of life. He or she is imbibed with the spirit of rationality. Attitudinal modernization leads to behavioral changes that enable a person to become modern.[46]

Although one could add some more characteristics, the above sum up the key components of the modernity syndrome. They are the kinds of qualities that are needed from the citizen of a modern society. In the final analysis, therefore, the individuals who are more modern in attitudes and values are those who act "to support modern institutions and to facilitate the general modernization of society."[47]

Thus, for societies to become modern, the transformation of individuals in psychological terms is a prerequisite, that is, transformation from traditionalism to individual modernity. A modern person is not typical to any particular culture or society. It is their number, however, which ultimately determines the state of a particular society. In the developing countries, their number, as a ratio of the population, is very limited and is confined mostly to urban centers. Evidence has shown, however, that "the means for bringing about greater individual modernization are . . . potentially within the reach of even the least-advantaged nations and communities."[48] There is no a priori reason to assume that in becoming modern the people of "traditional countries would lose whatever qualities had made them more friendly, humane, personal, warm, open, secure, or otherwise attractive and adjusted in their traditional mode. Modern [people] may be different, but they are not deculturated."[49] The role of modern individuals in the modernization process is crucial. Rapid economic growth and effective government cannot take root in a society without the widespread diffusion of those qualities in the population which have been explained earlier as the hallmark of a modern person. Diffusion of those qualities in the population is the essence of national development; in the present age they are not a luxury but a necessity for life.[50] In the same vein, John Stuart Mill argued over a century and a quarter ago that

a government cannot have too much of the kind of activity which does not impede, but aids and stimulates, individual exertion and development. *The mischief begins when, instead of calling forth the activity and powers of individuals and bodies, it substitutes its own activity for theirs*; when, instead of informing, advising, and, upon occasion, denouncing, it makes their work in fetters, or bids them stand aside and does their work instead of them. *The worth of a state, in the long run, is the worth of the individuals composing it*; and a state which postpones the interests of their mental expansion and elevation to a little more of administrative skill, or of that semblance of it which practice gives in the details of business; *a state which dwarfs its men*, in order that they may be more docile instruments in its hands for beneficial purposes—will find that with small men no great thing can really be accomplished; and that the perfection of machinery to which it has sacrificed everything will in the end avail it nothing, for want of the vital power which, . . . it has preferred to banish.[51] [Emphasis added]

THE SYSTEM AND THE INDIVIDUAL

Studies of modernization and development utilize two main approaches; one deals extensively with processes and functions at the institutional, societal, or national level, whereas the second is much more limited and emphasizes the cultural and ideational. Major studies of economic and political modernization have been conducted at the institutional, societal, or national level, and far fewer at the individual level. The first approach "stresses ways of *organizing* and *doing*, the second assigns primacy to ways of *thinking* and *feeling*. The first approach is concerned more with the *institution*, the other with the *individual*. The first is more narrowly sociological and political, the second more sociological and psychological."[52] The two are intimately related to each other, however. The nature of the political system and the state of the economic system, for instance, have a direct impact on the individual and determine how an individual is shaped; economic conditions profoundly affect people: " . . . [people] developing their material production and their material intercourse, alter, along with this their real existence, their thinking and the products of their thinking. Life is not determined by consciousness [alone], but consciousness by life."[53] The strength of the preceding argument is further illustrated by the work of Oscar Lewis and Edward Banfield. Their study shows that economic conditions (which are an outgrowth of several factors) are, in part, responsible for personality traits and group behavior, regardless of whether a person is oriental or occidental. Their description of personality traits and the structure of family relations and civic responsibility in Mexican and South Italian village families fits many Asian villages. Their study, therefore, overturns "stereotypes of religious and ethnic determinates of behavior. In Southern Italy and Mexico, we are not dealing with Buddhist, Confucian, or Muslim societies but with essentially Roman Catholic society and with an ethnic component which is almost totally different from that found in Asian societies."[54]

It is because of the impact of material conditions on life that economic development, which, of course, is the purpose of the entire developmental process, gains such an importance. Individuals, affected by the economic conditions, in turn affect the functioning and development of the economic system and thereby society itself. And for economic advancement many scholars have considered political modernization as essential.[55] It appears, therefore, that the whole process of development or modernization should be viewed as a triad relationship between the individual, the economic system or conditions, and the political system. In this triad relationship the individual plays the preeminent role.

IMPACT OF CHANGES IN TRADITIONAL VALUES
AND THE ROLE OF LEADERSHIP

For modernization efforts to be successful, the political system must carry out social and economic reform by state action. The political system must also be able to assimilate new social forces produced by modernization into the system harmoniously. If social groups that have acquired new consciousness due to modernization are alienated from the system, the result could be civil strife and secession.[56] In this entire process leadership plays a preeminent role.

Modernization demands the active participation of a country's entire adult population in the economic sphere. In particular, it requires a shift from traditional to nontraditional areas of employment. Studies have shown that when women move from traditional to nontraditional areas of employment or work, an appreciable decrease in their fertility rate takes place. This finding is significant for the developing countries, most of which suffer from overpopulation, which is one major factor thwarting developmental efforts.

When women enter nontraditional areas of employment, they are participating in work that was previously considered exclusive to men.[57] In traditional societies, even though women may be participating in the workforce, there is little incompatibility between such participation and a high birth rate because of the nature of the work performed. Thailand, for example, with 83 percent of all working women in traditional employment (agriculture), exhibits a positive relationship between female employment and fertility. In Singapore and Hong Kong, which are largely nonagricultural countries, a negative relationship exists between female employment and fertility. These two emerging industrial urban economies have experienced a sharp decline in birth rates: Hong Kong had a birth rate of 37.4 in 1956, 25 in 1966, and 18.3 in 1975, whereas Singapore had a rate of 44.4 in 1956, 28.3 in 1966, and 18 in 1975.[58] Japan's case also shows a strong relationship between the type of labor force activity and female fertility. "Japanese women in farming and fishing activities and those engaged as family helpers show the highest fertility among the labor force". The percentage of the female labor force in traditional employment areas has sharply declined, however; in 1955 it was 51.8 percent, and in 1979, 23.6 percent.[59]

Inherent in the notion of modernization is the process of change—that is, change from a traditional to a modern way of life. In the developing countries, the model of modernity is seen largely in the more developed countries. Yet a main feature of the traditional or developing countries is that "they are attached to beliefs and rules which guided past practices, and which are regarded as guides to right practice in the present . . . . the general disposition to accept what has been accepted in the past directs the course against modernity."[60] The change required to achieve modernity is, therefore, of such magnitude that it requires a shift from one historical era to another. The societies of the developing countries can thus legitimately be said to be in a state of crisis—a crisis of conflict between an old way of looking at life and a new one. Recognition and confrontation of a crisis are the first steps toward achieving such innovations which may resolve the crisis.[61] The existence of a crisis, whether in the social or scientific fields, indicates the need to invent alternatives, for the existing methods, practices, and views fail to solve the problems. "The significance of crises is the indication they provide that an occasion for retooling has arrived."[62]

The case of traditional versus modern can be analyzed in terms of what Thomas Kuhn has called a paradigm. The traditional and the modern approach to life can be called two different paradigms, for they represent two different worldviews that are both empirically observable and tested. Since the old worldview has been shown to be obsolete by the modern, there is a need to reject the older paradigm and to replace it by the new or modern one, for "the decision to reject one paradigm is always simultaneously the decision to accept another, and the judgement leading to that decision involves the comparison of both paradigms."[63] The transition to a new paradigm "is likely to occur only when the first tradition is felt to have gone badly astray."[64] All the available evidence about the state of developing societies suggests that the old system of organizing and governing the societies is no longer viable if the objective is to become modern progressive societies. In this context, it is useful to draw lessons from the scientific field regarding the process involved in the shift of paradigms. The similarities are noteworthy:

The transition from a paradigm in crisis to a new one from which a new tradition of normal science can emerge is far from a cumulative process, one achieved by an articulation or extension of the old paradigm. Rather it is a reconstruction that changes some of the field's most elementary theoretical generalizations as well as many of its paradigm methods and applications. During the transition period there will be a large but never complete overlap between the problems that can be solved by the old and by the new paradigm. *But there will also be a decisive difference in the modes of solution.* When the transition is complete, the profession will have changed its view of the field, its methods, and its goals. One perceptive historian, viewing a classic case of a science's reorientation by paradigm change, . . . described it as "picking up the other end of the stick", a process that involves "handling the same bundle of data as before, but placing them in a new system of relations with one another by giving them a different framework."[65]

Just as in scientific revolutions when change from one paradigm to another takes place, modernization is not achieved by merely extending the past with cosmetic changes into the present. Modernization means transformation from the old paradigm to the new one, the salient features of which are observable in the more developed countries where the new paradigm has faced history for a considerable period of time and is therefore well tested. In the process, the paradigm has also revealed its weaknesses which seem to be remediable.

Modernization does not mean merely tinkering with the path already being followed by the developing countries. It means the *transformation* of political, social, economic, intellectual, religious, and psychological systems. Transformation does not always mean the destruction of the past. Transformation is more subtle and more difficult than the destruction of the past, *and yet it is no less radical.* Modernization requires the willingness and ability of the elites to bring about the necessary changes.[66]

In both scientific and political revolutions (modernization qualifies to be termed a revolution because of the nature of change involved), the prime requirement is the awareness that "existing institutions have ceased adequately to meet the problems posed by an environment that they have in part created."[67] Just as scientific revolutions require the commitment and persistence of the scientists, modernization, to be successful, requires the honesty, commitment, and persistence of the ruling elites who exercise direct control on political resources,[68] which have profound impact on the social and economic systems.[69] "Resources have their origin in the *activities* and *attitudes* of members of the political community," and they derive their value from their scarcity and productivity.[70]

In the utilization of resources, regimes must make choices in the following policy areas: to cope with social and economic changes; to induce social and economic change; to remain in authority in both the present and the future; and to construct political and administrative infrastructure.[71] Many of the policies may be incompatible, and therefore choices must be made which serve as power constraints in the operations of a regime. Yet, in the final analysis, it is the elite's "conception of social and political causality [which] affects all choices," and it is the clarity of this conception or vision which influences a government's use of resources to induce change.[72] In addition, the less the regime is concerned with staying in power, the more likely that the regime's actions will be creative rather than reactive.[73] This makes a strong case for such political processes and institutions that ensure a smooth transfer of power so that incumbents are preoccupied not about staying in power, but about implementing progressive policies. The issue of what is progressive and what is regressive cannot be resolved here. Suffice it to say that it will depend on the vision of the people who run the affairs of the state and the people who form the society.

In order to satisfactorily deal with the changes attendant to the processes of modernization, a regime must continuously expand the political resources at its disposal. An important source for this purpose is what Lars Björk has termed the use of "cognitive images," which "underscores the importance of stakeholder participation in the change process."[74] Cognitive imaging operates both internally and externally, whether in an organization like a university or in a society or a country. It involves a shift in outlook among people which enables them to view the organization in a new way for themselves and, equally important, for the people external to the organization.[75] Björk explains the processes involved in cognitive imaging thus:

Creating the cognitive image of the future organization is a crucial element in gaining internal and external support for change and, as a social process, involves enlisting the support of individuals within the task environment, persuading them to share a similar view . . . , and translating that image into action. . . . Individuals who become associated with the social construction of the organization's cognitive image contribute to its viability. They provide information about the internal and external task environment, contribute to shaping the image, add to its legitimacy, assist in mobilizing support, confirm the correctness of the transformation decision, and continue to support the new public face created.[76]

In societies where governments encounter strong opposition and often fear the antagonism of religious functionaries or other vested interests that do not tolerate disturbing the status quo, the prime need is not to isolate such groups, but to win their support. Such support would require, first, the demonstration in practical terms that material benefits will be forthcoming to anyone who participates in the development process.[77] While in the initial stages of development the resources or wealth of a nation may be limited, the image and commitment of the government would be required that it sincerely follows the dictates of equity. "Economic growth and equity in sharing its fruits should be considered as complementary rather than conflicting objectives. Common sense requires that the claims of growth and equity be balanced."[78]

EVALUATING DEVELOPMENT AND ECONOMIC GROWTH

It is erroneous to confuse development with economic development and economic development with economic growth. Experience indicates not only that economic growth may fail to solve social and political difficulties but also that certain types of growth can actually cause them.[79] In the developing countries, in the initial period of economic growth those who benefit handsomely from the existing economic structure usually develop a vested interest in maintaining the system which is neither efficient nor suitable for rapid future growth. To achieve this, they solidify their control of the political system by joining forces with powerful groups in the country like landowners, religious leaders, and senior civil and military officials. In such a system, the rich become richer while the poor proliferate. The wealthy, in their shortsightedness, exhibit no real interest in change or development.[80]

The underlying notion behind the concept of development is "the realization of the potential of human personality";[81] and the ultimate aim of development is to increase total welfare.[82] What is often not realized is that "the social barriers and inhibitions of an unequal society distort the personalities of those with high incomes no less than of those who are poor."[83]   Economists have generally tended to evaluate economic growth in terms of gross national product (GNP), which is a highly suspect measure when evaluated in the context of developing countries. Growth in GNP is no indication that real development has taken place. The important question to be asked is how the national product is used, that is, who has benefited?[84]

In evaluating development, both the measures suggested by Dudley Seers and the arguments he advances are telling:

> The questions to ask about a country's development are . . . : What has happened to poverty? What has been happening to unemployment? What has been happening to inequality? If all three of these have declined from high levels, then beyond doubt this has been a period of development for the country concerned. If one or two of these central problems have been growing worse, especially if all three have, it would be strange to call the result "development", even if per capita income doubled.[85]

Seers rightly questions the validity of the classical economic argument that inequality is necessary to generate savings and incentives and thus to promote economic growth. When gross disparities exist between income distributions, the potential for savings is, in any case, low. A major obstacle to development in the underdeveloped countries is the high consumption levels of the rich whose "personal savings often flow abroad or go into luxury housing and other investment projects of low or zero priority for development."[86] Simon Kuznets advocates structural changes if economic growth is to take place: we cannot be certain of the extent to which economic growth by itself can modify political structure and the direction of change.[87]   Based on an historical analysis of economic growth, he argues that growth in any epoch is not only one of aggregate change but also one of structural change, which means substantial change in the way a society is organized. Political instability, authoritarian regimes, and an authoritarian structure that rests on familial and ethnic ties and the police are not the conditions under which economic growth can take place. Political structures and economic activity are interrelated. If a society's patterns of social and economic life are the same as those of the past in which modern economic growth, by definition, was absent, social and political structures will have to change before modern economic growth can take place.[88]

3

RELIGION AND MODERNIZATION

Historically, religion has played a major role in integrating societies; it has also been used to prevent change and to maintain the status quo, thereby limiting or thwarting progress. It has a powerful influence on the development process, both positive and negative, depending on a particular religious doctrine and how it is interpreted, disseminated, and applied.[1] In the following discussion we examine the role of religion in the modernization process, and to that end first make an assessment of the major religions of the world. Then we examine the role of religion in the Western experience of development and modernization, which can provide us useful lessons and help substantiate some of the arguments presented in this study.

In discussing the role of religion in societies, Donald Eugene Smith concludes that "it is widely, and correctly, assumed that religion is in general an obstacle to modernization."[2] This conclusion is seriously flawed. In considering the influence of religion in a society, it seems, much would depend on what a particular religion advocates or is based on. For instance, Judaism, Christianity, and Islam, which belong to the same tradition with much in common and have, at their core, a similar worldview, are likely to have a different impact on the modernization or development process than the Indic religions (Hinduism and Buddhism), which have a totally different worldview. Although societies can develop or modernize, in the material sense, without any religion, the issue is far deeper when it is viewed at the individual level. The question of human alienation, which was the central basis of Marx's thought and which he mistakenly attributed to the nature of work or a particular mode of production, seems to be related to human alienation from God. Marx related religion to alienation; religion, he said, was "born out of and sustained by alienation."[3]

Smith also considers "functional-valuation pluralism" and the secularization of polity as a basic and necessary condition for modern societies.[4] Not only is there no a priori reason for this to be so, but also we have already observed in

Chapter 2 the serious nature of the problems attendant to this approach. We will discuss it further in the context of Islam in the next chapter.

Table 3.1 presents the religious ideas and values of the major religions that are considered relevant to modernization, and that explain the importance of the nature of a religious system vis-à-vis modernization. These ideas and values are the doctrinal resources and, in some cases, the limitations of individuals subscribing to these religions.[5] However, religious ideas and values, howsoever progressive they might be, are by themselves no guarantee that a particular society will move forward or develop. Religious values and ideas provide broad guidelines, and although the contents of a particular religious system are of fundamental importance since they contain the seeds of development or destruction, in the last analysis, for the religious systems which are deemed to be progressive, it is the people who subscribe to those values and who interpret them one way or another in a particular historical era who are the ultimate arbiters of what becomes of those ideas and values. It is for this reason that the existence of a tolerant intellectual environment, in which it is possible to critically evaluate and interpret those values, ideas and practices which become established over a period of time, becomes of critical importance.

Religion has had a profound impact on human civilization. Human progress, wherever it has occurred, owes a heavy debt to the inspiration provided by religious ideas.   Samuel S. Cohen elaborates on the role of religion in development in the following manner:

. . . religion has been the axis on which civilization has turned. It has built empires and it has also torn them down. In its purity it has been the torchbearer and the vanguard of progress, the inspiration of the arts and sciences, and the life-breath of morality. When put into the service of bigotry, religion has been the scourge of humanity, the stumbling block of science, and the death knell of searching intellect.[6]

Religion provides meaning to life, and in the life of a person "meaning is constituted in the context of relations" to other people.[7] In the day-to-day life of a person, one has to make conscious choices:

Freedom of choice between good and evil, the ability to plan conduct according to a hierarchy of importance, cannot originate in the autonomous individual in autonomous situations. The choices are always "bound" and "transcendent" . . . .

The social proto-form of religion is determined by its fundamental function: to bestow meaning upon individual existence. . . . It is the condition for socialization, for the emergence of the person from the animal organism.[8]

When a society becomes segmented into more or less autonomous institutions like those of religion, politics, and economics (modern society), "the norms within the domains become increasingly 'rationalized,' i.e., determined by the functional requirements of the institution as such." Because of the autonomous

Table 3.1

Religious Ideas and Values Relevant to Modernization

Elements of Worldview	Hinduism	Buddhism	Judaism	Catholicism	Islam
I. The World					
A. Reality of world	*Ultimately unreal*	*Ultimately unreal*	*Real*	*Real*	*Real*
	Metaphysically unreal in dominant philosophical tradition	All existence is impermanent and substanceless.	World is created by God and is real.	World is created by God and is real.	World is created by God and is real.
B. Religious value of the material	*Ambivalent*	*Not valued*	*Valued*	*Not valued*	*Valued*
	Strong emphasis on renunciation of material things, but wealth and pleasure valid at certain stage of life.	Renunciation of material things necessary for serious religious life (in monastic order).	Wealth not incompatible with religious goals.	Strong emphasis on renunciation and asceticism. Rewards in the next life.	Wealth not incompatible with religious goals.
C. Significance of history	*Not significant*	*Not significant*	*Decisive*	*Significant*	*Decisive*
	History is cyclical, without significance, and ultimately unreal.	Metaphysically, similar to Hinduism. In practice, history taken more seriously.	A certain pattern of life must be established on earth. History moves toward divine culmination.	History moves toward divine culmination, but a person's highest fulfillment is in heaven.	A certain pattern of life must be established on earth. History moves toward divine culmination.

Table 3.1 (continued)

Elements of Worldview	Hinduism	Buddhism	Judaism	Catholicism	Islam
II. The Individual					
A. Reality of individual	*Illusory*	*Temporary*	*Eternal*	*Eternal*	*Eternal*
	Perception of individual existence based on ignorance. Salvation is absorption into Absolute, ending cycle of rebirth.	Cycle of rebirth. Nirvana achieved with extinction of the ego.	Each individual is created an eternal soul.	Each individual is created an eternal soul.	Each individual is created an eternal soul.
B. Spiritual equality	*Unequal*	*Equal*	*Equal*	*Equal*	*Equal*
	Individuals are inherently unequal, can progress spiritually through successive existences.	Individuals essentially equal, although conditioned by karma.	Spiritual equality of all souls.	Spiritual equality of all souls.	Spiritual equality of all souls.
C. Freedom—determinism	*Determinism*	*Freedom*	*Freedom*	*Freedom*	*Freedom*
	Individual action strongly conditioned by karma, but some freedom remains.	Strong emphasis on individual freedom and self-reliance despite doctrine of karma.	Emphasis on moral responsibility of the individual.	Emphasis on moral responsibility of the individual.	Emphasis on moral responsibility of the individual.

III. The Social Order

A. Divine pattern of society	*Divine pattern* — Divinely ordained caste order.	*No pattern provided* — Absence of detailed social regulations.	*Divine pattern* — Total society theoretically regulated by sacred laws.	*Divine pattern* — Integralist concepts of Catholic society, rooted in medieval period.	*Divine pattern* — Total society theoretically regulated by sacred laws.
B. Egalitarianism—hierarchical	*Hierarchical* — Rigidly hierarchical caste system, based on inherent inequality and degrees of ritual purity.	*Egalitarian* — Egalitarian assumptions, but not highly developed as positive principle of society.	*Egalitarian* — Strong emphasis on equality of believers.	*Hierarchical* — Hierarchical concepts in papal encyclicals until recently.	*Egalitarian* — Strong emphasis on equality of believers.

IV. The Political Order

A. Religious and political structures	*Differentiation* — Rulers and priests belong to different castes. But ruler is a divinity.	*Differentiation* — Roles of ruler and monk very different. But ruler is semidivine (future Buddha).	*Fusion* — Fusion of temporal and spiritual authority.	*Differentiation* — Strong corporate identity of church separate from ruler.	*Fusion* — Fusion of temporal and spiritual matters. Qur'an is the only spiritual authority.
B. Theory of clericalism (clerical domination of polity)	*No clerical theory* — No priestly challenge to ruler's power.	*No clerical theory* — None in Theravada countries, but such theory does exist in Lamaist Buddhism of Tibet.	*No clerical theory* — No theory of rule by rabbis.	*Strong clerical theory* — Tradition of papacy as temporal power. Papal states in Italy until 1870.	*No clerical theory* — Clerics not authorized.

Table 3.1 (continued)

Elements of Worldview	Hinduism	Buddhism	Judaism	Catholicism	Islam
V. Religious Truth and Authority					
A. nature of knowable truth	*Pluralist, relative* Each worshipper chooses his/her God. The absolute is unknowable.	Unitary but proximate Buddha professed agnosticism on various major metaphysical questions.	*Absolute* Revealed truth is final and perfect, although process of revelation continues.[a]	*Absolute* Revealed truth is final and perfect, although process of revelation continues.	*Absolute* Revealed truth is final and perfect.
B. Doctrinal development	*Unlimited doctrinal change* No credal norms exist to limit change, but doctrinal innovating produces only new sects.	*Static* Neither theory nor tradition of doctrinal development.	*Doctrinal change valid* Doctrinal development has occurred over the ages and continues.	*Doctrinal change valid* Since church is the infallible authority, doctrinal development continues through popes and councils.	*Doctrine is irrevocable but reinterpretation possible* Little change since medieval times.
VI. The Ecclesiastical Institution					
A. Internal corporate raison d'etre	*No corporate concept* No coherent ecclesiastical organization exists.	Strong corporate concept Sangha has a clear and self-contained reason for its existence. Exists to facilitate quest for Nirvana, totally apart from society or its needs.	*Weak corporate concept* Rabbis have no ecclesiastical authority except as expounders of the law—adminis-tration of law and education	*Strong corporate concept* Church has a clear self-contained raison d'ere. The sacramental life of church a religious end in itself, apart from relationship to society.	*Weak corporate concept* No one has ecclesiastical authority. Administration of law and education is state's responsibility.

B. External concept of clergy	No generalized concept	Extreme veneration	Respect	Extreme veneration	Clergy not authorized
	Some holy men worshiped but many not respected. Temple priests have low prestige.	Sangha venerated and worshiped as one of the Three Gems, along with the Buddha and Dharma (teaching).	Rabbis respected for their knowledge and piety but not venerated.	Pope is vicar of Christ, and all priests share his supernatural sacramental powers. Church is divine institution.	

ªThere are conflicting views on this point. See, for instance, Baeck (pp. 9, 14), op. cit., William E. Kaufman, *Contemporary Jewish Philosophies* (New York: Reconstructionist Press and Behrman House, 1976), p. 7, and Frederick S. Plotkin, *Judaism and Tragic Theology* (New York: Schocken Books, 1973), p. 4.

Sources: Adapted from Donald Eugene Smith, *Religion and Political Development* (Boston: Little, Brown, 1970), pp. 21-23; Philip S. Bernstein, *What the Jews Believe* (New York: Farrar Straus and Young, 1951); Leo Baeck, *The Essence of Judaism* (New York: Schocken Books, 1967); S. G. F. Brandon, ed., *A Dictionary of Comparative Religion* London: Weidenfeld and Nicolson, 1970), pp. 378-385; Milton Steinberg, *Basic Judaism* (New York: Harcourt, Brace and Co. 1947); H. Graetz, *History of the Jews* (Philadelphia: Jewish Publications Society of America, 1902); Samuel S. Cohen, *What We Jews Believe* (Cincinnati: Union of Synagogue and School Extension, 1931); Charles J. Adams, *A Reader's Guide to the Great Religions* 2nd ed. (New York: Free Press, 1977), pp. 283-344.

nature of institutions, norms become rational only in relation to them and therefore become "restricted in supra-institutional relevance."[9] And because the validity of ideas become relative, the structure of the worldview cracks and loses cohesion, for it juggles with ideas which are incompatible with one another.[10] In this operating environment, the individual lacks a coherent meaning of life and is provided with, at best, a very limited perception of life in which to operate.

THE STRUGGLES AGAINST RELIGION IN THE WEST

One of the main issues involved in the question of religion and modernization is the relationship between what has been termed in the West as "church and state,"[11] or between the religious establishment and the state when the issue is examined in the context of the world situation. The issue was given institutional recognition, and the separation legitimacy, most clearly through the American Constitution, keeping in view the peculiarly American situation. The separation of religion and state does not mean, however, that religion loses its validity and relevance and a critical evaluation on that score, although often that is how it is generally interpreted. Even in the field of science, religion retains its relevance, albeit religion not in the sense of rituals or dogma. Albert Einstein observed that there is such ordered regularity in the universe that there is no room for arbitrariness or causes of a different nature. A crucial and an all-important element of true religion is the faith, often not understood or recognized, that the regulations which govern the world of existence are rational and comprehensible to reason. As he put it, "I cannot conceive of a genuine scientist without that profound faith. The situation may be expressed by an image: science without religion is lame, religion without science is blind."[12] Einstein also warned that a teaching which suggests divine intervention in human affairs would not only be unworthy but also fatal.[13] If evidence for such a statement is required, the past several centuries of Muslim history provide incontrovertible proof. We will examine the issue in the next chapter.

Religion came under vigorous critical scrutiny in the West at the beginning of the sixteenth century, although the origin of the skeptical tradition dates back to the twelfth century when "the form of Averroes began to assume those gigantic proportions, which, at a later period, overshadowed the whole intellect of Europe."[14] However, almost at the same time, religious persecution became a major activity in Europe. At the beginning of the thirteenth century, Innocent III instituted the Inquisition with a call to princes to suppress heresy; in the fourteenth century, executions for heresy took place in many countries of Europe.[15] With the revival of Latin literature in Europe in the twelfth century, a feeling of doubt challenged credulity, and a curiosity for secular knowledge replaced in a small measure the prevalent passion for theology. The torpor of the preceding several centuries was replaced by a feeling of restless anxiety, a sense that something was wrong. Although orthodoxy suppressed many heresies, in each succeeding century they emerged with greater force and consistency.[16] Until then, Europe had no tradition of independent inquiry; Europe had learned to doubt in the twelfth century, yet doubt was not regarded as innocent. "The Church had cursed the human intellect by cursing the doubts that are the necessary consequence of its exercise. She had cursed even the moral faculty by asserting the guilt of honest error."[17]

With the revival of philosophy and growth of knowledge in the physical sciences, there emerged an intellectual atmosphere which grew increasingly hostile to the Church. The Church, however, was sternly inflexible. "Rebellion and doubt were, in her eyes, the greatest of all crimes; and her doctrine of evil spirits and of the future world supplied her with engines of terrorism which she was prepared to employ to the [utmost]."[18] In the fifteenth and sixteenth centuries, trials for witchcraft reached their climax; Europe was terror-stricken and in anarchy. It was the Reformation that eventually stemmed the rot. The Reformation created a multitude of churches where the spirit of qualified and partial skepticism which had often given rise to anarchy could exist with freedom and order. The Reformation rejected an immense array of dogmatic and ritualistic conceptions, which in the previous centuries had become the hallmark of Christianity. The Reformation, above all, diminished the power and influence of the clergy and thus paved the way for the development of the European intellect.[19]

The virtues of dogma were so ingrained in the minds of people by the ceaseless teaching of over twelve centuries that it required several centuries to weaken its hold over people. For a long time there was no realization in the Christian world that reason should be applied to theology, in the same way as in any other discipline. Faith was always presented as an abnormal intellectual condition, which required the suspension of the critical faculties.[20] In that age "doubt was almost universally regarded as criminal and error as damnable; yet the first was the necessary condition, and the second the probable consequence, of enquiry."[21] In that era, theology was the leading discipline and was infested with an incredible credulity that permeated all forms of thought. It was not until the seventeenth century that the preeminence of theology was arrested. The great secular writers of the age introduced a love of impartiality and free research that reached theology via natural science and metaphysics. Its result was that it destroyed or weakened some of theology's pronouncements. The philosophers of the seventeenth century taught people not to be credulous and to overcome their prejudices; they taught people to scrutinize their belief and to distrust the verdicts of the past; they taught, above all, love of truth for its own sake. "It was between the writings of Bacon and Locke that Chillingworth taught, for the first or almost the first time in England, *the absolute innocence of honest error*."[22]

Skepticism made wide inroads in the socially and politically influential classes of Italy, Germany, France, and England as a result of the Enlightenment.[23] Political conditions in Italy in the midfifteenth century were rather unique. Italy consisted of principalities, many of which were politically independent. The Church had a political entity—the central states of Italy were controlled by the Church. In addition, Italian cities and states were experiencing constant intervention from the outside. The emperor, who was a German, claimed suzerainty over Italy since theoretically he was a Roman ruler. If that was not enough, the kings of France and Spain also intervened in Italian affairs. The papacy, corrupt as it was, also had direct impact on Italian politics. The religious professions of the rulers of the Church and their actual conduct were contradictory to the extreme. All of them, for instance, had bastard children. While this contrast has always existed in every society in almost every age, "at no time in human history has it been greater than during the Italian renaissance."[24] In the middle of the fifteenth century, the Church was seething with corruption.

From the twelfth century onward, popes and Christian emperors and kings were embroiled in a long controversy over who possessed ultimate authority in a state. In 1516 Martin Luther, a professor of theology at the University of Würtemberg, Germany, began his lectures on St. Paul's Epistles to the Romans. The Epistles which he discussed and criticized included Romans 9 to 16 of Chapter 13:1-8, which essentially taught people to be subservient to rulers, be they emperors, kings, or popes; they taught people to be fearful of rulers and to pay dues to them; they taught, above all, that the powers of the rulers were ordained by God and therefore could not be challenged. The rulers were, therefore, free to do what they desired.[25]

The above-mentioned verses had been the subject of intense debate before 1516. In Italy, Machiavelli was well aware of them. He had seen how kings and popes alike had derived self-serving meanings from them no matter what happened to the state. He was fully aware how in his own time religion was being exploited for political purposes at the cost of the welfare of the state.

Later, in Europe, the verses from Romans became the source of "one of the most vigorous and penetrating controversies of all time over the nature, the source, the extent, and the limits of political authority, the obligations and rights of subjects, and the power and responsibilities of rulers."[26]

Within a year after his lectures of 1516, Martin Luther challenged the pope's right to issue indulgences. Within four years he refused to obey the pope, rejected all of his authority, and burned the volumes of canon law. A year later he stood before the Holy Roman Emperor, the chief prince of Christendom, and other assembled rulers at Worms, Germany. "There, charged with disobedience and asked to revoke his pamphlets, he asserted the sovereignty of his conscience against all the 'higher powers,' temporal or spiritual."[27]

Machiavelli's political outlook was strongly influenced by his observations of

Italian Renaissance politicians. In explaining how Machiavelli viewed religion and politics, Mulford Q. Sibley has argued that, although Machiavelli completely separates politics from religion and morality, it "does not mean that there is or ought to be no morality in politics but rather that he assumes politics to have a morality peculiar to itself."[28] It is not clear, however, how politics can have a morality of its own. To say that politics should have a morality of its own is to say that it should not have any morality since morality has, after all, been historically gleaned from religion. Although Machiavelli acknowledged the importance of religion, for him it was merely a political weapon; hence his advice to rulers to at least have the appearance of being religious.[29]

Machiavelli considered the division of Italy into many principalities and the decline of military discipline as the main causes for the ills of Italy, and for both of these he held the Christian religion responsible. The papacy was neither so strong that it could hold its dominion over all the states of Italy, nor so weak that any single state could bring about the unification of Italy, since the papacy was always able to seek outside help to perpetuate its rule or to prevent any state or principality from getting stronger.[30]

Machiavelli's thought has had enormous impact on Western political thought. Ernst Cassier has viewed the modern Western world as an outgrowth of Machiavelli's political thought; as Machiavelli desired, the state is now autonomous and has severed its connection with religion or metaphysics and, as a consequence, ethics.[31] Leo Strauss is of the opinion that the substance of Machiavelli's thought is universal and not merely Florentine or Italian. He forcefully argues that Machiavelli was a teacher of evil and that his teaching is immoral and irreligious:

They [scholars] are satisfied that Machiavelli was a friend of religion because he stressed the useful and the indispensable character of religion. They do not pay any attention to the fact that his praise of religion is only the reverse side of what one might provisionally call his complete indifference to the truth of religion . . . they misinterpret Machiavelli's judgement concerning religion, and likewise his judgement concerning morality, because they are pupils of Machiavelli . . . they do not see the evil character of his thought because they are the heirs of the Machiavellian tradition; because they, or the forgotten teachers of their teachers, have been corrupted by Machiavelli.[32]

In the eighteenth-century Enlightenment, religion was viewed as irrelevant or even an obstacle to progress. Edward Gibbon saw a cause-and-effect relationship between the rise of Christianity and the fall of the Roman Empire. Some of the French philosophers thought that "religion obstructed the progress of knowledge, social justice, and international peace, and even contaminated morals."[33]

The indictment against religion in the West was the joint effort of the French philosophers, English deists, German professors and Italian anticlericals. It was based on three main points. First, "By their fruits ye shall know them, and the fruits were mostly rotten." Voltaire felt that the Church had historically been the enemy of intellectual progress; he considered "Christianity (including Protestantism) to be the great foe of western civilization, promoting superstition instead of reason, war instead of peace."[34] Second, Christian credentials were questioned, which dated back to the Middle Ages when the imposture theory was propounded. This theory held that religion was born because of man's desire to dominate: "Battening on men's ignorance and fears, impostors (priests and tyrants) invented religion to 'lull to sleep the people in fetters'."[35] Third, the indictment questioned the authenticity of the bible.[36] Although the Enlightenment was, on the whole, anti-Christian, it was not antireligious.

The philosophers of the Enlightenment argued that faith was not necessary to believe in a Supreme Being and that reason itself clearly demonstrated the existence of a Supreme Being. They emphasized the dignity of humans rather than their wretchedness, and in doing so they "rendered the Christian doctrine of Atonement superfluous . . . . Salvation was by works, not by faith."[37] This seems to be a more powerful reason for the development of the West than Weber's thesis of the sanctification of the profit motive. The Enlightenment shifted the focus on God in human affairs to humans and thereby produced a major breakthrough in human thought. It placed power squarely in human hands and created the powerful belief that people had the capacity to carve out their own destiny and that mankind had the capacity to grow in virtue. It inculcated the spirit of rationality and made people aware of learning lessons from the laws of nature which could empower them to harness nature so as to create a great kingdom of mankind on earth, morally and intellectually better than what had been before. It was a mighty faith, and although it was partly derived from the humanism of the Renaissance, it differed substantially from it. The humanism of the Renaissance had believed that fate ruled half or more than half of human actions. "But the Enlightenment proposed to take fate by the throat and eliminate it from human affairs except for certain unavoidable vicissitudes of personal life and the final intrusion of death."[38]

The Enlightenment thus gave birth to the idea of progress and with it to secularism. It rejected the pessimistic and providential view of history that had been widely prevalent in Christian circles for over a millennium: that both nature and mankind were decaying from that pristine state in which God had created them. Galileo denied theologians the right to interfere in matters about which they had no knowledge; Bacon refused to give to faith things that were not faith's; John Locke acknowledged that divine revelation was a matter of faith, "but whether it be a divine revelation or no, reason must judge"; Pierre Bayle (1647-1706), who was called the "advocate-general of the *philosophes* by Voltaire," hated priestcraft more than atheism and found prevalent conceptions of religion to be morally wanting.[39] The above is only a small sampling from scores of philosophers who were highly critical of religion and found it to be interfering with human progress. Their criticisms were, of course, confined mainly to Christianity. One of the main points to note here is the exercise of the critical faculty. With such widespread and open criticism of religion and those who tended to appropriate it, the misuse of religious power was checked to a considerable extent.

In addition, beginning in 1760, theology also began to be transformed. Jacob Salomo Semler, following the Protestant principle of depending solely on the meaning of the text, investigated various texts philologically to determine the authenticity of the orthodox dogma. He found that in several cases passages of the texts had been distorted in the process of transmission. The Church Fathers, influenced by Greek philosophy, had repeatedly distorted the meaning of such texts that made the traditional dogmatics possible. This awareness led to the possibility of eliminating particularly objectionable items of dogma. The new critical theology also frankly acknowledged the possibilities of corruption in texts through historical circumstances. It recognized that dogmatic analysis of word-meaning leads to insoluble controversies, and it provided an all-important insight that "the sense of a text can be made clear only from the situation in which it was written. Thereby the spirit of the times and . . . the . . . peoples must also be taken into consideration."[40]

Hegel devoted a considerable portion of his work to the question of religion. Although he was concerned primarily with speculative thought for which Marx took him to task, and although his philosophy of religion is questionable, his writings provided food for thought for theology in two important ways:

First, that a mere unthinking faith is not truly a faith at all: to accept the myths and symbols of religion on a superficial and literal level without understanding their content is to possess merely a "blind" faith that is really dehumanizing, for man has the capacity to think, and it is only through the use of that capacity that man can attain a rational faith . . . .

Secondly, . . . what Hegel did achieve . . . was to recognize the extremely narrow restrictions that had been imposed on Christian symbolism, even to the point where its truth had been lost: he recognized that Christianity had been turned into what Tillich calls an "unbroken mythological" religion, that is, one in which the myths and symbols are taken to be literal; and having recognized this restrictiveness, Hegel broke free from it.[41]

Hegel attacked revealed religion. Throughout his life he was preoccupied with the concepts of freedom and reason, and he felt that religion was undermining freedom and moral autonomy. He described Judaism and Christianity as "positive religions" that are characterized "by laws and commands which, imposed upon the individual, throw him into a condition of enslavement. All that positive religion demands is mindless conformity to dead formulae. A mechanistic obedience is the inevitable result."[42] He preferred the bygone democratic states of Greeks and Romans who obeyed laws that they themselves had made. The condition of "positivity" (dogmatism) emerged not because people submitted to laws, Hegel argued, "but because they did not make their own laws." It was for this reason that the Jews lacked dynamism: "a burden of statutory commands . . . pedantically prescribed a rule for every casual action of daily life and gave the whole people the look of a monastic order."[43] Such criticisms drew attention to humans and their faculties. Religious positivity led to

loss of political freedom. As the seeds of positive religion were to grow in the teaching of institutional Church so they furthered political submission: "The Church taught men to despise civil and political freedom as dung in comparison with heavenly blessings of eternal life." Consequently Church members opted out of political life, they had no say in civil affairs and were therefore called upon to obey laws not of their making and lead a life not of their own choosing.[44]

Hegel, however, recognized the importance of religion, for it is "a means to education and (a higher) mentality." He even advocated religion as the basis of the state in the sense that a true religion would uphold individual freedom. The state must therefore be based on this principle.[45] Yet, religion is subordinate to the state because "by working at the process of government rather than by submitting to authoritarian religion man has embodied reason in the structure of law and government."[46] Hegel also saw the need for the state to serve as a check on religion because the state is aware of the objective realities:

. . . while the church and state differ in form they do not stand opposed in content, for truth and rationality are the contents of both. . . . In contrast with the Church's faith and authority in matters affecting ethical principles, rightness, laws, institutions, in contrast with the church's subjective convictions, the state is that which knows.[47]

Hegel viewed society as a "secularized civil union" and his thought contributed to the "secularization of all aspects of life, society, and religion" in the West. He argued that religion should be limited to and seek meaning in the sphere of thought.[48] In the midnineteenth century, when Germany was the center of intellectual activity in Europe, scientific materialism came to the forefront of intellectual activity. Although the scientific materialists rejected German idealism, especially Hegel's thought which was considered to be very abstract, ironically, "the formulations of scientific and dialectical materialism, both rooted in the impact Feuerbach's work had on German society in the 1840s, grew originally from deep within German idealism."[49] German philosophers Karl Vogt, Jacob Moleschott, and Ludwig Bucher made it their primary task to correct one of the greatest errors of humanity—unquestioned acceptance of and belief in authority. Approaching the matter sometimes theoretically, and even denouncing the very principle of authority, what they sought was to oppose the political and religious institutions of their time.[50]

Opposing Hegel, Feuerbach argued that an individual's conception of nature was dependent on the act of sensation that was as primary a human experience as self-consciousness.[51] What Feuerbach was pointing out was that sense experience or the reality of things was of paramount importance and that reflections were not equivalent to actual sensations as speculative philosophers tended to suggest.[52] In other words, he was drawing attention to the reality of human conditions and focused on them in real terms instead of "intellectualizing the experience of sensation" which Hegel and other idealists had been engaged in.[53] Subsequently, Marx would build on this thought. Feuerbach also pointed out that speculative philosophy was actually based on real experiences of human life, but instead of dealing with them, it transferred them "to the realm of thought and there made into a separate, ideal reality." In effect, what had happened was the intellectualizing of "the experience of human needs," which gave birth to theology: "The element of alienation, of setting something over and above man that should be man's, increases as religion comes to reflect on itself, . . . as it becomes *theology.*"[54]

The German materialists were deeply affected by Feuerbach whose views on social and political matters were directly related to his opposition to the religious ideas of the day. The scientific materialists' social view was similar to Feuerbach's and for the same reasons: "their opposition to the German religious establishment of the 1850s."[55] Feuerbach traced the origins of German materialism back to the Reformation "which took its stand against false, unreal, 'theological' authority," and he argued that Christianity no longer corresponded "to the theoretical or the practical man." As he stated, "it no longer satisfies the mind, nor does [it satisfy] the heart, for we have other interests for our heart than eternal heavenly bliss."[56] He described the "other interests" as follows: "Unbelief has taken the place of belief, reason the place of the Bible, politics the place of religion and the church, earth the place of heaven, work the place of prayer, material want the place of hell, man the place of the Christian."[57]

Scientific materialists, profoundly affected by Feuerbach, worked toward eliminating transcendence by emphasizing realism and naturalism. Natural science was associated with materialism with the message that, whereas science dealt with the real and true, the claims of tradition, whether religious or philosophical, were unproven. Discounting the claims of philosophy, Feuerbach had insisted that "there was a natural relationship between the *a priori*, authoritative, illusory and artificial categories of idealism, and the qualitatively similar justifications of religious, political, and social authority."[58] Kant had argued that "defense of God, the soul, and immortality was theoretically necessary and in practical life unavoidable." The materialists, rejecting his ideas and insisting that the senses were the ultimate source of knowledge, blamed Kantian doctrine for giving them a feeling of impotence; they regarded the spiritual to be "an epiphenomenon or even a fiction."[59] Others, however, found fault with materialism for postponing the metaphysical problems and clinging "to the closed circle of causal law, in order . . . to open its polemic against religion."[60]

Following Feuerbach, Marx wrote a stunning criticism of religion that was carried further by other Marxists. Another philosopher who figures prominently in his criticism of religion and whose thought profoundly affected the intellectual currents of the time was Nietzsche. We will consider Nietzsche first and then the Marxists together.

Nietzsche rejected absolute morality and considered all moral codes to be "systems of deportment founded on human conditions in accordance with the environmental needs of a people." He felt that all morality was subject to revision, amendment, and cancellation, and he argued that all human institutions should be open to change, given the changing conditions of societies.[61]

To be sure, serious problems plague Nietzschean philosophy, such as the denial of absolute truth, the doctrine of "perpetual recurrence," and the idea that there is no goal of life.[62] Nonetheless, his criticisms of religion were, on the whole, insightful. He praised the ability to contradict and to endure contradiction, "the attainment of *good* conscience in hostility to the accustomed, the traditional and the hallowed"; he called it "the step of all steps of the emancipated intellect."[63] Nietzsche sought to replace the commonly accepted "divine will" in human affairs with the human will, which he called the "will to power." He sought an affirmation of life instead of the rejection of life that distorted religious doctrines tended to produce.[64] He considered religion to be an impediment to human progress, and argued that development could occur only if the negative influences of religion, which had their origin in antiquity, were overcome. The prevalent religious doctrines, however, indirectly provided an impetus for development by creating the spiritual tension that needed to be conquered.[65] He protested that the prevalent Christian practices had made

a caricature of man . . . : he had become a "sinner," he was caged up, he had been imprisoned behind a host of appalling notions. He now lay there, sick, wretched, malevolent even toward himself: full of hate for the instincts of life, full of suspicion in regard to all that is still strong and happy . . . . In physiological terms: in a fight with an animal, the only way of making it weak may be to make it sick. The Church understood this: it ruined man, it made him weak, but it laid claim to having "improved" him.[66]

In the contemporary world, however, the indictment of religion qua religion, which continued for several centuries in the West, has been seriously questioned. Scholars have observed that when the "power curve" shoots up and the "spiritual curve" plummets, an explosion of sorts occurs in society. Paul Tillich pointed out that the decay of religious belief in the West has led to anxiety, despair, emptiness, and meaninglessness.[67] In the same vein, other philosophers have pointed out the "disastrous effects on civilization of the breakdown of the idea of man's creation in God's image. When this idea faded with the humanist and positivist movements of modern times . . . man lost his essential dignity, and his humanity turned into the inhumanity of modern machine-civilization."[68] Philosopher C.E.M. Joad attributed the ills of modern civilization to the denial of "objective values (truth, beauty, goodness, God) which are located in an order of reality not subject to time and space."[69] He argued that when this happens, human ego swells to such a degree that it starts imagining that "nothing is impossible to it. At the same time, however, it necessarily turns in on itself and becomes morbidly subjective, for it lacks objective standards, 'creeds and codes' by which to be guided."[70]

MARXIST ANALYSES OF RELIGION

Whatever the validity of the criticisms of religion by Marx and other Marxists who followed him, often highly questionable, they were correct in their penetrating insight that "religion *is* very largely what it *does*."[71] It immediately points out to be vigilant, first of all, about what a particular religious doctrine contains and is based on, and second, how it is interpreted, understood, disseminated, and applied. It also highlights the importance and necessity of critically examining a religious doctrine at all times which will serve as a powerful check on unwarranted and objectionable creeds creeping into it. Here again the appeal is to the primacy of human intelligence, that is, reason.

Marx laid great emphasis on human consciousness which, he argued, was directly affected by the material conditions, which were therefore vitally important. He described "the consciousness of man as the supreme divinity."[72] He called for people to examine the present state of affairs rather than to glorify the past; as he put it," without parting there is no progress."[73] And when religion "becomes a political quality, an object of politics," it must be discussed openly.[74] Marx wanted people to take matters into their own hands and not resort to a "vale of woe" which prevalent religious ideas caused them to do. People, he argued, were in a state of illusion through religion, which he designated as "the opium of the people." His criticism of heaven, he pointed out, was actually a criticism of the earth, the criticism of religion a criticism of right, and the criticism of theology a criticism of politics.[75]

Marx's criticism of religion was trenchant, and he repeatedly exhorted the German nation and the state to pay attention to the plight of their society rather than to wait for the bliss after this life:

The criticism of religion ends with the teaching that *man is the highest essence for man*, hence with the *categoric imperative to overthrow all relations* in which man is a debased, enslaved, abandoned, despicable essence, relations which cannot be better described than by the cry of a Frenchman when it was planned to introduce a tax on dogs: Poor dogs!

They want to treat you as human beings.[76]

Engels described religion as "nothing but the fantastic reflection in men's minds of those external forces which control their daily life, a reflection in which the terrestrial forces assume the form of supernatural forces." Along with the forces of nature, he argued, human beings also allowed the social forces, which were created by themselves, to dominate and control them as if they were unalterable.[77] Material conditions directly affected religious and political phenomena, and it is for this reason that they gain such an importance. Material conditions, he explained, have a profound impact on the human thought-process.[78] The Marxist critique of religion, Trevor Ling points out, is correct wherever it is maintained that priests of some kind possess a special kind of expertise to understand the true nature of people, and therefore an exceptional ability to direct their affairs. "Wherever religion is not of this disposition, the Marxist critique may be inappropriate."[79]

Marx's criticism of religion was essentially based on German Protestantism of the early nineteenth century; he felt that members of the Prussian state bureaucracy were engaged in using "theological ideas as a means of justifying the economic inequalities of their contemporary society. The Prussian state was, as Marx saw it, a committee to defend the interests of the property-owning elite. . . . this is the essence of Marx's critique of religion."[80] Marx's criticism of religion, however, was by no means objective, and his association with religion was limited and shortlived.[81] For Marx religion was the beginning of all criticism for two reasons: "First, it was the only effective means available at the time for launching a 'relentless attack' on 'existing conditions,' and second, it was of primary importance pedagogically and therapeutically for the benefit of the working class just then awakening to revolutionary activity."[82] The Young Hegelians with whom Marx was associated for some time considered the regime of Friedrich Wilhelm IV (1840) as reactionary and repressive. In the then "theoretical" Germany, religion and politics were the two major pursuits. Open criticism of the regime was impossible, however. They, therefore, attacked priestcraft to destroy the traditional religion and to smite the regime. That is why Marx said that religion was "the table of contents of theoretical struggles."[83]

Marx had noted the decline of religious authority since the time of the Protestant Reformation all over Europe, especially among the elites. But no longer was it confined to the upper classes. When the French Republican Convention of 1793 abolished Christianity as an institution of state, and subsequently when religious tests and civil and political matters of the same nature were gradually repealed all over Europe, along with the Italian movement of 1848, it indicated the direction of the popular mind in Europe. This era may be described as the "era of democratic revolt against ecclesiastical authority."[84]

Marx took pains to emphasize that human consciousness is always a social product. He considered religion to be "a mode of consciousness both false and perverted; the happiness it offers, bogus and illusory . . . . In order to progress from these irrationalities to rationality . . . religion must be abolished, its disastrous effects transcended."[85] But did Marx really understand religion apart from the fact that it had historically been abused in the social, economic, and political realms? Delos B. McKown has shown that Marx's etiology of religion is "ill-informed and illogical."[86] And Marx, Engels, Lenin, and Kautsky never addressed the issue of death, which is as important as life itself. They focused entirely on life, and ignoring death, they only attempted to understand one part of life, which cannot be understood without understanding the implications of death.[87]

Despite serious flaws in the Marxist approach and understanding of religion, it has the merit of approaching religion functionally. This approach makes it possible to study the religious phenomena objectively.[88] The Marxist critique of religion was correct in pointing out that religion must be judged on the basis of what it does to a society.

CONCLUSION

Religion is a very powerful force. It can work both positively and negatively, depending on the content of a particular religious doctrine, and its interpretation and application. It is a serious matter that requires the full exercise of human intellect. For this reason it needs to be studied and applied carefully and intelligently.

In the course of the development history of the West, religion has played a major role. Philosophers have wrestled with profound issues and have critically examined their relevance in the operations of societies. Religion hindered progress as long as it remained dogmatic, unexamined, and an exclusive domain of some people. In the process of analysis, it provided useful insights that allowed societies to move forward. The tension between religion and society at large is a healthy one and need not be deplored. It may well be that some religious doctrines are antithetical to progress or development. If this is the case, serious questions must be raised as to the validity of those doctrines. Needless to say, this presupposes a critical approach to religious doctrines and the existence of a tolerant intellectual environment in which it is possible to critically evaluate and interpret those ideas, customs, and practices that become established over a period of time.

Beyond doubt, religion becomes an obstacle to progress when it is politicized or becomes an object of politics. The same is true when the religious establishment controls or attempts to control the functioning of a society. The Western experience leaves no doubt on this score. However, secularization, as commonly understood, is not a necessary condition for development; in fact, it has very grave consequences.   The acid test of a religion is, based on its substance, how it is interpreted and applied in a given society.

4

ISLAM AND
MODERNIZATION

It has been well over a century since the conditions existing in Muslim societies became the focus of attention of some of the leading thinkers of the Muslim world. They have examined the role of the existing interpretations, conceptions, and practices attributed to Islam, and their relationship to the backward and stagnant conditions existing in Muslim societies. Muslim scholars who have examined this issue, however, have been relatively few; and their works have largely remained out of the reach of the general public; in the educational institutions, their works, important as they are, have not formed part of the curriculum. The major reason for which seems to be that the state is not aware of the serious nature and the repercussions of the issues involved; nor does it seem to care. As a result, the issue of the existing ideas attributed to Islam and their relationship to the existing conditions in the societies is not seriously discussed at all as if the problem does not exist. Ghulam Ahmad Parwez, a modernist writer of Pakistan, explains the situation thus:

The question as to why . . . [Muslims] are so down-trodden, backward, and humiliated, needs very deep thought and attention. In the first place, in Muslim societies this question is not considered worth raising collectively, and if sometimes it becomes a subject of conversation, it is either ignored or subjected to emotionalism. Those who claim monopoly of religion, get very angry on this question; and they dismiss it by saying that "such noises are raised by Westernized, materialistic, and irreligious elements of the society for whom the purpose of life is only to live in comfort and convenience; such people do not accept 'spiritualism,' and they have no concern with God and Prophet Muhammad. The true people of God have their eye on the next world, which is the real home of mankind. This world is like an inn. . . . A traveller visiting an inn never worries what kind of structure the inn has; he has to merely spend a night in the inn and move on the next morning." [1]

Such discourse is presented as Islamic education and its effect is that the people are conditioned accordingly in their conduct and in their beliefs about Islam. Parwez also points out that in many parts of the world there are large Muslim populations; most of the Muslim societies are functioning as independent countries. Their condition, as compared to the more developed countries of the world, is very weak and humiliating; they are alive at the mercy of the countries of Europe and America; most of the essential things of life are received by Muslim countries from the more developed countries of the world. Many Muslim countries receive economic aid from foreign countries. Muslim countries are located in different parts of the world; their geographical conditions are different, climates are different, modes of living are different, temperaments are different, and even languages are different. But, they have only one thing in common: they are all [supposedly] Muslim. They have one religion.[2]

The above is an accurate description of Muslim societies in the present world. The influence of the propagated religious ideas on societies is profound. Marx's conclusion that social conditions determine people's ideas seems flawed; the reverse can be equally true. Weber, agreeing with Marx that ideas do not govern people's conduct, strongly qualified the statement to the point of canceling it when he said that very frequently the world images which are created by ideas determine action.[3] The study of Islamic society is the study at root, of how religious ideas, the way they have been interpreted, advocated, and propagated, have shaped it. Weber was against monocausal theories, and his "pluralist view of causality ruled out any search for final or ultimate causes."[4] But as Bryan S. Turner has said, Weber's alternative is not compelling. Pluralist causal explanations, by rejecting attempts to establish primary causal relationships, either end up as truisms, in which everything influences everything else, or leave no way to determine if any causal relationship exists in a particular situation. The result is that explanations rarely go beyond plausible descriptions. Weber's own explanations are not of this pluralist nature. We find "a strong determinist element in Weber's explanations, particularly of Islam, which places him very close to Marx's own explanatory schema."[5]

In the case of Islamic societies, the prevailing religious ideas gain urgency and primacy in the study of these societies because "Islam is a complete code of life,"[6] and thus directly, and strongly, affects all aspects of life. It is for this reason that the explanation for the conditions of the contemporary Muslim countries need to be sought through the religious ideas prevalent in these countries. Religion thus becomes the single most important variable in the explanation of societal phenomena of Islamic countries.

Islamic societies, in the last several centuries, have themselves been the worst representatives of Islam, which has given rise to the idea that Islam is antithetical to development, that it is static. Even Kemal Ataturk of Turkey seems to have eventually reached this conclusion, or had not fully examined and understood the matter, which led to his large-scale and swift attempt to secularize Turkish society. But his conclusion, like those of many other scholars who advocated secularization as the *sine qua non* of modernization, was mistaken, as will be shown in the following section of this chapter.

In what follows in this chapter, I will attempt to show that inherently there is nothing in Islam which is against development or modernization. That, in fact, Islamic societies have been, generally, static and have not developed in the manner they should have is due essentially to the failure in understanding and application of the Qur'anic doctrine in its totality. Claims are made in the Muslim world by the ruling elites that their societies are Islamic, but when one critically scrutinizes these societies on the basis of the Qur'an, that is, its principles and guidelines, apart from noticing some rituals and traditions, one finds it extremely difficult to take the claims seriously. Thus, Jamal al-din al-Afghani pointed out that "Muslim peoples grew weak because the truth of Islam was corrupted by successive waves of falsity. . . . Muslims are weak because they are not really Muslim."[7]

Fazlur Rahman explains the problem faced by Muslim societies by pointing out that "the conventional repetition of such usual 'information' about the Qur'an as the 'Five Pillars' or the inheritance laws has kept understanding of the Qur'an at the most superficial level."[8] The most serious problem with Qur'anic scholarship, both by Muslim and non-Muslim scholars, has been that a synthetic exposition of the Qur'an has not taken place. "Most [works] deal only with certain aspects of the Qur'an, and none is rooted in the Qur'an itself. . . . None has presented the Qur'an on its own terms, as a unity . . . . "[9] And as far as Muslim scholarship on the Qur'an is concerned, it suffers from "two problems: (1) lack of a genuine feel for the relevance of the Qur'an today, which prevents presentation in terms adequate to the needs of contemporary man; but even more (2) a fear that such a presentation might deviate on some points from traditionally received opinions."[10]

Examining the condition of Muslim societies over a century ago, Syed Ameer Ali observed the following, which aptly describes even the present-day conditions of the Muslim world:

The present stagnation of . . . [Muslim countries] is principally due to the notion which has fixed itself on the minds of the generality of [Muslims], that the right to the exercise of private judgement ceased with the early legists, . . . and that a Muslim . . . should . . . abandon his judgement absolutely to the interpretations of men who lived in the ninth century, and could have no conception of the necessities of the twentieth.

. . . Canons were invented, theories started, traditions discovered, and glosses put upon [the Prophet's] words utterly at variance with their spirit. And hence it is that *most* of the rules and regulations which govern now the conscience of so many professors of the faith are hardly derived from any express and positive declarations of the [Qur'an], but for the most part from the lego-religious books with which the Islamic world was flooded in the later centuries.

. . . *"the [Muslims] have abolished the [Qur'an] in favour of the traditions and decisions of the learned"* . . . *a large part of what [Muslims] now believe and practise is not to be found in the Qur'an at all.*[11] [Emphasis added]

SEPARATION OF RELIGION AND STATE AND ISLAM

In his analysis of religion and modernization, Donald Eugene Smith argues that secularization has played a universal role in the past century and a half in the development of modern polities. Secularization in general means: (1) to separate the polity from religious ideologies and ecclesiastical structures, (2) the *expansion* of the polity to perform those regulatory functions which were previously performed by the religious establishment, and (3) to emphasize temporal goals and rational, pragmatic efforts, or secular political values.[12] The first aspect of secularization is, however, questionable insofar as it relates to separation of religious ideology from the polity. In some societies the separation of religious ideology is not only not likely to occur, but is actually harmful were it to occur. The decisive factor in the development process is the ideology or the religion itself.[13] In Turkey, for instance, Atatürk attempted radical secularization but with little success. The secular measures had a very slight impact in the countryside. The more distant the area was from the capital or from the major cities, the less chance there was that its inhabitants were even aware of the change.[14] After Atatürk's death in 1938, resistance to secularization became more noticeable in the countryside. During and immediately after the Second World War, financial hardship led to a feeling of discontent which changed people's indifference to the nonreligious outlook of the Republican People's party (RPP) to resentment against the party, which was considered antireligious. Local religious leaders and others with grievances against state officials or the RPP fanned this resentment and accused the government of imposing secularism on the population.[15]

The central idea of the social philosophy of Ziya Gökalp, the Turkish philosopher who formulated the theoretical basis of the Turkish nation-state and measures for its implementation, was the evolution, "both of society and of the factors, including religion, that determine it."[16] He argued that evolution presupposed differentiation with mutual interaction. In primitive societies, he reasoned, all institutions are based on religion, which gives them value and power. In organic societies, however, religion should be confined to institutions which are relatively spiritual. He argued that religion becomes harmful when it is extended to worldly or secular (especially material) institutions, for it prevents these institutions from adapting themselves to the necessities of life.[17]

As Ervin I. J. Rosenthal notes, Gökalp did not underrate religion as a great social force. In fact, he "proposed positive measures designed to spread its influence as a character-building element of great value for individual and society."[18] He wanted to bring all religious matters under the authority of the central government, thus making a radical departure from past practices when religious leaders had a monopoly on such matters. He attributed the decline of Islam to the confusion of perfect principles with the backwardness of judicial methods and practices, and he felt that a separation of functions would be beneficial to both fields and therefore to religion itself. He was fully aware that "people can neither entirely drop the religion they hold sacred, nor can they dispense with the necessities of contemporary civilization. Reason demands, not that one be sacrificed at the expense of the other, but that an attempt be made to reconcile the two."[19] A separation of functions does not mean relegation of religion in any manner.[20] Nor does it mean, as far as Islamic societies are concerned, that religious education be banished. On the contrary, religious education can be so meshed with secular education that each person is given the opportunity to be well conversant with the fundamentals of religion, which, in the case of Islam, means the *study* and not merely the veneration of the Qur'an which hitherto has generally been the case. This would be in keeping with the requirements of the Qur'an which does not recognize any priestly class and instead places emphasis and responsibility on the individual. Regarding this an insightful critic observes that the downfall of Muslims started when Islam became a habit with them and ceased to be a socioeconomic program of life. Their indolence and cultural decay offered a free field to priests who disguised their priesthood in the name of ulema or religious leaders. "Islam, the religion of free thought, the religion which once banished priesthood, became priest-ridden."[21]

In this context, it is interesting to make a comparison with Christianity in which a priestly class has historically existed. The Renaissance and the Enlightenment were basically attempts to free society from the power and influence of the priestly class which was getting in the way of progress or development; it eventually resulted in the separation of religion and state in the West. The separation does not mean that religion has lost its value; the basic societal values are still derived from religion. The separation has actually meant to keep the priestly class in check; at the same time, it has enabled people to question and criticize the pronouncements of this class or to ignore them whenever necessary. This has served as a powerful mechanism to ensure that the mistakes of the past are not repeated. The important point which emerges from the above is that, whereas in Christianity a priestly class exists, through the separation of religion and state its power and influence have been greatly checked. In Islam, which does not recognize any priestly class, such a class in the form of ulema or religious leaders in recent centuries has existed and continues to exert its influence.

The separation of religion and state, in the Islamic context, therefore, actually means to neutralize the power and influence of a class which has no legitimate reason, on the basis of the Qur'an, to exist in the first place. The separation does not mean that religion loses its importance. It is only to regulate the religious activity of a society in a more effective way. Separation of religion and state in the Islamic context only means, since there are no ecclesiastical structures, that the state, in order to regulate religious affairs of the society in a responsible and careful manner, creates a separate religious institution, like the Ministry of Religious Affairs which exists in some countries. But at present a serious mistake is made by the state when the Ministry of Religious Affairs is staffed and controlled by religious leaders.

Given the past history of a millennium of Islamic societies, the state needs to be very cautious that the existing religious organizations or groups, be they religious educational institutions or religious political parties, do not perceive and interpret the existence of a separate religious body to mean a free hand in religious matters, for it can lead to fanaticism. For this reason, the state's representative bodies will need to supervise and provide guidelines, especially as they relate to religious education. This seems necessary and inevitable given the historical display of gross irresponsibility and credulity by the Islamic religious functionaries and educationists. Here it is presupposed that the representatives themselves have received modern education and are fully conversant with the Qur'an. The religious institution needs to be a separate and clearly defined structure, but a structure which is counterbalanced and checked by the authority of the state, as is the case with the other institutions of state. In other words, the religious institution is to be subordinate to the state. Most importantly, the state will need to demonstrate, in order to regulate religious affairs in a constructive manner, that it is not afraid to carry out the needed reforms in the religious sphere.

The creation of such an institution presupposes that the people who come to occupy places in such a body have, like members of representative bodies, received modern education which included the study of the Qur'an; and they are open to discussion, debate, and criticism. This institution is not meant to be staffed by the traditional religious leaders or the ulema, for that would defeat the very purpose of creating such an institution. It also presupposes that for such a mechanism to develop successfully, the government is a representative one where issues, procedures, and criteria for the selection of members to the institution, and matters pertaining to the institution, can be openly discussed and resolved.[22]

In Islamic societies religion cannot be separated from everyday life, and there is no basis whatsoever for a religious class or clergy to exist. For Islam, life is an indivisible unity in which the spiritual and the mundane go together. According to Islam, life is to be lived with a spiritual attitude which sublimates all that it touches. The Qur'an recognizes neither kings nor priests.[23] What this means is that *each* individual is solely responsible to know what Islam entails. For this to occur, however, a comprehensive synthesis is to be arrived at on the Qur'anic doctrine to dispel many of the existing notions and practices which are readily explained away as Islamic. The seriousness and magnitude of the problem, insofar as it relates to the individual, is apparent from the fact that the most basic ailment of humanity has been the concept that the "average person," "the masses," are no good. They are bound to live in moral wretchedness and mental blindness, and therefore must follow the lead of those enlightened and exalted souls who alone are capable of rescuing them because they have already "made good" their humanity. While the grotesque and heinous features of the Hindu caste system are derided the world over, all societies are guilty of such practices.[24]

Instead of depending on the religious leaders who have so far considered religion as their special and exclusive domain, the need in Islamic societies is for universities to "produce scholars of the highest quality in Islamic studies, capable of interpreting Islam and presenting it as a body of thought that can meet the challenge of modern times and fulfill the requirements of a modern scientific society."[25] To carry the process further, it is essential that "the modern historical and literary criticism as current in the west must be fearlessly applied to the religious sources and to the historical literature."[26]

Although through the process of differentiation religious structures acquire a distinct appearance, it does not mean that religion loses its relevance; religion continues to exert its influence on the polity; it is only that the two spheres are well demarcated for practical purposes, that is, to avoid confusion and to regulate the two spheres effectively. In any society the dominant religion or religions are likely to exert their influence and provide the values to regulate society. Even among those countries where religion and state are supposed to be separate, there are differences in the way religion affects the political and cultural life of the society.[27] In societies where there is no separation of religion and state, religion and state interact at the symbolic, institutional, and legislational levels.[28] The need for separation of religion and state in a pluralist society like the United States arose primarily because the intention was to prevent any special relationship between the state and any of the ethniccultural groups that constitute its population. Separation is one means to assure the loyalties of the various religious and ethnic groups to the larger political system.[29] In societies where the overwhelming majority of the population subscribes to one religion, it is religion which unites the people and helps overcome cultural-ethnic differences.[30]

An intelligent and responsible discussion of religious issues must be allowed by the society; this is necessary because many of the religious practices and traditions attributed to a particular religion are often nothing more than interpretations made by some people and are therefore open to distortions from the original intent of religious injunctions; also, since different religious communities have interacted in the past several centuries, the inter-borrowing of social practices and traditions has occurred in varying degrees and forms.[31] Marx was to the point when he said that "criticism of religion is the premise of all criticism," for if one cannot openly criticize religious practices and traditions in vogue at a particular time, a substantial portion of human activity is likely to go unchecked. Moreover, since religious practices and traditions have a profound impact on every sphere of human activity, it is essential that criticism is never made a taboo. The truth or falsity of religious phenomena, like any other phenomena, must stand or fall on its own merit. Explaining the causes of the failure of Islamic societies to deal successfully with the problems of modernity, R. J. Werblowsky forcefully argues that in the Islamic case it is not the result of a genuine struggle but rather a failure to come to grips with the real challenges of modernity. The ulema are the least educated in modernity. A major cause of this failure is the impossibility in many parts of the Muslim world to discuss problems in an open and frank way. Official censorship, fear, hypocritical forms of social conservatism, and vested prejudice preclude open discussion.[32]

Islam makes no distinction between the temporal and the spiritual. That is, the two do not exist in isolation but are strongly welded together. This is so because reality cannot be understood otherwise. As Weber pointed out, when a society is organized on a secular basis, an individual's grasp of reality is very provisional, because of which a person grows tired of life. What an individual seizes is always very provisional and not definitive; therefore, death becomes a meaningless occurrence. And since death is meaningless, life becomes meaningless.[33]

Weber noted three phases in the development of secularization: "disenchantment, fragmentation and conflict between partial world-views."[34] Weber, acknowledging that rationality and bureaucratic organization had made it possible for humans to gain control over nature and effectively organize society, was very concerned about modern values, social consciousness, and the subjective experience of a rational society. Because of secularization, Weber argued, the social and private world had become fundamentally meaningless. While rational organization, scientific knowledge, and legal codification can provide us with appropriate means to achieve temporal goals, they cannot help us choose between absolute values or between competing goals.[35]

Weber noted that modern Western society, due to advance of science and the specialization of knowledge in different fields, postulated "countless world-views and interpretations of reality, but precisely because these interpretations are infinite, they cannot lay claim to any absolute value."[36] The result was that there was "no longer any natural or inevitable boundaries for an individual's life";[37] in other words, just because an individual's life became limitless, it became a life lived in a vacuum, so to speak. Weber also reasoned that, whereas rational capitalism was an outgrowth of Protestantism, it would no longer be confined to the Protestant worldview. Paradoxically, it was Protestantism which had made the demarcation between the sacred and the secular, and in doing so it had written its own death-warrant.[38]

Shorn of any ultimate values, capitalism would grow, Weber argued, without any intrinsic meaning. Economic activities would become self-propelled without any need for legitimation or religious meaning. Capitalism, left to itself, produces a society that is run by machinelike rational procedures without any intrinsic meaning. Secularization is the social product of capitalism and Protestantism. Capitalism, with rationalization as its base, produces institutional and cultural differentiation, leading to specialization in different social spheres. While social life as a whole becomes more calculable, each sphere of life such as politics, economics, religion, and morality becomes autonomous. The resultant institutional changes transform human experience in which the individual is forced to make choices between values which are partial and shifting. This leads to an existential crisis in terms of the meaning of life. Since values lack an authoritative base, choices are ultimately arbitrary and irrational. In a secular society, religion is confined to interpersonal rather than public relations.[39]

Modernization and development in the West has led many scholars to conclude that secularization is the *sine qua non* for development to occur anywhere. Weber, Peter L. Berger, and Alasdaire MacIntyre, for instance, have related secularization to industrialization. In other words, industrialization is not possible without a society becoming secular, or it is the secularization of a society which paves the way for industrialization. But, as Bryan Turner observes, we can distinguish between secularization as the outcome of basically economic changes in Western Europe and secularization as a state policy enforced by the state in Russia, Eastern Europe and China. Therefore, as far as the process of secularization is concerned, it must be treated with suspicion.[40] In addition, we must also explain the tenacious persistence of religion in Eastern Europe and Russia during the communist rule.[41]

In Islamic societies, far-reaching changes will undoubtedly be required in the traditional approach and understanding of Islam, and in those practices which have been wrongly attributed to Islam. This does not mean that the societies need to or will become secular in order to continue the evolutionary process of development. In this context, Muhammad Iqbal has forcefully argued that in Islam the spiritual and the temporal are not two distinct and independent domains. The nature of an act, no matter how secular, is determined by the attitude of mind behind the act. It is the invisible mental background which ultimately determines the character of an act. Islam is a single indivisible reality. This point is extremely important and far-reaching. The ancient mistake was made when the unity of man was broken into two distinct and separate realities which somehow have a point of contact, but which in reality are opposed to each other. In truth, however, matter is spirit in space-time reference. In Islam, it is the state's responsibility to transform the ideal principles of equality, solidarity, and freedom into space-time forces and to realize them in a definite human organization. The ultimate reality, according to the Qur'an, is spiritual, and it must manifest itself in temporal activity. The spirit finds its opportunity to operate in the natural, the material, and the secular. "All that is secular is therefore sacred in the roots of its being. . . . The State according to Islam is only an effort to realize the spiritual in a human organization."[42]

The purpose of religion, Iqbal further explains, is to have a direct impact on life. Religion is essentially a mode of living and is the only serious way of handling reality. It serves as a check on our concepts of philosophical theology, or at least it makes us suspicious of the purely rational process through which these concepts are formed.[43] Religion "in its higher manifestations is neither dogma, nor priesthood, nor ritual."[44] It is religion alone when grasped in its totality, which can provide value and meaning to the material conditions of life. It is directly concerned with the life processes. Otherwise, it has no meaning except that it can be used as a license to do evil and then seek "salvation" through prayers or by observing some religious ceremonies or rituals. In other words, spiritualism by itself is as bankrupt as the lack of it, or secularism.

The Qur'an is geared toward the practicalities of life and declares itself to be the most comprehensive guidance for mankind, both assuming and subsuming earlier revelations. The Qur'an, from the time of its revelation, had a practical and political application. It was not meant to be merely a devotional or personal pietistic text. The Prophet Muhammad's actions were devoted entirely to the moral improvement of people rather than to the private and metaphysical.[45]

The Qur'an is fundamentally concerned with the conduct of humans. It repeatedly emphasizes that no real morality is possible without the regulative ideas of God and the Last Judgment. Their very moral function requires that they exist for the regulation of life and cannot be intellectual postulates merely to be "believed in."[46] Later medieval Islam, in the form of Sufism (mysticism) made God the exclusive object of experience instead of deriving values from this experience to regulate the social world. Medieval Christian theology, on the other hand, was concerned primarily with certain doctrinaire issues related to God and did not go beyond them;[47] yet it had the effect of sharpening human intellect when philosophers confronted and debated politico-theological issues, which subsequently paved the way for material progress in the West, as noted in the previous chapter. But in opting for secularism, the West, in effect, made material progress meaningless. The bane of modernity through secularism is far worse than either medieval Islamic Sufism or medieval Christian theology, for secularism destroys the sanctity and universality of all moral values. The effects of this phenomenon have just begun to make themselves felt, most palpably in the West, but also in other parts of the world. Secularism is intrinsically atheistic.[48]

THE TWO DIMENSIONS OF LIFE AND THE QUR'AN

In Islamic societies, Islam has hitherto been generally explained and understood by the ulema to mean an otherworldly attitude by observing the rituals of Islam. The present world has been explained away as meaningless or at best not worthy of much attention. This explanation or attitude of mind is totally against the whole of Qur'anic doctrine. It actually militates against the very spirit of the Qur'an as will be seen in this section. Indeed, one is wonderstruck when one studies the Qur'an and evaluates the state of affairs in Islamic societies.

The major weakness in the application of the Qur'anic doctrine has been in its interpretation. Not that the interpretation is difficult, but the chief problem has been that since the medieval period Muslims have not paid attention to the basic questions of method and hermeneutics in studying the Qur'an.[49] There has been a general failure to understand the underlying unity of the Qur'an; instead, emphasis has been on the isolated words or verses of the Qur'an. As a result, laws have often been derived from verses which were not at all legal in intent. The failure to understand the Qur'an as a deeper unity prevented the development of a definite weltanschauung, and for this the greatest penalty was paid in the realm of theological thought. As a consequence, Islamic intellectualism has remained truncated. This approach to the Qur'an has not ceased in modern times; in fact, in some respects it has worsened. Some Muslims advocate the adoption of certain key modern Western ideas and institutions, without an underlying and clearly defined and understood weltanschauung, whereas others completely reject modernity. At the same time, there is a proliferation of "apologetic" literature that is engaged in self-glorification rather than reform. Under these circumstances, the development and application of an adequate hermeneutical method is essential.[50]

The importance of an adequate method to interpret the Qur'an cannot be overemphasized. It is the lack of such a method and a lack of understanding of the Qur'an which gives rise to fatalistic and bland statements like the following: "Islam, in its general and wide sense, means that man should give himself up to God, surrender his soul completely to Him and leave everything, however small, in His hands. In its specific, religious sense, Islam . . . [urges mankind] to submit themselves wholly to God and surrender to His Divine Will in every detail of their everyday life."[51] The whole question of human accountability is thus brushed aside, and, in effect, God is made responsible for human actions. To advocate that the Qur'an suggests absolute determinism of human behavior, denying an individual free choice, is not only to deny almost the entire content of the Qur'an, but also to undercut its very basis. The Qur'an repeatedly makes it clear that it is an invitation to people to come to the right path.[52]

The Qur'an also makes it abundantly clear that human creation is purposeful:

Those [are believers] who remember God standing and sitting and lying down and reflect upon the creation of the heaven and the earth [and say]: Our Lord! You have not created all this in vain (3:191); We have not created the heaven and the earth and whatever is between them in vain (38:17); We have not created the heaven and the earth and whatever is between them in sport. If We wished to take a sport, We could have done it by Ourselves [not through Our creation] — if We were to do that at all (21:16-17); . . . Do you then think that We have created you purposelessly and that you will not be returned to Us? The True Sovereign is too exalted above that (23:115); Does man think that he will be left wandering [at his own whim]? (75:36).[53]

It follows therefore that human actions are accountable. There is no scope for predeterminism in Islam insofar as human actions are concerned. But this idea was propagated by the Ash'arite school of theology, pantheistic Sufism, and above all by the strong fatalistic doctrines of the Iranians, the echoes of which are still heard in Muslim countries.[54]

A related idea to predeterminism is that of submission, which scholars like Wallerstein and Weber equally falsely attribute to the Qur'anic doctrine. They thereby imply that that is the cause of the backwardness of Islamic societies.[55] Submitting or surrendering to the Will of God or "the limits of God" is not the same thing as being submissive or inactive. The Qur'an explains that when God creates a thing, He puts into it its nature and the laws governing its nature whereby it falls into a pattern and becomes part of the cosmos. Since everything in the universe behaves according to its ingrained laws, that is, obeys the "command" of God, the whole universe is Muslim, for it surrenders to the Will of God. Mankind is the only exception to this universal law, for it is endowed with the capacity of free choice in obeying or disobeying the command of God. The command of God is expressed in the laws of nature. But nature does not and cannot violate natural laws, that is, the command of God. The entirety of nature surrenders itself to the command of God. The fundamental difference between mankind and nature is that, whereas God's commands to nature (the natural laws) disallow disobedience, commands to mankind include the element of choice. Hence, God's command to nature becomes moral command to mankind. This makes mankind unique among God's creations, and, at the same time, it charges mankind with a unique and grave responsibility.[56]

The basis of Islamic movement at its inception was the unity of God and the amelioration of the condition of the poor. Later Muslim jurists and present-day rulers and reformers in the Muslim countries, however, have abused the "principle of graduation"—that is, reform should be carried out gradually when conditions are ready for it. But the conditions for reform are never going to arise unless they are changed by a conscious effort.

In the legislation of the Qur'an and the decisions of the Prophet, the historical context or the "situational contexts" were all important. Their full import was never realized by the later Qur'anic commentators and jurists.[57] Although early Muslim scholars displayed a great deal of ingenuity and freedom in interpreting the Qur'an on the basis of ijtihad (personal reasoning) and qiyas (analogical reasoning), there was no well-thought-out system of rules for these practices and early Muslim legal schools sometimes abused this freedom. For this reason, in the late eighth century C.E., al-Shafi'i succeeded in getting general acceptance for making the "traditions from the Prophet" the basis of interpretation rather than ijtihad or qiyas. The real solution, however, was to understand the Qur'anic injunctions strictly in their context and background. The basic thrust of the Qur'an, which is apparent from its very early passages, is toward socioeconomic justice and egalitarianism. Now all that follows in the Qur'anic legislation in private and public life has social justice and the creation of an egalitarian society as its end. Even the so-called "five pillars of Islam", around which Islam has been made to revolve in the last several centuries has this end in view. To insist on a literal interpretation and implementation of the Qur'anic rules, without due regard to the social change that has already occurred and is occurring in various parts of the world, amounts to deliberately defeating the moral-social purposes and objectives of the Qur'an.[58]

The literal interpretation of the Qur'an over the past several centuries, which continues almost unabated in the present in Muslim countries, has done the greatest harm to Muslims. The classic example of the literal interpretation and application of the Qur'anic injunctions and statements is the present-day kingdom of Saudi Arabia. This is not the place to examine the Saudi society. Suffice it to say here that, whereas the Saudi government proclaims that the Qur'an is its constitution, no serious effort has been made for a systematic exposition of the Qur'anic doctrine so that it could be intelligently applied. As a consequence, interpretations and regulations are made arbitrarily, for instance, segregation of the sexes (a phenomenon observable in all Muslim societies), about which the Qur'an does not say a word. This grotesque practice, which is believed in, practiced, and presented as an "Islamic way of life" is sufficient, by itself, to devastate the societies.

Whereas the overwhelming emphasis of the Qur'an is on the establishment of a social order based on socioeconomic justice and ethical values (derivable from the Qur'an), the major part of Islamic history up to the present time has neglected its importance and urgency. Instead, all emphasis has been placed first on "minimal Islam"—that is, the profession of faith, prayer, fasting, zakat (tax, of the same ratio which the Qur'an stipulated fourteen centuries ago in totally different conditions), and pilgrimage—and second on "negative or punitive Islam"—that is, certain punishments specified in the Qur'an for certain crimes like murder, adultery, and theft. These various items were arbitrarily linked together and focused on in isolation. Thus, Islam was made the sum of these items. As far as the integral teaching of the Qur'an and the historic struggle of the Prophet were concerned, which provided the sociomoral context for these provisions and institutes and cemented them together, it had already been lost sight of.[59]

It is the simplistic approach to Islam, presently incarnated in neorevivalism or neofundamentalism, which is a major obstacle to reform in Islamic societies. Its first principle is anti-Westernism and opposition to classical modernism, as if it possessed all the right answers to life. The neofundamentalist's pet issues are the ban on bank interest, the ban on family planning, not changing the status of women, the unrestricted authority of religious leaders, the collection of the zakat (tax), and similar matters. For the neofundamentalist, Muslims must be just the opposite of the West. As for neorevivalism, it lacks serious intellectual endeavor and suffers from intellectual bankruptcy; its style is cliché mongering. Like the neofundamentalist, it picks on certain selected issues that would most "distinguish" Muslims from the West. The neorevivalist is a shallow person steeped in superficiality and is rooted neither in the Qur'an nor in the traditional intellectual culture. Because he lacks intellectual depth, he ceaselessly chants that Islam is "very simple" and "straightforward" without knowing what it means. The Qur'an, as compared to theology, is, of course, simple and straightforward. But in another and more meaningful sense, the Qur'an is as complicated as life and requires careful and intelligent study.[60]

The Qur'an does provide guidelines in different spheres of life, but these can be gleaned and correctly understood only if the sociohistoric situation in which the Qur'anic message was delivered is fully kept in mind. It also presupposes a profound intellectual effort to understand the Qur'anic message in its totality, so that the spirit of the Qur'an is not violated. If it is violated, it can have devastating effects as the prevalent conditions of Muslim societies testify, which are a consequence of subverting human minds through distorted and often patently false interpretations of the Qur'an.

Muslims often state that the Qur'an gives us "the principles" that are embodied in concrete solutions through the sunna or our reasoning. As Fazlur Rahman has pointed out, this is considerably less than half-truth and is dangerously misleading. The Qur'an, in fact, does not give many general principles. Mostly it gives solutions and rulings on specific issues; and, it does provide, either explicitly or implicitly, the rationales behind those solutions or rulings from which one can draw general principles. This is the only way to obtain the real truth about what the Qur'an teaches. Building an authentic set of Islamic laws and institutions involves a three-part process that requires a radical departure from past and present practices. In arriving at general principles from the Qur'an, one must first give due consideration to the socioeconomic conditions then existing, for the general statements or principles are embedded in actual cases or rulings, which the Qur'an discusses, from which they must be disengaged. Second, these general statements or principles must be placed in the context of the general principles on which the entire teaching of the Qur'an converges. The third step is to move from this general level to the specific legislation now sought, keeping in view the present societal social conditions and developments in the world.

Islamic religious teachers and most scholars, and as a consequence the general Muslim populations the world over, have failed to understand, and indeed would be shocked to learn, that certainty does not belong to the meaning of particular verses but to the Qur'an as a whole. That is, certainty of meaning belongs to a set of coherent principles or values where the entire teaching of the Qur'an converges. For centuries, Muslims have had a fixation on isolated words and verses of the Qur'an. The laws and teachings of the Qur'an have been treated in a discrete, atomistic, and totally unintegrated manner, even though the Qur'an itself repeatedly states that it is a highly integrated and cohesive body of teaching.[61]

The simplistic and atomistic approach to the Qur'an has led Muslims the world over to focus on the rituals of Islam and often to arrive at meanings that violate the spirit of the Qur'an when seen in its totality. Thus, for instance, as Sayyid Ahmad Khan pointed out over a century ago, we see "an exaggerated preoccupation with personal prayer in traditional Islamic practice."[62] He wanted Muslims to be self-conscious individuals and to take personal responsibility for their actions. He thought it wrong for prayers to be taken as a recourse for direct intervention from God and pointed out that countless prayers had not changed the world.[63] No doubt the Qur'an exhorts the believers to "establish prayers," apparently to make people God-conscious and to have positive psychological effects on human personalities so that their actions acquire a direction and meaning based on a realization of human accountability to God and powerlessness vis-à-vis God.

Thus, although prayers and attention to God are in the spiritual domain, their effects are meant to be felt in the physical world based on human actions. In addition, prayers of course help alleviate human afflictions and are the source of hope under utter despair: "And who other than Him responds to the distressed one when he calls Him and He relieves him of the distress and Who has made you [mankind] His viceregents on earth? Is there, then, a god beside God?—little do you reflect! (27:62. Translated by Fazlur Rahman, 1980, p. 6.)* That one of the main purposes of the Qur'an is to make people God-conscious is clear from the entire message of the Qur'an. This is further explained when we consider that at the time of the Qur'an's revelation, pagan Arabs used to worship and ask all kinds of deities and even humans to do things for them. Hence, God asks:

---

* Citations from the Qu'ran in the following pages, except where specifically mentioned, are from the translation by Muhammad Marmaduke Pickthall, *The Meaning of the Glorious Qur'an* (Karachi: Taj Co., Ltd.).

Attribute they as partners to Allah those who create naught, but are themselves created. And cannot give them help, nor can they help themselves?" (7:191, 192 and elsewhere). Lo! those on whom ye call beside Allah are slaves like unto you. Call on them now, and let them answer you, if ye are truthful! (7:194 and elsewhere). Have they feet wherewith they walk, or have they hands wherewith they hold, or have they eyes wherewith they see, or have they ears wherewith they hear? Say: Call upon your (so-called) partners (of Allah), and then contrive against me, spare me not! (7:195 and elsewhere).

But prayers and other rituals of Islam have been advocated by the religious teachers in such a manner as to almost take the place of action. This is evidenced from the fact that, in religious congregations, prayers are routinely offered for God's intercession in the political and economic spheres. On the contrary, the Qur'an is so action-oriented and so emphasizes the accountability of human actions that "it insists that 'last minute' declarations of faith and pleas for forgiveness are absolutely rejected."[64] What those action will be, are left entirely to humans within the overall framework provided by God in the Qur'an when He explains human nature which swings between contradictory extremes. The contradictory extremes are not a "problem" to be resolved through theological thought but tensions that must be lived with if a person is to be truly "religious," that is, a servant of God. This is the framework provided by God for human action. The contradictory extremes, like utter powerlessness and "being the measure for all things," hopelessness and pride, determinism and freedom, are natural tensions within the human nature for proper conduct. And since the purpose of these tensions is to maximize moral energy, the Qur'an demands that one must not violate the balance of opposing tensions, for it would lead to moral nihilism.[65]

The present state of Muslim societies is perhaps best explainable as being due to moral nihilism reached through persistent advocacy, over a long period of time, of such doctrines as determinism and powerlessness or divine intervention in human affairs. In this process, massive illiteracy and an unenlightened educational system have, of course, played a major role. In addition, Muslim societies have been suffering from the false and self-deceptive belief that they have an abundance of spirituality and that all they need to do now is to acquire material technology.[66] The lack of spiritual development, however, is evidenced by the fact that the Qur'an is still interpreted by the ulema, or religious teachers, according to the conditions as they existed in Arabia fourteen centuries ago. In addition, in a dichotomous educational system, which is prevalent in all Muslim countries, and which demarcates between religious and secular education, the overall effect is no different from that found in secular societies.

Another indicator of the lack of development in spiritual thought, and by extension thought in general, is the peculiar relationship of religion and politics in Muslim societies and the pitiable subjugation of religion to politics. As a result, the effects of politics waged in these countries are as pernicious as those of secularism. Instead of attempting to genuinely interpret the Islamic principles or values that are to be realized through political or government channels, Islam is distorted and exploited for party politics and group interests; the result is that Islam becomes a sheer slogan and is reduced to demagoguery. The crowning feature of this demagoguery, of which the so-called Islamic parties are the most blatantly guilty, is the slogan that in Islam religion and politics are inseparable, through which the masses are duped.[67]

For modernization to evolve in Muslim societies in a meaningful way, therefore, a massive effort at educational reform would be a prerequisite. The first step for such a reform to occur lies in the sphere of Qur'anic interpretation, for religious ideas have a profound impact on an individual's worldview, on life itself. This is by no means an easy task, but it is the only way if Muslim societies are to embark on a progressive path and breakaway from highly retrogressive and self-destructive thought systems. For the modernization of old Islamic learning and the Islamization of the new one, the original thrust of Islam "must be clearly resurrected so that the conformities and deformities of historical Islam" can be judged by it.[68] This resurrection can occur only if the Qur'an's social and legal enactments are studied in the light of its general moral teaching and principles, and against their historical background.[69]

The confusion existing in Muslim societies regarding what Islam really advocates and demands of Muslims is due essentially to the lack of a proper method of interpretation. Both the Muslim modernist and the fundamentalist agree and state that Muslims must go back to the original sources of Islam—the Qur'an and the sunnah of the Prophet Muhammad—but both have lacked a clear enough method of interpretation. The neorevivalist, lacking any method of interpretation, has only reacted on certain important social issues to the classical modernist who, also lacking any method, attempted to solve ad hoc issues which were historically of Western inspiration in the light of the Qur'anic teaching, often with remarkable plausibility. The premodernist revivalist, who knew the traditional parameters of Islam, was correct in pointing out that Muslim societies had become permeated with such superstitious practices which were a form of *shirk* (raising someone to share in God's status) and therefore must be eradicated. The premodernist revivalist, however, could not go beyond this, for he also lacked any method of Qur'anic interpretation. As Fazlur Rahman has pointed out, there has never been any systematic attempt to understand the Qur'an in the order in which it was revealed. This method can rule out most arbitrary and fanciful interpretations of the Qur'an. And because the Qur'an was not treated as a coherent whole by most Muslim thinkers, the metaphysical part in particular received the wildest interpretations. The majority of the orthodox became dusty-dry literalists with no real insight into the depths of the Qur'an.[70]

The first condition for the reformation and modernization of Islamic societies is that the state must bring about educational reforms. The first step in that direction would be an obligatory *study* of the Qur'an as a textbook, starting at the high school level and carried out *independently*. This would bring home to everyone the importance of a systematic and intelligent study of the Qur'an, and at the same time break the monopoly of religious teachers and religious institutions, so to speak, over the Qur'an. At the same time, a textbook, not a commentary, needs to be produced which explains (again keeping in mind the socioeconomic and historical conditions under which the Qur'an was revealed) what the Qur'anic injunctions and statements mean, when viewed in the overall message of the Qur'an.[71] This approach would prevent literal and isolated interpretation of Qur'anic verses. This seems essential because of the many fanciful ideas and beliefs, as noted above, in circulation in Muslim countries. This task cannot be left in the hands of the ulema, just as lawmaking cannot be left to them, in whose hands it has remained so stagnant, uninspired, and undeveloped.

In a modern system of government in Islamic societies, legislative assemblies whose members have received modern education and who have first-hand knowledge of the Qur'an would be fully capable of producing Islamic law. Such individuals would emerge as a matter of course in a society where a new system of education, as explained earlier, is in place. In addition, of course, the need is to systematically work out Islamic ethics from the Qur'an and to make such works accessible to the public.[72] All of this would help ensure that the grossly distorted ideas about Islam which exist in Islamic societies are removed.

For Islamic societies to develop or modernize in the material sense, what is required is the intellectual development of the societies concerned, which means that the emphasis of developmental policies needs to be in the educational sphere. We will examine this aspect of the development process of the countries under study in the following chapters. In the educational sphere, there is also the necessity of working out an Islamic worldview so that issues related to life can be meaningfully understood. This means an interplay of philosophy and religion or theology, a necessary intellectual activity that was banished from Islamic societies centuries ago. Two Muslim philosophers, al-Farabi (A.D. 873-950) and Avicenna (A.D. 980-1037), following Aristotle and other Greek philosophers, constructed the main framework of a philosophy which advocated that (1) the world is eternal, (2) God cannot know individuals, and (3) there is no bodily resurrection.[73] Islamic theologians attacked the philosophers for such views, and their attack was spearheaded by al-Ghazali (A.D. 1058-1111), who argued that in the three questions the philosophers were opposed to the belief of all Muslims.[74] Through his arguments, al-Ghazali was successful in demonstrating how limited a role is left to the philosophers' God if the world were deterministic and eternal, and how different this role is from what Islam explains.[75]

Al-Ghazali wanted to reestablish the role of a personal, powerful, and omniscient God, which he felt could not be reconciled with the basic metaphysical and logical theses that the philosophers accepted and defended.[76] While his criticism of the philosophers was apt on several counts, based on the teaching of the Qur'an, where he and other theologians went wrong were to instil and leave the legacy of the influence of a personal God on the events of the material world.[77] Religious teachers have continued to emphasize this doctrine up to the present time, based on a literal and an isolated interpretation of some of the Qur'anic verses.

Notwithstanding serious problems with the philosophers' position on some metaphysical issues, the theologians failed to appreciate that the philosophers had learned a new way of thinking from the Greeks. Philosophers had learned a system of constructive logical thought that provided its users with great conceptual power.[78] Theologians came to view philosophy as antithetical to religion. Al-Farabi, however, had attempted to point out that their philosophical activity, far from undermining religion, was undertaken in defense of the faith.[79] Moreover, theologians failed to realize that what interested the philosophers was the form of the argument and not the conclusions or its premises. In their works, which were directed at other philosophers and not the general public, they were not really discussing Islam. This did not mean that they were not devout Muslims; it was only that they were writing philosophy. Al-Farabi argued that religion could not go against demonstrative knowledge available through philosophy since religion is a reflection and a more digestible form of that knowledge. The truth of religion is based on revelation, whereas the truth of philosophy is based on demonstrative reasoning. "In both cases the means of defence can be dialectical, but the means of gaining knowledge of more than just that one's opponent is mistaken are different."[80]

By banishing philosophy altogether as a system of thought, life in Muslim societies became stereotypical and stagnant, which was a necessary consequence, for the growth of human thought and imagination was arrested. In medieval Islam, philosophy gave violent affront to the orthodoxy, and since then philosophy has been a *disciplina non grata* in most of the Muslim world. But the philosophy that the medieval Muslim philosophers were engaged in was only one form of philosophy with which, however, the fate of all philosophy was decided by the orthodox. This caused great harm to orthodoxy, which thereafter suffered from a lack of ideas and their challenge, and to philosophy. Philosophy, however, is an essential intellectual activity for its own sake and for other disciplines. It not only inculcates and sharpens the analytical-critical abilities, but it also generates new ideas that become important intellectual tools for various disciplines, including religion and philosophy. Philosophical activity is so critical in the life of a society that if it deprives itself of philosophy, it commits intellectual suicide. To argue that all philosophy must necessarily go against theology or its suppositions is to play not only a naive game but a dangerous one as well.

According to the Qur'an, knowledge, that is, the generation of ideas, is an activity of the highest possible value. Indeed, the Qur'an asked the Prophet to continue to pray for "increase in knowledge." The Qur'an emphasizes the need to delve into the universe and into history, and to ponder over issues related to life and death. To ban or discourage pure thought, therefore, is not compatible with the demands of the Qur'an. In the last several centuries, however, the distorted Islam propagated and practiced in the Muslim world has been made into a mystery by the religious circles;[81] its effect has been that, given the sacredness attached to this distorted Islam, Muslims in general have been literally afraid to think for themselves in all walks of life. A necessary part of thought is to ask questions. To prevent this from occurring, religious teachers have resorted to all kinds of ruses, a major one of which is to make the distorted Islam an exclusive domain of the ulema so that its mystery is maintained.

Significantly, none of the Muslim countries carries out the study of the Qur'an in a systematic manner in the classroom, at any level—not even in those institutions that specialize in Islamic education. The usual practice is for the religious teachers to teach children to recite the Qur'an when they are of schoolgoing age, that is, those who go to school. When they complete its recitation within a year or two, a celebration-of-sorts is made that so-and-so had "finished" the Qur'an. In some cases, such "finishing" of the Qur'an may take place a few more times in adolescence or by the time a person reaches adulthood. Subsequently, it is the religious teacher who "teaches" in the mosque, verse by verse, or through sermons, whatever his understanding of the subject matter is. In addition, of course, the Qur'an is "finished" collectively in the mosque every year during the month of Ramadan through recitation, which is preceded by long sermons and narration of traditions by the religious teachers. Some individuals, however, prefer to study the Qur'an on their own during this period and otherwise. All of this activity revolves around men, barring the early period of childhood. Women, of course, do read the Qur'an on their own, but it generally involves recitation rather than an understanding of the Qur'an. It also seems to indicate a deliberate attempt and practice of keeping women uninformed about matters pertaining to the Qur'an, or else the Qur'an would have been taken to the classroom a long time ago, where questioning minds would have questioned several issues and practices. As a result, generally, in Islamic countries an air of mystery or gross misunderstanding exists about the Qur'an.

Even when traditional Islamic education has been reformed, it has tended to "simplify" the traditional syllabus by dropping heavy doses of medieval theology, certain branches of philosophy (such as logic), and a plethora of works dealing with Islamic law. In this "simplification," however, the discipline of hadith is accentuated. In some cases, greater emphasis is placed on the Arabic language and literature and on principles of Qur'anic interpretation. Most astonishingly, as far as the Qur'an is concerned, it is not part of any systematic study.[82]

One aspect of modernization, or of the benefits of modernization, is to have a better quality of life, which requires that a person strive for prosperity. Now, the Qur'an does not advocate an ascetic way of life or a life of poverty. It does not oppose the acquisition of wealth, although it comes down heavily against those who hoard wealth or who make wealth and things related to it the purpose of life. It repeatedly exhorts Muslims to spend wealth for the benefit of everyone so that society does not become polarized at two extremes—those who have an abundance of wealth and those who live in poverty. That, indeed, is one of the major reasons for its prohibition against usury. Ironically, while one hears a ceaseless chant in Muslim societies that usury is a sin, that it has been prohibited, not much thought is given to the idea behind the prohibition. Gross socioeconomic inequalities are ignored as if they do not matter, and they are explained away simply as God's will. Yet the Qur'an's emphasis on creating a social order based on socioeconomic justice is totally disregarded. The Qur'an exhorts Muslims

"to spend in the cause of Allah" and thus establish credit with God, so that God may repay you manifold, rather than invest money in usury in order to suck the blood of the people (30:39; 2:245; 5:12, 18; 57:11, 18; 64:7; 73:20). . . . "Satan inspires you with [fear of] poverty [for investing in society] and commands you obscenities; God, on the other hand, promises you forgiveness and prosperity [for such investment] (2:268)." Indeed, *the Qur'an holds that one major cause of the decay of societies is the neglect into which they are cast by their prosperous members.*

. . . With regard to distributive justice, the Qur'an laid down the principle that "wealth should not circulate only among the rich" (59:7).[83]

As for wealth itself, the Qur'an places a high value on it, "which it terms 'the bounty of God . . .' (62:10; 73:20; 5:20; cf. 24:22; 27:16; 30:33) and 'good . . .' (2:18, 215, 272-73; 11:84; 22:11; 38:32; 50:25; 68:12; 70:21)."[84] The Qur'an considers peace and prosperity among the highest blessings of God:

How accustomed have the Quraish [the mercantile tribe of Mecca] become to their winter journey [to Byzantium] and their summer journey [to the Indian Ocean] [so that they take them for granted]. Let them, then, serve the Lord of this House [the Ka'ba] who has given them plenty instead of hunger, and peace instead of war (106:1-4).[85]

To be successful in this world is vitally important according to the Qur'an, and one measure of success is prosperity. Societies that are not successful in this world are, in effect, punished by God. Individuals' fates in this world are bound up with the state of a society. Thus, a two-way process is involved here: individuals must do good for the society and vice versa. It is a collaborative, participatory, and joint effort. Embedded herein, therefore, are the roots for establishing a democratic system of government, a government that is accountable to the people. It is absolutely essential that the society be successful in every sense of the word. Otherwise, individuals, because of their place of birth and residence, become society's victims. This is what is implied when God mentions about punishment in this world (59:3 and elsewhere). Disgraced and poverty-stricken societies are certainly not successful (2:61, 85; 3:56, and elsewhere).

The Qur'an repeatedly makes it clear that the criteria of Judgment on the Last Day will be based on human beliefs (faith) and actions, that is, "good works" (2:25, 62, 82, 110, 139, 217, 281, 286; 3:57, 115; 4:57, 124, and elsewhere). In other words, faith, or beliefs by themselves, howsoever correct they might be, are not sufficient. Although faith, or correct beliefs, in the eyes of the Qur'an, are necessary, human actions ("good works") are equally important; that is, one without the other is not sufficient: "Whoso denieth the faith, his work is vain and he will be among the losers in the Hereafter" (5:5,10,93 ; 6:88,158, and elsewhere); "And He it is Who created the heavens and the earth . . . [so] that He might try you, which of you is best in conduct . . . " (11:7). Of course, individuals and societies can prosper without any faith, as the Qur'an makes abundantly clear through the following verses, but such prosperity is of no consequence when evaluated in the overall scheme of things:

Whoso desireth the life of the world and its pomp, We shall repay them their deeds herein, and therein they will not be wronged. Those are they for whom is naught in the Hereafter save the Fire. (All) that they contrive here is vain and (all) that they are wont to do is fruitless. (11: 15, 16). Lo! those who believe and do good works and humble themselves before their Lord, such are rightful owners of the Garden; they will abide therein (11: 23).

That the worldly things are important, albeit not singularly, is apparent when the Qur'an calls on Muslims to ponder over things related to the world and the Hereafter (2:219, 220). And further:

. . . He whom Allah sendeth astray, for him there is no guide. For them is torment in the life of the world, and verily the doom of the Hereafter is more painful. . . . (13: 33, 34).
. . . ye will indeed be asked of what ye used to do (16:93).
Whosoever doth right, whether male or female, and is a believer, him verily We shall quicken with good life. . . . (16:97).
. . . and every soul will be repaid what it did, and they will not be wronged (16:111). And every man's augury have We fastened to his own neck, and We shall bring forth for him on the Day of Resurrection a book which he will find wide open. (And it will be said unto him): Read thy book. Thy soul sufficeth as reckoner against thee this day. Whosoever goeth right, it is only for (the good of) his own soul that he goeth right, and whosoever erreth, erreth only to its hurt. . . . (17:13-15).
And whoso desireth the Hereafter and striveth for it with the effort necessary, being a

believer, for such, their effort findeth favour (with their Lord) (17:19).
Lo! We have placed all that is in the earth as an ornament thereof that We may try them: which of them is best in conduct (18:7).

For a society's conditions to change for better, that is, to be prosperous, the first condition that the Qur'an stipulates is that necessary changes must occur in the thought processes of its people (as a whole and not merely in a few people), for it is the thought processes that give shape to actions: "Lo! Allah changeth not the condition of a folk until they (first) change that which is in their hearts . . . " (13:11). Similarly, the downfall of a society is directly related to the prevalent thoughts in a society at a particular time:

. . . Allah never changeth the grace He hath bestowed on any people until they first change that which is in their hearts. . . . (Their way is) as the way of Pharaoh's folk and those before them; they denied the revelations of their Lord, so We destroyed them in their sins [i.e., through their actions]. . . . (8:53, 54).

As the above makes clear, changes in a society, both in the positive and negative directions, occur when thoughts or ideas, whatever they are, are widespread in a particular society. This links up with the Qur'anic idea and emphasis on socioeconomic justice. In other words, a small proportion of a society may be relatively well off, but its cumulative effect on the society as a whole is nil or negligible. A society in such a state can exist for a long period of time, but the important point here is that the society as a whole has failed; it has stagnated or degenerated.

THE TRADITIONS OF ISLAM

Thus far, we have been primarily focusing on the Qur'an to determine what it says about the regulation and conduct of life. We have also examined the question of Qur'anic interpretation. Now we need to briefly examine issues related to Muslim hadith/s (tradition/s), for when ulema and some political leaders in Islamic countries talk about the creation of an Islamic society, or an Islamic way of life, after mentioning the Qur'an, in the same breath they invoke the word sunna, or the traditions of the Prophet's behavior.

A hadith proper is the record of a saying attributed to the Prophet Muhammad or a description of his actions. Over of a period time, these records were compiled and collected, which together came to be designated as the so-called hadith literature. Several of these collections acquired so much prestige that they were made sacrosanct and vested with an authority second only to the Qur'an. The hadith is studied with great reverence in the religious schools everywhere in the Muslim world and is the basis of thought and action in different spheres of life. The point of view developed among the people is necessarily of the late Middle Ages when research into the origins and evolution of the hadith literature virtually came to a standstill.[86]

Scholars have shown, however, that a major portion of the hadith literature was fabricated.[87] The issue is so sensitive among the traditionalists that a mere mention of this fact evokes hostility from them. Earlier, it was stated that in Muslim countries the Qur'an is not studied in a systematic manner at any level, not even in the traditional schools. In contrast, the hadith literature is taught in the traditional schools, not with a critical approach but as if its authenticity had been established once and for all. Thus, what goes for Islam in the Islamic territories is essentially not what the Qur'an teaches, but is derived primarily from the hadith literature or ideas, customs, and practices wrongfully attributed to Islam. The invocation of hadiths in the sermons delivered in mosques is a common observation; the impact of ideas thus propagated can be well imagined. As questionable as the bulk of the hadith literature is, it is remarkable how strong its hold is even on the "educated" Muslims throughout the world. In July 1975 the Muslim Students' Association of the United States and Canada held a seminar on the hadith to celebrate the twelve hundredth anniversary of Bukhari; over one thousand Muslims of all ages and nationalities attended. Subjects like the indispensability of hadith in Islam and its role in Islamic law and in understanding the Qur'an were discussed. All the speakers emphasized the importance of studying the hadith.[88]

Systematic criticism of hadith transmitters is estimated to have begun around 130/747. G. H. A. Juynboll believes that before the chain of transmitters came into existence nearly seventy-five years after the Prophet's death, traditions and legendary stories were transmitted haphazardly and mostly anonymously.[89] Once the chain of transmitters came into existence, the names of older authorities were provided when a new transmitter required one. "Often the names of well-known historical personalities were chosen but more often the names of fictitious persons were offered to fill in the gaps in *isnads* [transmitters] which were as yet far from perfect."[90] In the subsequent compilation of traditions, traditions that related to legal decisions were especially raised "to the level of a more prestigious authority, mostly the prophet, by supplying the necessary links."[91]

With the passage of time, traditions of all sorts attributed to the Prophet, his Companions, and their Successors mushroomed in different parts of the Muslim empire. As Juynboll points out, as far as the first four caliphs are concerned, the number of prophetic sayings directly attributed to them are very few, but "the younger Companions are credited with a colossal number of traditions."[92] The first systematic compilation of traditions was done by Bukhari (d. 256/870), which "means that more than one and a half centuries had elapsed since the [transmitters] had come into existence before a compilation was made that was generally considered sound."[93] He is said to have sifted through 600,000 traditions to collect 7,397 "sound" ones, many of which are repeated in different contexts. The final count of his collection is 2,762 traditions. Another person who is credited with having collected "sound" traditions is Muslim bin Al Hajjaj (d. 261/875). His collection is said to be identical to Bukhari's except for some variation in the transmitters.[94]

Besides these two "genuine books," there are the following four which have also been elevated to canonical rank: *Sunna* of Abu Daud (d. 275), *Jami* of Abu Isa Muhammad al Tirmidhi (d. 279), *Sunna* of Abu Abd Allah Muhammad bin Maja (d. 283), and *Sunna* of Abu Abd Al-Rahman al Nasa'i (d. 303). Out of these four, Abu Daud's collection alone contains 4,800 traditions that are said to have been selected out of half a million. Besides these six, several others are in circulation.[95] The proliferation of so many traditions was a major consequence of, among other reasons, intergroup rivalries that developed in the early period of Islam. Thus, we read from Ibn Abi l-Haddad (d. 655/1257), himself a Shi'ite, who candidly admits of fabrications:

Know that the origins of fabrications in *fada'il* traditions [reports containing the alleged merits of certain people or institutions] were due to the Shi'a, for they forged in the first instance traditions concerning their leader. Enmity towards their adversaries drove them to this fabrication. . . . When the Bakriyya (i.e. those favoring Abu Bakr) saw what the Shi'a had done, they fabricated for their own masters traditions to counter the former . . . When the Shi'a saw what the Bakriyya had done, they increased their efforts . . . .[96]

Earlier we observed that in Muslim countries no systematic study of the Qur'an is carried out on a regular basis. We also observed that, for the Qur'an, success, in every sense of the word, in this life is vitally important. We have now found that the bulk of the so-called Islamic traditions, which have historically been elevated in importance second only to the Qur'an, are in fact forgeries and distortions. Yet, these traditions not only form the basis of a major portion of the Islamic curriculum in the traditional Islamic schools, but also regulate the conduct of Muslims in everyday life because of their pervasiveness. Therefore, Muslims have an urgent need to critically evaluate their intellectual Islamic past on the basis of the Qur'an. Because they have developed a peculiar psychological complex vis-à-vis the West, that past is defended as if it were their God. In that past, the greatest sensitivity surrounds the hadith.[97]

CONCLUSION

In analyzing the phenomenon of modernization and development, many writers have emphasized secularization as the *sine qua non* for modernization. Islam, however, does not distinguish between the temporal and the spiritual; the two are welded together. Secularism, therefore, has no place in Islam. Islam seeks to have a direct impact on life; it is directly concerned with the life processes. Islam is not supposed to be a ritual or dogma; it seeks to provide value, meaning, and direction to life.

The Qur'an does not recognize any priestly class; it is squarely addressed to each person. However, in the course of history the ulema have assumed the role of clergy. By giving a literal interpretation of isolated Qur'anic verses and by making the hadith literature sacrosanct, this class has grossly distorted the message of the Qur'an. It is due to practices such as these that no systematic exposition of the Qur'an has ever taken place, with the consequence that the teachings of the Qur'an are grossly misunderstood. This misunderstanding is further compounded and reinforced by the so-called traditions of Islam, a vast majority of which are believed to be forgeries and distortions. The prevalent ideas and practices attributed to Islam are largely derived from such traditions.

The Qur'an calls for active participation in worldly affairs; it sanctions the generation and possession of wealth. Therefore, no conflict exists between the Qur'anic doctrine and what can be termed a modern way of life.[98] Systematic exposition of the Qur'anic doctrine or, to put it another way, the Islamic worldview is required, however. For Islamic societies to become progressive, changes in Muslims' ideas about Islam must occur. To begin with, that requires the study of the Qur'an as a required text in schools, beginning at the high school level and carried out *independently*. Concomitantly, the bulk of the hadith literature, which is of questionable validity, must be weeded out. This can occur only if it is critically examined.

Nothing in the Qur'an prevents a person, male or female, from living life in a vigorous manner. In the eyes of the Qur'an, a society's failure in this world amounts to having been punished by God. A measure of a society's success is material prosperity, albeit not singularly but mediated by the overall message of the Qur'an. To put it another way, a Muslim society's failure in the material sphere is proof of its failure in the understanding and application of the Qur'anic doctrine. Such a society, on the terms of the Qur'an, can hardly be designated as Islamic.

Just as the evolution of Western societies began with the exercise of the critical faculties, especially with regard to religion, the evolution of Islamic societies from a more or less stagnant condition can systematically begin only if the critical faculties of the mass of the society are awakened and employed. This essentially means a critical appraisal of all that has traditionally been accepted as Islamic. This appraisal is not a onetime effort but a continuous process that underscores the importance of modern education. A few changes here and there through development projects will simply not do because over the centuries (say, since the tenth/eleventh) the Muslim community has developed a temperament whereby it accepts small changes without really moving forward.[99]

With reference to bringing about changes gradually, Muslim jurists in Islam's earlier history and many present-day reformers have abused the "principle of graduation" in Qur'anic legislation.[100] This lends credence to the idea that the ruling elites in Muslim societies are not serious, or honest, in bringing about the necessary changes. They also do not seem to know how to bring this about.

Reducing Qur'anic legislation simply to some penal legislation and maintenance or reinvocation of some highly questionable traditions and practices essentially undermines the whole of the Qur'anic doctrine. To argue that developing Islamic countries face a multitude of internal and external problems, and hence the process of development must be slow and gradual, is a defeatist argument. The issue is a thousand years old. Such an argument amounts to saying that the societal problems are unmanageable and that the ruling elites are simply incompetent to deal with them. Such an argument, moreover, suggests a vested interest by the ruling circles in maintaining the status quo. The foremost requirement for Islamic societies to be able to develop or modernize is the intellectual development of the societies concerned. In this endeavor, the Qur'an has the most important and critical role to play.

5

THE RELIGIOPOLITICAL
SYSTEM OF PAKISTAN
AND MODERNIZATION

In this and the following two chapters we will analyze the religiopolitical systems and their impact on the modernization efforts of the countries under study. Already in Chapter 4 we have seen that, based on the teaching of the Qur'an, nothing in Islam is antithetical to development or modernization. We have also observed that gross misunderstanding exists in Islamic countries about the Qur'anic doctrine, especially in the minds of the ulema or the religious teachers. And since religious education has been in the hands of the ulema for the last millennia, they have created and cemented deep misunderstandings about Islam among the populations of these countries. The study in this chapter, as also in the subsequent two chapters, is therefore not an examination of Islam or how Islam has fared in the modern world. The study is of societies that are recognized as Islamic. It is a study of the treatment of Islam at the hands of these societies. *It is not an examination of Islam at all.* Chapter 4 has dealt with that part, insofar as it related to this study. In fact, none of the Islamic societies, as a whole, anywhere in the world, come close to be designated as Islamic, when evaluated on the basis of the Qur'an.

The background of the struggle and the creation of Pakistan have been covered in detail in numerous books and articles.[1] It was demanded and achieved on the basis of Islam, with social and economic considerations in mind. And it was meant to be a modern, progressive, country. Thus, the founder of Pakistan, Quaid-i-Azam Muhammed Ali Jinnah, in a broadcast in February 1948, stated that Pakistan's constitution would be of a democratic type embodying the essential principles of Islam. He then said: "Islam and its idealism have taught us democracy. It has taught equality of man, justice and fairplay to everybody. . . . In any case Pakistan is not going to be a theocratic state—to be ruled by priests with a divine mission."[2]

The question of Islam's role in Pakistan was taken up by the Constituent Assembly, as we will see shortly. Jinnah was also fully aware of the negative influence of the religious leaders and functionaries on the Muslims. He had publicly stated the problem as far back as 1938 when he addressed the Muslim League session at Calcutta. Explaining the efforts made by the Muslim League in organizing Muslims all over India in the preceding six months during which the party successfully organized them, as they never were in the previous century and a half, he informed the gathering: "We have to a certain extent freed our people from *the most undesirable* reactionary elements. We have in no small degree removed the *unwholesome influence and fear* of a certain section who used to pass off as Maulanas and Moulvis [ulema and religious leaders; emphasis added]."[3] In the preceding century and a half of colonial rule in the subcontinent, Islam continued to be understood and practiced as it had been since the medieval period in the Muslim territories. The Muslim rulers of the subcontinent, after losing power, had eventually accepted British rule on the condition that their "religious obligations would be respected."[4] But as far as the critical appraisal of religious practices and traditions was concerned, it went largely unattended, although Muslim scholars raised the issue, as we will see in a later section.

The methodology used to carry out the analysis in this and the following two chapters is based on the following six indices. Each country will be examined, as far as possible, within this framework to give uniformity and consistency to the study.

1. State position and policies regarding Islam and religious leaders' responses.
2. Modernist intellectuals' views of religious matters and practices.
3. State responses to modernist intellectuals' views of religious matters and practices.
4. State responses to religious leaders' views and demands regarding Islam.
5. Religious educational system.
6. Assessment of the development plans and modernization goals of the state.

STATE POSITION AND POLICIES REGARDING ISLAM AND RELIGIOUS LEADERS' RESPONSES

In his conception of Pakistan, Jinnah had gone much beyond the traditionally understood and accepted ideas about Islam; he was concerned about the higher ideals of Islam. These were echoed when he addressed the Constituent Assembly. Emphasizing that the partition of the subcontinent was inescapable and inevitable given the constitutional problem, and therefore minorities were bound to be in the two states, he pointed out that if the people of Pakistan wanted their country to be happy and prosperous, they should concentrate on the well-being of the people. They must not get bogged down in religious controversies. In the affairs of the state, he argued, everyone was an equal citizen, with equal rights, privileges, and obligations and with no regard to a person's religion, color, caste, or creed. If people followed this principle, there would be no end to the progress they would make. He wanted religion to be kept out of politics.[5]

Jinnah was fully aware why the struggle for Pakistan and its eventual triumph had taken place. He himself had educated the masses about the necessity of creating Pakistan. The president of the All-India States Muslim League, at the conclusion of the thirty-first session of the All-India Muslim League on December 26, 1943, stated: "We want Pakistan for the establishment of the Quranic system of government. . . . The object . . . [is] to enable the Muslims . . . of . . . Pakistan . . . to make their life worth living and plan their educational, social, economic and political uplift from the purely Islamic point of view." The speaker emphasized socioeconomic justice in the new state, and addressing Jinnah said:

Quaid-i-Azam! We have understood Pakistan in this light. If your Pakistan is not such, we do not want it. ("Is this a challenge to me?" asked the Quaid-i-Azam smiling.) No, Sir, I am not challenging you. I wanted to explain to the audience through this "challenge" the nature of the Pakistan we visualize.[6]

The point is that Jinnah was aware of the general direction Pakistan should take. But he was not willing, quite correctly, to drag the country into religious controversies. At the same time, he was not calling for a secular state as some writers have suggested.[7] Much earlier, in 1925, Jinnah had observed that the intellectual, moral, and religious resources ought to be utilized in making the life of the people comfortable and happy.[8] Moreover, he along with the other members of the Muslim intelligentsia knew that in the last five hundred years religious thought in Islam had remained stationary. There was a time when Western thought received inspiration from the world of Islam, but that time had long since passed. Western intellectual culture is only a further development of some of the most important phases of the culture of Islam. During the last several centuries of intellectual stupor in the Muslim world, which continues in the present age, the West has seriously been thinking on those issues which were of great interest to the philosophers and scientists of Islam. Ever since the schools of Muslim theology were completed in the Middle Ages, infinite advance has taken place in human thought and experience.[9]

Jinnah's vision was concerned with the bigger issues that faced Pakistan. He referred to these issues when he said: "educational planning, economic planning, social planning. These are very big questions."[10] The prevalent educational system itself was in such a state that one observer described it as having taught the people "humble servility, self-negation and absence of ambition. "[11]

The Constituent Assembly took first major step in making the constitution when it passed a resolution in March 1949 on the aims and objectives of the constitution, which came to be known as the Objectives Resolution. The main points of the resolution were: (1) sovereignty over the entire universe belongs to God; the authority which He has delegated to the state of Pakistan through its people is a sacred trust and is to be exercised within the limits prescribed by Him; (2) the state shall exercise its authority and powers through the chosen representatives of the people; (3) the principles of democracy, freedom, equality, tolerance, and social justice, as enunciated by Islam, shall be fully observed; (4) Muslims shall be enabled to order their lives in the individual and collective spheres in accord with the teachings and requirements of Islam as set out in the Holy Qur'an and the sunna; (5) fundamental rights, including equality of status, of opportunity and before law, social, economic and political justice, and freedom of thought, expression, belief, faith, worship, and association will be guaranteed, subject to law and public morality.[12]

The purpose of all these clauses was to ensure "that the people of Pakistan may prosper and attain their rightful and honoured place amongst the nations of the world and to make their full contribution towards international peace and progress and happiness of humanity."[13] Thus, from the outset, Pakistan's leading political figures recognized the importance for Pakistan to develop, prosper, and progress.

The debates about Islamic provisions, as far as Muslim members of the Constituent Assembly were concerned, were essentially between those (the ulema, or their representatives) who insisted "on the course as before—sometimes without knowing what that course was, but sensing it as good"—and those who were aware of the pitfalls in the old course, while at the same time recognizing new possibilities.[14] The resolution itself reflected the prime minister's strong effort to accommodate, as far as possible, the views of the ulema, who had exerted strong pressure behind the scenes.[15] Emphasizing that Pakistan was achieved to build "up a country and its polity in accordance with our ideals," and, emphasizing further that the people of Pakistan firmly believed that "all authority should be exercised in accordance with the standards laid down by Islam so that it may not be misused," prime minister Liaqat Ali Khan minced no words when he emphatically stated that this was, however, not a resuscitation of the dead theory of Divine Right of Kings or rulers because in accordance with the spirit of Islam authority had been delegated to the people, and to no one else, and that only the people would decide who would exercise that authority. Because this was so, the resolution eliminated any danger of establishing theocracy. Acknowledging that theocracy in its literal sense meant the government of God, Liaqat pointed out to the delegates that it was obvious that in that sense the entire universe was a theocracy. In its technical sense, however, theocracy had come to mean a government by priests who were specially appointed by those who claimed their authority from a sacerdotal position. Denouncing such an idea as absolutely foreign to Islam, Liaqat warned that any individuals who used the word "theocracy" with reference to the polity of Pakistan were either suffering from a grave misapprehension or indulging in mischievous propaganda.[16]

Liaqat felt it was necessary to elaborate and emphasize the above because "to the *ulama* . . . the acknowledgement of God's sovereignty meant . . . a formal commitment on the part of politicians to rule in accordance with the elaborate system of Islamic law (Shari'a) as preserved and interpreted by the ulama."[17] The inclusion of the sunna in the preamble to the constitution seems, however, to have been a major mistake, for two reasons. First, it permitted the ulema to have a wide say in the lawmaking process because they alone claimed to have been well versed in the sunna literature and therefore most competent to interpret Islamic law.[18] Second, whether or not the ulema are competent to interpret what is written in the hadith (sunna) literature, as we have seen in the previous chapter, a major portion of the literature is believed to be fabricated.

A woman member of the Constituent Assembly, Begum Shah Nawaz, raised the issue regarding the inclusion of the sunna in the constitution when she said: "I would have been much happier if the word 'Sunnah' were not there, because I believe the word Qur'an would have been sufficient."[19] Because of the strong pressure exerted by the ulema, all three constitutions produced in Pakistan have included the word sunna along with the Qur'an; its implications are very serious. Such a provision attempts to ensure that life in Pakistan would be regulated on the basis of traditions, or rules and regulations, which were accumulated over a thousand years ago. It is the first major obstacle in Pakistan's quest for development, for it prevents fresh thinking in all spheres of life.

The essence of the Qur'an is God-consciousness, which, if achieved, is the ultimate safeguard against human potential for evil. As Liaqat put it, "it is God-consciousness alone which can save humanity."[20] It was in this spirit that the preamble of the resolution declared that "all authority must be subservient to God" and acknowledged, first of all, God's sovereignty.[21] For the ulema, however, the sovereignty of God connoted, for all practical purposes, the sovereignty of the sharia, and for this reason they would include the sunna along with the Qur'an, its subtle but powerful implication being that life in an Islamic state must continue to be governed by rules and regulations formulated and collected by the third Islamic century.

The fundamentalists, lacking in serious thought, could only nostalgically and in vague terms talk about the "golden era" of Islam.[22] They can therefore be seen as indulging in a moral shortcut that perpetuates intellectual confusion and leads to social defeat. In their quest for Muslim identity, they have resorted to some strange distinctions that serve no constructive purpose, but instead prevent their victims from fully participating in the modern world.[23]

The intellectual confusion of the counterreformists in Pakistan is evidenced by the fact that for nearly seven years they had tied up the Constituent Assembly in a facile debate about the sovereignty clause. This clause shows mass confusion among the fundamentalists regarding the Qur'anic statement that "to God belongs the kingdom of the heavens and the earth" and the idea of political sovereignty. Such confusions among the religious teachers are pervasive and have bedeviled all public fields in Pakistan. A classic example is the fundamentalist contention that modern banking is unlawful in Islam because the Qur'an banned usury (riba). However, the Qur'an imposed this ban because it was an extremely cruel and exploitative system.[24]

The effect of the fundamentalists' assault on the modernists in Pakistan was to put them on the defensive and to confuse them.[25] This became one of the main obstacles to the development process in Pakistan, for lacking any clearly stated goal and direction, politics in Pakistan came to mean the sum of ad hoc arrangements and the prevalence of the status quo in which the landlord class continued to exploit the peasantry. Jinnah had emphasized the doctrine of economic justice and had accused the landlords of "the socioeconomic ruination of the peasantry," but Jinnah died too soon for the goal to be spelled out into concrete policies. The goal still remains obscure and bereft of any policies and planning. The main reason why this situation exists and why Pakistan has not been able to define its Islamic goals in meaningful and concrete terms is the terribly confused ideological situation in the country.[26]

From the Qur'anic statement that "to God belongs the kingdom of the heavens and the earth," which is repeated throughout the Qur'an and hence speaks about its importance, the fundamentalists could only derive the meaning of sovereignty, which, as already stated, is not the issue at all. It has a profound ethical meaning and warning, that is, since the heavens and the earth belong to God, it is not any individual's or group's possession. It therefore calls for socioeconomic justice and equity.[27] The fundamentalists have failed to grasp the seriousness of the meaning of this verse, and the impact it should have on human conduct and thereby on society itself. To them the sovereignty of God means "the supremacy of His will as embodied in the Islamic Canon law" or the sharia.[28] The problem with the Islamic canon law is that it is " not based upon the Qur'an and *sunnah* alone, but also upon many other historical, local, and customary sources."[29] We have already noted that fabrications were created in the sunna (tradition) literature, although some of the traditions are true. Therefore, to call this body of law the "Will of God" is not only a gross distortion, but also a major obstacle to the reform and development of the society. The ulema's understanding of sovereignty has profound consequences for the society. The greatest mischief created by their assertion is to confuse the religio-moral and political issues. By such an assertion the fundamentalists imply that God is politically sovereign, and sometimes they explicitly state this idea. The term sovereign is of a relatively recent coinage and denotes that element or elements in a society to which rightfully belongs coercive force so that it can obtain obedience to its will. Obviously, God is not sovereign in this sense; only people are sovereign, and "only their 'Word is law' in the politically ultimate sense."[30]

Hidden under the ulema's conception of sovereignty of God is the idea that it would give recognition to their own institution, for they claim, without any justification, an exclusive right to interpret Islam and to enact "Islamic laws." The slogans and outcries regarding Islam by the ulema are a subterfuge for "the political recognition of their own institution."[31] This is substantiated by the fact that many ulema claim that Islamic legislation is their prerogative. This claim is absolutely false, however, as is borne out by the early Muslim history. Originally, ijma (consensus of opinion) was meant to be the consensus of the community, and not merely of the ulema, until well after the second Islamic century when the concept of ijma of the ulema replaced that of the community.[32] Contrary to what the ulema proclaim, the Qur'an is not a book of laws but rather a text that provides divine teaching and guidance:

Such quasi-laws as do occur in the Qur'an are not meant to be *literally* applied in all times and climes; the principles on which these legal or quasi-legal pronouncements rest have to be given fresh embodiments in legislative terms. In this process of legislation the twin principles of *Ijtihad* [individual opinion] and *Ijma* [consensus of opinion] play the most crucial role. . . . *Ijtihad* means that individuals "exercise themselves" to think out new solutions of problems on the basis of Islamic principles. . . . It is sometimes asserted by those who call themselves "ulama" that a peculiar unknown kind of capacity is required for exercising *Ijtihad,* including, so it is said, the study of a certain prescribed course of books or materials. This assertion is not only historically groundless but patently false. What is required is a good acquaintance with Islam . . . and a power of thinking.[33]

Earlier, we stated that religious leaders in Pakistan tend to equate their institution with Islam and to believe they possess a special expertise in explicating Islam or exercising ijtihad. But any competent person or persons, whatever their vocation, can perform ijtihad. Ijtihad really means an attempt at thinking, and everyone is endowed with the capacity to think.[34] The contention by many of the ulema that the ijma of the previous Islamic religious doctors cannot be repealed or amended is absolutely false. "Indeed, 'the closing of the door of Ijtihad' and the irrepealability of earlier *Ijma* were the twin doctrines whereby Islamic progress committed suicide."[35] The ulema continued to confuse the population with their peculiar understanding of Islam.

The Basic Principles Committee of the Constituent Assembly appointed the Board of Talimaat-i-Islamia to advise on Islamic matters. The appointment of a Board of experts was precisely what the ulema demanded earlier. But the powers of this board were limited to advising only, and then, too, could be exercised only if any matter was referred to it.[36] This board and the ulema of the country insisted on their right to interpret the sharia, which modernist politicians rejected.37   The board and the ulema wanted to "reestablish the system as it was under the Rightly-Guided Caliphs, when there was hardly any such group known or functioning as the ulama."[38]   Although the ulema raised and debated many issues, their primary occupation was with the sharia. To this end, the ulema, at a conference in January 1951, formulated twenty-two principles of an Islamic state. One principle required that the state provide for "Islamic education in accordance with the requirements of the various *recognized schools* of thought."[39] These schools of thought and what they entail have been described in the previous chapter.   The ulema were not content with an important clause of the Directive Principles of State Policy, which stated that "the teaching of the Holy Qur'an to the Muslims should be made compulsory."[40] That itself was a major step for the Muslims of Pakistan to understand, at first hand, what Islam was all about and to remove the distorted and mythical elements propagated by the religious circles, but it has never been implemented. Without such a step, the contention by Muslim scholars that in Islam the mundane and the spiritual are inseparable becomes meaningless. This would have been a major move away from secularism.

In Islam the ultimate control and direction of the religious life of the society are vested in the state. This includes such matters as how the mosques are to be manned and run, how the religious schooling is to be conducted, and what religious subjects are to be taught. If this is not done, a bifurcation of functions into secular and religious takes place, which is the essence of a secular state. All Muslim societies have inherited this dichotomy of society into the religious and political authority.[41]

In the constitution-making process in Pakistan, the ulema did not offer any proposals of substance; their contribution was essentially negative. Their main concern was that the personal law, which has retarded growth in Muslim countries for centuries, must remain unchanged. To that end they invoked the sharia time and again. They wanted "to keep this most sacrosanct part of the Sharia as untouched as it had been throughout the British raj."[42]

The modernist politicians were, to a considerable degree, conciliatory toward the ulema, but their emphasis was, correctly, on policy rather than on law.[43] Thus, the first prime minister, Liaqat Ali Khan, emphasized that an Islamic society was one with "no inner conflicts, where a man gets just reward for his toil and where there are no parasites".[44] He also stated that a government's most important duty, which was based on Islamic principles, was to end all exploitation.[45] When his administration proposed land reforms, a group of ulema made a statement to the press to the effect that the zamindari system (the feudal system of landholding) was not un-Islamic.[46] Liaqat retorted that the government was "not bound to accept the interpretation which vested interests may give to laws of Shariat simply to serve their own selfish ends."[47] Clearly, then, the ulema did not have any idea how to address a myriad of socioeconomic and political issues facing the country. While they incessantly talked about

Islam, they did not know its deeper meanings. The ulema's overemphasis on theoretical matters diverted public attention from the practical implementation of Islam's socioeconomic programs. The result was that the idea of an Islamic state remained a political slogan.[48]

The religious establishment was essentially operating at the theoretical level; they were more concerned with the form than the substance of what it meant to be an Islamic state. Thus, they wanted the state to be declared Islamic, which the first constitution, adopted in 1956, declared it to be. Such declaration, by itself, is of no consequence, however, since the overwhelming majority of Pakistan's population is Muslim. It is the interpretation of Islam which is the critical issue—whether it is a progressive interpretation or a reactionary one. It is on this basis that the world will judge it.[49] One real hope for Pakistan was that it would aim at making itself an ideal Islamic state. Since its population is almost entirely Muslim, it must "pursue Islamic ideals or no ideals at all. For practical purposes, the alternative to the Islamic state is complacency or corruption."[50]

Constitutional debates regarding Islam in the early years of Pakistan's history had one overall positive effect: the respective positions of the religious establishment and the modernists were brought into the open. In the aftermath of the political instability that characterized the period from 1956 to 1958, the military regime, which came into power in 1958, abrogated the constitution. In the new constitution that was promulgated in 1962, two points are noteworthy. First, the phrase "the Qur'an and the sunna" which was used ⁄in the old constitution, was replaced by the word "Islam"; second, the word Islamic was deleted from the *Islamic Republic* of the old constitution.[51] The modernists wanted, correctly, to get rid of amorphous traditions that were the only source of the sunna. They argued that much of the tradition literature was either fabricated or simply reflected partisan prejudices, and therefore, could not be relied on. Moreover, applying the sunna would mean reinstating those rules and regulations that were formulated when the hadith literature was accumulated. This, they argued, would be an anachronism in modern society. As far as the Qur'anic formulations were concerned, they could be independently interpreted and applied to modern institutions. They also wanted to avoid any reference to the sunna, for it could raise questions of sectarian interpretations that could lead to conflicts within the community.[52]

The new government instituted a Constitution Commission to examine the causes of the failure of parliamentary government in Pakistan and their prevention in future, once a democratic form of government was reestablished. The commission made a number of observations of general importance. Their observation regarding the role religion played in society is revealing:

The impression among the people in general seems to be that, as long as prescribed forms of worship are observed, it does not matter if one is careless or indifferent or even corrupt in his profession or service, private or public. This attitude which is very disturbing, appears to have grown from before independence. . . . nowadays the tendency is to put in the barest minimum of effort necessary. This is not confined to people of no education or the half educated but extends also, with honourable exceptions, to the elite and the politically relevant section of society.[53]

The commission went on to cite the general lack of "moral training" in the populace and to call for an overhaul of the education system.[54] Soon after the incorporation of the new constitution, issues relating to Islam reemerged; the influence of the ulema on the establishment also became noticeable. The law minister, extolling the "great Imams" who had "contributed to the laws of Islam," stated that the professional judges "in the present state and courts [were] not competent to give their final judgement in regard to controversies which pertain to the complex questions of the interpretation of Muslim laws."[55] According to him, it was "a matter which would require certain types of people [i.e., the ulema] who would be more devoted to religion, who would understand the spirit of religion better."[56]

In the amendment to the constitution, the first amendment act of 1964, Islam was declared to mean "as set out in the Holy Qur'an and Sunnah"; the name of the country was again changed from the Republic of Pakistan to the Islamic Republic of Pakistan.[57] The government took some other measures regarding Islam, which will be discussed in a later section. In the third constitution of the country, adopted in 1973, we again see the hand of the ulema in invoking the sunna: "Muslims shall be enabled to order their lives in the individual and collective spheres in accordance with the teachings and requirements of Islam as set out in the Holy Qur'an and Sunnah."[58] All three constitutions have also stated that the state will "bring the existing laws into conformity with the injunctions of Islam as set out in the Qur'an and Sunnah, and that no law contradictory to such injunctions was to be enacted."[59]

The foregoing analysis has shown the religious establishment's preoccupation and propagation of the sharia or the sunna. The words mean virtually the same, for their source is basically the same—the hadith literature. In the course of constitutional development, reference was often made to Islamic ideology. Islamic ideology is, in fact, an offspring of political theology, which is a medieval concept and a medieval approach to political theory and practice.[60] It is a spiritual concept in which the principles of brotherhood and social justice form the basis of a modern society and state. But giving political theology a modern name, Islamic ideology," "is not sufficient to transform Islamic law as it evolved in the Middle Ages (when it remained largely ideal theory divorced from political reality) into a twentieth century" system of law and government.[61]

The ulema's idea of an Islamic society and Islamic ethics can be gleaned from the following statement, which the Central Committee of the Jamaat-i-Islami made in 1984. It reflects the influences of the celebrated "traditions."

Open violation of Islamic ethics, rebellion from Islamic teachings has now reached an alarming point in our society. The public media organizations, with the connivance of certain corrupt officers, are bent upon converting our society into a mixed and shameless one. Vulgar songs, semi-nude and immoral advertisements, programs of dance and music, encouragement of mixed gatherings on television, particular unreserved [*sic*] dialogue delivered by boys and girls, the color editions of newspapers full of huge colored pictures of women and feminine beauty are only a few examples of this condemnable conspiracy. This dangerous wave of vulgarity has now gripped the country. Performances by foreign troupes attended by certain very important government officials, fancy dress shows, vulgar stage plays in the name of art, mixed gatherings, country-wide virus of VCR, dancing and musical programs, printing of girls' pictures in the newspapers in the name of sports, mixed education, employment of women in certain government departments to make them attractive and the day-by-day rising process of seating men and women under one roof in government and business offices and even in local councils are all "red" signs of dangers against the society and Islamic ethics. This meeting condemns all these things very strongly and demands to the government that it should take immediate steps to stop such shameless, vulgar, and obscene activities and fulfill its promised safety of *chaddar* and *chardiwari*.[62]

MODERNIST INTELLECTUALS' VIEWS OF RELIGIOUS MATTERS AND PRACTICES

Our point of departure for examining the views of modernist scholars of Pakistan will be the mideighteenth-century religious scholar of Muslim India, Shah Waliy Allah. This is necessary because Pakistan, though created only four and a half decades ago, has its intellectual roots in the preceding history of the subcontinent.

The greatest impact of Waliy Allah's thought on the Muslims of India was from his belief that an individual had the right to form an independent judgment on a legal question. "To most of the traditional theologians the individual scholar had no such right: the last word on the subject had been said by the end of the tenth century, and since then the 'gates of ijtihad'—the gates on the path leading to independent judgment—had been closed."[63] He saw the need of growth and change in a healthy society. Although a theologian, he thought of society in sociological terms. Religious injunctions, he pointed out, were to be observed not exclusively because of their divine origin, but because of the benefits they conferred on the individual and the society. Islamic commandments were not designed as tests for rewards and punishments (although in an ultimate sense the concept of reward and punishment holds); the purpose of the commandments was social.[64]

Waliy Allah called on the theologians to search for pure religion in the hadith literature and the Qur'an, and to apply it to their own time and place.[65] He argued that no religious tradition could exist in a vacuum, and, therefore, it was vitally important to recognize the sociohistorical conditions surrounding a religion. Although Islam had emerged in Arabia, it did not mean, he reasoned, that it was forever tied to Arabic customs and procedures. In formulating sharia, Waliy Allah felt it was imperative that attention be paid to the cultural background, the mental aptitude, and the social usage and practice of the society in which a person is born.[66]

Waliy Allah did not believe that it was either possible or particularly Islamic to ask for a literal return to the conditions of the early caliphate.[67] It was Waliy Allah who, for the first time in Indian history, translated the Qur'an into Persian, the language of the aristocracy;[68] few people in India understood Arabic. The Arabs believed it was a sin to translate the Qur'an into any other language, a position they have maintained until recent years. Even now many Arabs contend that the Qur'an cannot be understood in any other language except Arabic, a position that is totally unwarranted.

Until Waliy Allah translated the Qur'an, around the mideighteenth century, very few Muslims of the subcontinent would have read and understood the Qur'an. Not knowing the Qur'an directly, it was easy for the Muslims to be influenced by and to adopt Hindu customs and traditions. Waliy Allah openly criticized the influence of the Indian environment on the practice of Islam in India.[69] His two sons subsequently translated the Qur'an into Urdu, the language that was rapidly replacing Persian in India. Their action was to prove even more revolutionary than his own translation, for the Qur'an was now made accessible in the language of the common people.[70] Such an access, however, has been relatively recent and has had limited effect because of the lack of literacy in the Indo-Pakistan subcontinent and because of the dichotomous system of education.

The ulema's ideas about Islam have also been highly conditioned by their contact with the Arabs, particularly Saudi Arabia, owing to the annual pilgrimage to that country. In addition, for centuries they have been conditioned by the al-Azhar University of Egypt. The Saudis are well known for their literal interpretation of the Qur'an and for deriving meaning from the Qur'anic verses out of context.[71] The only real contribution from Saudi Arabia in the reformation of Islam came from Muhammad ibn 'Abd al-Wahab in the eighteenth century, and only in one respect. Wahab and his followers, known as Wahabis, regard the visiting of tombs as idolatry and prohibit it with great severity.[72] Other than that, their tenets do not differ from orthodox Islam; they have no place for reason in religion.[73]

After Waliy Allah, a century was to pass before Sayyid Ahmed Khan emerged, in the second half of the nineteenth century, as the leader of the modernization movement.[74] He organized social and educational reforms along with a new approach to and interpretation of Islam. His religious orientations, however, were the least popular and the most criticized elements of his reformist program within Islamic religious circles.[75]

In the period beginning around the last quarter of the nineteenth century up to the creation of Pakistan, several Muslim scholars had written on Islam. In this section we will focus only on the most outstanding of them all, namely, Sir Sayyid Ahmed Khan, Chiragh Ali, and Sir Mohammad Iqbal. In the period following the creation of Pakistan, two prominent figures emerged—Ghulam Ahmed Parwez and Fazlur Rahman. Of these, we have covered the views of Fazlur Rahman on Islam to a considerable extent in the preceding chapter. He is by far the most outstanding scholar on Islam in the contemporary world. Here we will examine the views of Parwez only. In this period too, a number of other modernist writers emerged in Pakistan, but the views of Parwez and Rahman capture the thrust of the modernist scholars' arguments.

Sayyid Ahmad Khan (1817-1898) argued that the Qur'an was the only infallible source of law for the Muslims. He considered much of the hadith (the Prophet's traditions) as either apocryphal or relevant only to the Prophet's day and age. Of the remaining two classical sources of law, he rejected the validity of ijma (consensus of the theologians) but broadened the meaning of ijtihad (use of individual reasoning) as the birthright of every intelligent Muslim. Individual reasoning, he argued, could be utilized for the revitalization and modernization of Islamic law and life. His religious ideas have had a powerful impact on all religious thought in Muslim India and Pakistan and is the partial source of modernist movements in Islam (in Indo-Pakistan). Much of fundamentalist thought takes a defensive position against it.[76]

Although some of Sayyid Ahmad's religious ideas are questionable, his analysis of the prevalent ideas about Islam among the ulema was penetrating and insightful. The conclusion he reached was that the causes of Muslims' backwardness were rooted in the prevalent religious ideas and social practices that were based on those ideas. He took the ulema to task for their view of Islam, which was "nothing more than a parody of the teaching of the Qur'an and the holy Prophet," and who, "instead of analyzing the causes of decline, had begun to assert that the social and economic backwardness of the Muslims was not a religious problem at all, for the primary object of a Muslim should be the welfare of the hereafter and not this mundane transitory world."[77] He emphasized that the increase in human knowledge and modern life demanded that people solved their problems in the light of their own experiences instead of relying on what the ancient thinkers had said.[78]

Sayyid Ahmad felt that Muslims were obliged to accept and follow those traditions of the Prophet which referred to religious injunctions, but as far as the rest of the literature on traditions was concerned, it needed to be examined critically so that one could "discard all those which are found to contradict the Qur'an, human experience and reason."[79] He reasoned that in social, economic, and cultural affairs Muslims should adopt anything that is suitable, as long as it conforms to the fundamental spiritual values of Islam. A particular form of dress, how food is to be eaten, and similar matters are not to be decided on the basis of traditions or usage in the days of the Prophet. The forms of social, political, economic, and cultural institutions, he argued, cannot be based on the standards as they existed in early Islam. He considered it to be "the height of absurdity . . . to consider such worldly matters as unchangeable as the eternal verities incorporated in the Qur'an."[80]

Sayyid Ahmad revolted against the blind imitation of the traditions and decisions of the ancient jurists. He strongly, and rightly, believed that there was no need of theologians. It was equally unnecessary, he said, to study the fourteen subjects on which the ulema had based their knowledge. All that was required was an intelligent study of the Qur'an.[81]

Explaining the rigidity of the ulema's mind, he argued that "the original error had been a confusion between things of the spirit (*din*) [i.e., spiritual things], and things of the world."[82] True religion, he pointed out, should always be carefully distinguished from temporal affairs because, whereas true religion is unchanging, the affairs of the world are always changing. In the early period of Muslim history, the ulema used their personal opinions to give judgments on worldly affairs, which was a valid approach.[83] The causes of the Muslims' stagnation and backwardness are, however, rooted in the fact that subsequently these opinions became identified with unchanging truth. This made the ulema lawgivers in the same sense as the Qur'an. For all practical purposes, their opinions became the Will of God. Islam thus became equated with the personal opinions of lawyers, and the legal system became a rigid and unchanging system. What was worse, the legal system (fiqh) was considered a form of revelation. It was also considered so comprehensive that the ulema thought there was no need for any civil, criminal, or trade code apart from this system. This belief was one of the major reasons for the decay of Muslim societies all over the world. And the fault of the ulema has been their dogged unwillingness to reexamine and change this antiquated system.[84]

Sayyid Ahmad made an outstanding contribution in reawakening the Muslims of the subcontinent. Yet, his efforts to change Muslim thinking on several important issues "made him a kind of arch-fiend in the eyes of many of the ulema. They counterattacked regularly by accusing him of many forms of heresy. The ulema of the present-day Pakistan still often refer to him as an instance of disruptive bad thinking."[85] Systematic study of his writings in the educational institutions of Pakistan is unheard of. His commentary on the Qur'an, which generated great controversy among the Muslims of the subcontinent in the last quarter of the nineteenth century, was made to "disappear." As Aziz Ahmad and G. E. von Grunebaum have said, it is a scandal that his commentary should now be out of print. "His critics blame him for posing questions and voicing fears that were baseless. This is not altogether true."[86]

In 1878 Sayyid Ahmad had established a modern college at Aligarh; its establishment meant that Muslims had generally accepted his fundamental thesis to educate themselves in modern knowledge. But the opposition from the ulema was so great that he had to compromise on one basic issue. He had to agree to allow the traditionalists to conduct such religious education as they wanted. A result has been that the universities, both prior to and since the creation of Pakistan, have not been centers in which religious ideas like those of Sayyid Ahmed Khan could be systematically studied. Whatever new ideas have emerged are the result of the independent efforts of individuals.[87]

The Aligarh movement, started by Sayyid Ahmad Khan, gave rise to a number of intellectuals who supported and elaborated his ideas, although there were some who moderated and compromised with the orthodoxy. Among all of them, including Sayyid Ahmad Khan, Chiragh Ali (1844-1895) stands out for taking a more drastically radical stand. Chiragh Ali was "a scholar of rare caliber in that early phase of Islamic modernism."[88] Two of his works written in English were well known to late nineteenth and early twentieth century Western scholars like Ignaz Goldziher and Alfred Guillaume who benefited from his ideas and who, like him, have questioned "the authenticity of the contents of even some of the classical collections of hadith."[89] In that period of great orthodoxy, Chiragh Ali had the courage to point out that the six collections of hadith that the ulema have historically revered and given a status second only to the Qur'an are "not based on critical investigation of the text in the modern sense and as containing much more apocryphal material than the Muslims are generally ready to concede."[90] He forcefully argued that the Qur'an did not profess to teach a social and political law.

Some aspects of the civil and political law which were the most corrupt and abused such as polygamy, divorce, concubinage, and slavery have been noticed in the Qur'an. These and other immoral practices were checked and removed by the Qur'an. Because of the weakness and immaturity of the pagan and barbarous Arabs, the Qur'an even allowed some judicious, reasonable, helpful, and harmless accommodations for a time. These accommodations were eventually set aside when, under its influence, the people's condition began to improve.[91] To reach still higher levels of development, it was essential that Muslims continuously ponder over the teachings of the Qur'an to draw fresh meanings and inspiration for new situations in the ever changing world. This, however, was not done, which eventually led to the stagnation of Muslim societies. A major reason was that Muslim societies, in their ignorance and the fear created by the ulema, drew only literal and fixed meanings. Regrettably, this condition prevails in the present world.

Chiragh Ali pointed out that the more important civil and political institutions of the Islamic law based on the Qur'an "are mere inferences and deductions from a single word or an isolated sentence. Slavish adherence to the letter and taking not the least notice of the spirit of the Qur'an is the sad characteristic of the Qur'anic interpretations and deductions" of the Muslim doctors.[92] In a brilliant analysis of Muslim law, Chiragh Ali has shown how most of the deductions of the early legists were fortuitous interpretations. To interpret the Qur'an in legal and juridical terms, "apart from the doctrinal, moral, prophetical and historical interpretations, the words, sentences and their uses" were divided and subdivided by the early doctors according to a schema they had devised.[93] Some of the Muslim compilers picked out verses that they termed as "law verses," and they "compiled separate treatises in which they have made an abstract of all such verses of the Qur'an. They have applied them to the different heads of the various branches of the canon and civil law, giving their fanciful processes of reasoning and the deductive system of jurisprudence."[94] With regard to the legal system that the ulema the world over decry so vehemently and that is referred to as sharia, Chiragh Ali observed:

It has been said there are about two hundred out of six thousand verses of the Qur'an on the civil, criminal, fiscal, political, devotional, and ceremonial (canon or ecclesiastical) law. Even in this insignificant number of the . . . (law verses), a thirtieth part of the first source of the law, is not to be depended upon. These are no specific rules, and more than three-fourths of them I believe, are mere letters, single words, or mutilated sentences from which fanciful deductions repugnant to reason, and not allowable by any law of sound interpretations, are drawn.[95]

Refuting the notion that "the Qur'an has so encrusted the religion in a hard and unyielding casement of ordinances and social laws, that if the shell be broken, the life is gone," Chiragh Ali pointed out that what the Qur'an teaches is certain doctrines of religion and rules of morality. The rules of morality addressed, among many other aspects, such civil institutions of the ancient Arabs as infanticide, polygamy, slavery, arbitrary divorce, concubinage, degradation of women, drunkenness, gambling, extortionate usury, superstitious acts of divination, and idolatry. These all have either been condemned or reformed.[96]

With regard to the traditions or the sunna, which the ulema insisted that the constitution of Pakistan specifically mention, Chiragh Ali had drawn attention to the fact that most of the traditions are spurious. The sifting of the mass of traditions that had been collected by the third Islamic century was not based on any critical, historical, or rational basis.[97] Although most of the Islamic civil, political, and canon laws are based on traditions, the Prophet Muhammad had never enjoined anyone to collect traditions of any kind, nor did his Companions think of doing so.[98] Recourse to traditions was made much later in order to defend every religious, social, and political system to please a ruler. In this process, the Prophet's name was abused to support all kinds of deceptions, lies, and absurdities, so that the passion, caprice, or arbitrary will of the despots were satisfied.[99] We have already seen in Chapter 4 that other scholars subsequently reached similar conclusions. In the contemporary Muslim world, the practice continues in which the leading despots now are the ulema who continue to terrorize and mislead the populations.

Muhammad Iqbal, who provided the vision for creating Pakistan, was well aware that the causes of the Muslims' backwardness were rooted in the stagnation of religious thought. For Muslims to be able to develop, therefore, it was crucial "to rethink the whole system of Islam without completely breaking with the past."[100] He pointed out that modern knowledge was indispensable for the development of Muslim societies. Muslims must learn to approach modern knowledge with a respectful but independent attitude; they must appreciate the teachings of Islam in the light of that knowledge which may mean arriving at meanings different from before.[101] Since the actualities of the world change, he argued, Muslims must learn to accept the change. The world's changing realities force our being into fresh formations. It is our reflective contact with the changing situations in the temporal world which gives us a vision of the nontemporal. Humanity cannot afford to ignore the changing world. The Qur'an opens our eyes to the great fact of change. To build a durable civilization, he said, we must appreciate and control the changes taking place before our eyes.[102]

Iqbal believed that a fresh orientation of Islam was a legitimate demand. Modern knowledge as developed in the West is indispensable toward that end. In other words, education in Muslim societies must consist of both modern education and the study of the Qur'an. It is for want of this combination that, emotionally, people in Muslim societies are divided into two groups. A large majority of the people, as a result of illiteracy and credulousness, hold very conservative views and are not prepared to accept change in any form.[103] The second group, because of the secular nature of education, is generally not known to carry out a serious study of the Qur'an, which is the base of Islam. While this group, as the other, has a profound reverence for the Qur'an, very little is known by both as to what the Qur'an contains.

Iqbal pointed out that the ultimate fate of a people depends on the worth and power of each individual in a society; he eschewed false reverence for past history. A false reverence for past history and its artificial resurrection were no remedy for the deterioration of a people. To counteract the forces of decay the development of self-concentrated individuals is required. They alone reveal the richness and depth of life. They disclose new standards that make us aware that our environment is not wholly inviolable and needs revision. The legal interpreters of Islam in the thirteenth century and later tended to over-organize out of a false reverence of the past. This was contrary to the inner impulse of Islam.[104]

Iqbal, like Sayyid Ahmad Khan, taught liberalism and moderation. Their liberalism had resulted from the recognition that modernity was an existential fact and was therefore not to be avoided since Islam taught that the realities of life were to be faced. Iqbal called for the revival of ijtihad (independent judgment) which he regarded as the principle of movement in the structure of Islam and which equipped the Muslims with the philosophy of what he called *permanence-in-change.* He longed for the emergence of new ulema from among the modern Muslims who would approach modernism with an open mind. Spiritually, he argued, Muslims were living in a prison-house of thoughts and emotions, which during the course of centuries they had woven around themselves. Islam, as he put it, "requires emancipation from the medieval fancies of theologians and legists."[105]

Answering the question of whether materialist outlook was inimical to Islam, Iqbal observed that Islam had had too much of renunciation. It was time that Muslims faced the realities of life. Materialism is also an effective weapon against mulla-craft (mulla or mullah refers to the religious teacher in the mosque and has pejorative connotations because of the primitive education and outlook of the individual) and Sufi-craft, which deliberately mystify people to exploit their ignorance and credulity. As far as the spirit of Islam is concerned, it is not afraid to come into contact with matter. Indeed, the Qur'an specifically states that one should not forget one's share in the world. Iqbal viewed the materialist outlook as a form of self-realization. The inventions of the mythmaking religious teachers are largely responsible for the stupidity of the average Muslim.[106]

Iqbal considered it a dangerous situation in which the ulema supervised the legislative activity in a Muslim country. He thought that the remedy against erroneous interpretations of Islamic law was to reform legal education in Muslim countries, by extending its sphere and combining it with an intelligent study of modern jurisprudence.[107] Based on independent judgment, penetrative thought, and fresh experience, he argued, Muslims must courageously undertake the work of reconstruction before them.[108] The ulema's preoccupation with the opinions and thoughts formulated centuries ago in the Islamic history is due to that intellectual laziness which, especially in the period of spiritual decay, turns great thinkers into idols. If the ulema continue to uphold the fiction that the doors of independent judgment closed in Islam around the third Islamic century, modern Islam is not bound by this voluntary surrender of intellectual independence.[109] As far as Islamic traditions of legal import are concerned, Iqbal fully agrees with the penetrating thought of Shah Waliy Allah. Waliy Allah had pointed out that in the prophetic method of teaching, the law revealed by the Prophet takes special notice of the habits, peculiarities, and situation of the people to whom he is specifically sent. The Prophet aims at all-embracing principles, and therefore,

can neither reveal different principles for different peoples, nor leave them to work out their own rules of conduct. His method is to train one particular people, and to use them as a nucleus for the building up of a universal Shari'at. In doing so he accentuates the principles underlying the social life of all mankind, and applies them to concrete cases in the light of the specific habit of the people immediately before him. The Shari'at values [injunctions] . . . resulting from this application (e.g., rules relating to penalties for crimes) are in a sense specific to that people; and, since their observance is not an end in itself, they cannot be strictly enforced in the case of future generations.[110]

Iqbal pointed out that in the course of history the moral and social ideals of Islam have been gradually de-Islamized. These ideals were corrupted through local influences and the pre-Islamic superstitions of Muslim nations. These ideals are now more Iranian, Turkish, or Arabian than Islamic.[111] For Muslims to be able to move forward, the only alternative is to restore Islam's dynamic outlook on life and to rediscover the original verities of freedom, equality, and solidarity. Muslims must rebuild their moral, social, and political ideals out of their original simplicity and universality.[112]

A world of difference exists between Iqbal's perspective on the finality of Muhammad's prophethood and what the traditionalists have understood from it. The traditionalists have grossly misunderstood the idea, and this misunderstanding has distorted the traditionalists' entire thinking:

For the traditionalists a comprehensive life-system had been passed on; faithfulness consisted of dutiful adherence to unchanging patterns. For Iqbal, the "spirit of the message" of the message was a dynamism from which had followed the birth of inductive intellect, the abolition of castes and priests, and the destruction of hereditary kingship. To manifest that spirit in the present would mean to exhibit comparable world-transforming energy and intelligence.[113]

The idea of finality, moreover, incorporates the Qur'an's emphasis on reason and experience, and the study of nature and history. "In Islam prophecy reaches its perfection in discovering the need of its own abolition. This involves the keen perception . . . that in order to achieve full self-consciousness man must finally be thrown back on his own resources."[114] Islam sought to inculcate individuality. Self-negation was dangerous since it could breed otherworldliness and passivity. Good religion sought to affirm the strengthening of individuality; a strengthened individual would also be creative. Growth toward God does not entail destruction of individuality; on the contrary, it requires the strengthening of true individuality. If an individual does not take the initiative, if he or she does not develop the inner richness that is bestowed on a person, if a person ceases to feel the inward push toward the advancement of life, the result is that he or she is reduced to the level of dead matter. A being whose movements are predetermined cannot produce goodness.[115]

The emphasis on individuality and creativeness does not, however, mean that religion loses its significance. An individual must at the same time transcend himself or herself; otherwise, individuality is reduced to self-centeredness. Such transcendence is possible only through religion: "The most intense and self-transcending experience possible is a religious one. Also only such experiences can make [people] capable of that kind of virtuous action which is necessary if

[they] are to become capable of responsible corporate life."[116] Self-transcendence, in fact, links up with the idea of equality, which the Qur'an emphasizes so heavily. Creativeness is a response to concerns that are not self-centered. Therefore, strong individuality is possible only in those individuals who are capable of forgetting about themselves as they try to solve problems and serve people.[117]

Iqbal had observed that, according to Islam, the principal fact that stands in the way of people's ethical progress is fear. The central proposition that regulates the structure of Islam is that there is fear in nature, and the object of Islam is to free people from fear. We can extend this point further by saying that undue fear inhibits growth in human societies. In Islamic societies we have the classic example of the creation and spread of fear. The ulema, by instilling in the minds of the people the idea that the hadith literature (which is the source of the traditions and customs, or the sharia, or the sunna) was sacrosanct and binding on Muslims in all ages, have created the fear among Muslims that, if they did not follow those traditions, they would not only undermine Islam, but they would also cease to be Muslims. This explains why the vast majority of even educated Muslims, including political leaders, silently accept ulema's invocation of sunna, hadith, shari'a, or traditions (which mean the same thing), whenever they make reference to Islam or the Qur'an.[118]

Iqbal emphasizes the importance of freedom for people to think and act. Goodness is not a matter of compulsion; freedom is a condition of goodness. Goodness requires "the self's free surrender to the moral ideal and arises out of a willing cooperation of free egos."[119] Iqbal pointed out that it is vitally important for societies to succeed in this world, and a great measure of success is certainly prosperity. One of the most important teachings of the Qur'an is that nations are collectively judged and suffer for their misdeeds in this world. To bring this point home, the Qur'an constantly cites historical examples and urges the reader to reflect on the past and present experience of mankind and to learn from it.[120] Although this is one of the most essential teachings of the Qur'an, the ulema have failed to pay any heed to it or have simply failed to understand it. Instead, their emphasis has been on otherworldliness, and a preoccupation with prayers and the sharia or the traditions that were collected in the third Islamic century.

Ghulam Ahmad Parwez, an important modernist writer of Pakistan, takes the prevalent conditions in Pakistan seriously and critically. He firmly believes that "the religious leaders are basic obstacles to the creation of a new and prosperous Pakistan; that the religious leaders care nothing for the problems of the poor; they are only yes men for the rich landlords."[121] He points out that the whole structure of medieval law and theology, which has persisted up to the present age, is totally wrong. He forcefully argues that since the time the hadith collections were made, two kinds of religion have existed under the name of Islam, one based on the Qur'an and the other based on the hadith literature.

The purpose of the hadith literature was to establish a system in which an answer to every question is given. Parwez's main thesis is that the Qur'an is the authority that refutes the traditionalists. He also maintains that the sharia was always wrong because it was accentuated to the level of revelation by the ulema, and because it was articulated at a time when the Muslim territories were ruled by kings, whom he views as corrupt. He also argues that "all the traditional practices such as prayer, fasting and pilgrimage have been wrongly understood."[122]

Parwez rejected the idea that the collection of traditions is in any way a manifestation of the Qur'an. "Such a principle of belief," he said, "is against the Qur'an."[123] He argued that "if religion had been confined to the Qur'an, there would have been no scope for un-Qur'anic ideas to become Islamic. . . . until these traditions are rejected, real Islam cannot come to the fore."[124]

STATE RESPONSES TO MODERNIST INTELLECTUALS' VIEWS OF RELIGIOUS MATTERS AND PRACTICES

Thus far, the state has largely ignored the views of modernist intellectuals. Most modernists contend that the hadith literature/traditions/sharia/sunna pose a major obstacle to development in Muslim societies; it has prevented fresh thinking from emerging in these societies. They have found the religious leaders' role in the society to be negative and retrogressive. The dichotomous system of education, secular and religious, has further contributed to stagnation and maintenance of the status quo in Pakistan and other Muslim countries.

Until 1958, Islam's role in the new state was debated quite extensively but no fresh ground was broken. The ulema's rallying cry then and subsequently has been the enforcement of the sharia, which they describe as

a complete scheme of life and an all embracing social order where nothing is superfluous, and nothing is lacking. . . . These directives touch such varied subjects as religious rituals, personal character, morals, habits, family relationships, social and economic affairs, administration, rights, and duties of citizens, judicial system, laws of war and peace and international relations. In short, it embraces all the various departments of human life.[125]

In 1960 the state appointed a constitution commission to give its recommendations for a new constitution. In its deliberations, although the commission seems to have been influenced by groups like Jamaat-i-Islami (a religious political party), it nevertheless "recognized the difficulty of identifying the authentic *hadis* [hadith] by which *sunna* could be determined in legal terms."[126] Although the commission accepted the modernist scholars' argument dating back to Shah Waliy Allah that the situational context must be kept in mind, it did not call into question the authenticity of the hadith literature. This shows (1) the influence of the ulema and, more importantly, (2) the fear of the ulema in raising the issue. The commission was content merely to recommend the creation of an international commission of Muslim countries, which should advise "as to whether instructions given by the Prophet with reference to local conditions should necessarily be followed literally in the various countries regardless of the local customs to which people of these countries have all along been accustomed, or, only the principles have to be adopted."[127]

The commission seemed to be indefinitely postponing the issue, for it suggested that before changes were made in the general laws of Pakistan, "a synthesis had to be made between different schools of Muslim juristic thought as well as other legal views in the modern world of Islam."[128] The commission would not have been unaware that "most Muslim countries, except theocracies like Saudi Arabia, would be either lukewarm or hesitant to accept such commissions in their lands; and if countries such as Turkey . . . and Tunisia did set up such commissions, their recommendations were bound to range from secularism to liberalism."[129] This was a manifestation of a situation in which the state wavered and merely attempted to ignore the issue. The issue, however, is very serious and affects the lives of the people in several ways, and negatively.

In 1953, when the state had instituted a court of inquiry to inquire into the religious disturbances that had become serious, the court sought to draw the state's attention to the seriousness of the issue between orthodoxy and modernism and their consequences. The court stated that Muslims find themselves in a state of helplessness, uncertainty, and confusion, and are waiting for someone to come and help them. It called for a bold reorientation of Islam to separate the vital from the lifeless so that a Muslim could become a citizen of the world from the archaic incongruity he or she had become. This lack of bold and clear thinking, the court observed, had created the situation they were investigating. The court noted that opposing principles, if left to themselves, could only produce confusion and disorder. As long as Islam was pressed "into service to solve situations it was never intended to solve, frustration and disappointment must dog our steps," the court argued.[130]

It is ideological confusion, primarily because of reliance on the hadith literature or the sharia, false ideas attributed to Islam, and gross misunderstanding of the Qur'anic doctrine, which manifests itself in the way the society is organized and run. It is vitally important that this ideological confusion be resolved or corrected if society is to move forward and not remain suspended in stagnation.[131] The authors of the court of inquiry mentioned above attempted to bring the importance of this point home when they concluded:

If there is one thing which has been conclusively demonstrated in this inquiry, it is that provided you can persuade the masses to believe that something they are asked to do is religiously right or enjoined by religion, you can set them to any course of action, regardless of all considerations of discipline, loyalty, decency, morality or civic sense.[132]

We can illustrate this point and the seriousness of its implication for the society by means of only one example. Because the religious teachers propagate the idea that birth control is un-Islamic or that God will provide the means of livelihood for everyone, and similar other ideas, the result is a population explosion in Pakistan. An international organization affiliated with Pakistan for family planning for several years recently reported that all birth control efforts in Pakistan have failed.[133] The population is growing at a rate of 3.1 percent, and it is feared that at this rate of increase the entire development effort will be neutralized.[134]

The state had been aware of the importance of Islam in the country right from the beginning. It was also aware, until the middle of 1977, that the matter was far more complex than the simplistic ideas of the ulema. This awareness was indicated when the state decided to create two institutions: (1) The Advisory Council of Islamic Ideology, and (2) the Central Institute of Islamic Research. In creating the Advisory Council of Islamic Ideology, the second constitution had stated: "The President shall, in selecting a person for appointment to the Council, have regard to the person's understanding and appreciation of Islam and of the economic, political, legal and administrative problems of Pakistan."[135]

Because of the nature of the educational system in the country, it was not easy to choose members of the Council.[136] Of the eight members chosen, five were Mawlanas [ulema], that is, those who were the products of seminaries and thus represented the religious establishment.[137] The state had apparently foreseen this problem, for the scope of the Council was limited to advising only. Furthermore, in order to have a check on the Council's deliberations, the state appointed to the Council two former justices of the Supreme Court of Pakistan, one being the chairman, and the director of the Central Institute of Islamic Research. The law minister also indicated this when he said on July 30, 1962: "Though the first principle is that no law should be repugnant to Islam, there are 15 other principles which have no direct relationship with Islam and [are] in the nature of an enunciation of human rights recognized by the United Nations[,] of which Pakistan is a member."[138] The purpose of this Council, the law minister explained, was to generate a process to apply Islam to the present conditions that were different from the time when Islamic jurisprudence originated and developed.[139]

The Central Institute of Islamic Research was established in 1960; after the promulgation of the 1962 constitution, it was renamed the "Islamic Research Institute." A notification of the central government explained its objectives in these terms: (1) to define the fundamentals of Islam "in a rational and liberal manner and to emphasize, among others, the basic Islamic ideals of universal brotherhood, tolerance and social justice"; (2) to interpret Islam "in such a way as to bring out its dynamic character in the context of the intellectual and scientific progress of the modern world."[140]

Two more objectives related to research in other areas. These were all progressive steps and bode well for the future. The president in his inaugural address underscored the need to be clear about the basic principles and how they were to be implemented, so that there was no confusion regarding the alterable and the unalterable. He also pointed out that, if people failed or refused to bring about adjustment between Islam and the requirements of modern life, the fear was that the Muslims would drift away from Islam.[141]

Soon after the second constitution was promulgated, the president appointed a commission on national education with a view to integrating religious education at different levels with secular education. Based on the commission's recommendations, religious education was made compulsory up to Class VIII. This education was understandably of an elementary nature and can hardly be called religious education. For some inexplicable reason, at the high school level where a student can be expected to have the faculties to study the Qur'an, the commission completely shied away and made no such recommendation. In effect, then, the students were not to know what Islam taught and for all practical purposes were to remain ignorant, save for the rituals. With regard to the religious seminaries, they were to continue as before, with some modification of their syllabi and inclusion of modern subjects. However, no reforms took place, and the seminaries continued to function as before.

The commission accepted the dual nature of the educational system and did not recognize the dangers of such a system. It favored the view that "modern educational institutions should exist side by side with the religious seminaries."[142] The practice has continued up to the present. An element of mystery surrounds the religious education, and the state has so far conceded, without critically examining the issue, that it is the prerogative of the ulema. The seminaries only produce such individuals who assume the role of priests. And because of massive illiteracy in the country, the ideas generated and propagated by them have a powerful but negative effect on the society.

The modernizing regime of Ayub Khan had made it clear that it was not in favor of traditional Islam.[143] Its thinking was also reflected through the Central Institute of Islamic Research under the directorship of Fazlur Rahman. He had pointed out that the conservatives in Pakistan, that is, the religious teachers, were engaged in "uncompromising cynicism."[144] Thus, when President Ayub Khan promulgated the Muslim Family Laws Ordinance on March 2, 1961, which was a progressive step in the social life of the country, the ulema attacked it as thoroughly un-Islamic. This law was based on the recommendations of a seven-member commission set up in 1955; of the seven members, six were modernists and one represented the religious establishment who totally disagreed with the recommendations of the commission and wrote a lengthy note of dissent.[145]

The government was moving cautiously to ensure that Pakistan did not become a religious state of medieval applications. For this purpose, it was necessary to educate the country and to persuade the people that for a state to be Islamic did not mean that it had to be backward and stagnant, as the religious teachers wanted. President Ayub Khan had indeed "warned Muslims against being trapped by people who, in the garb of religion, were trying to achieve political power."[146]

There was a "consistency with which certain interpretations espoused by the more conservative religious elements in Pakistan" were being replaced by modern interpretations.[147] This situation was reversed by the state when the archconservative religious merchants* captured state power through General Zia, who led them.

During General Zia's eleven-year military rule, Pakistan became a theocratic state against the wishes of a majority of its population which found itself helpless against the vast coercive power wielded by the military. In the process, great damage has been done to the evolutionary process in the country through state sponsorship of fundamentalism.[148]

The manner in which the state has reacted to modernist intellectuals as well as religious merchants shows great ideological confusion. For a meaningful national development to occur, this ideological confusion will have to be faced and resolved.[149] Simply stated, an honest and thoughtful answer has to be given to the questions: What does Islam mean and, second, what does it demand from an individual and society? The Qur'an provides the answer, as we saw in the previous chapter, and reliance has to be on the Qur'an alone to get the answer; only then can the ideological confusion be resolved.

STATE RESPONSES TO RELIGIOUS LEADERS' VIEWS AND DEMANDS REGARDING ISLAM

Earlier in this chapter, we discussed some of the main ideas of the religious establishment regarding Islam, or their understanding of it. Their main thesis is that Islamic law as it was worked out in the earlier centuries of Islam is "binding on all and for all times."[150] Although the ulema mention the Qur'an as a source of Islamic law, they rely heavily on the sunna or the hadith literature and the decisions of the early jurists of Islam.[151] The ulema claim that they alone have the knowledge to authoritatively interpret Islam; others "are conversant neither with the language of the Qur'an and the sunna nor possess any insight in Islamic traditions. None of them has seriously devoted even a day

---

* The term was apparently coined by Maulana Mawdudi who, being a leading member of the ulema, surprisingly, used it in his writings.

of his life to the study of Islam and its vast literature."[152]

Before we examine the state's responses to the religious establishments' views and demands regarding Islam, a brief look at the religious circles and religious life of Pakistan is in order. In Pakistan two major groups of religious leaders have emerged, the ulema and the pirs (holy men). In almost every mosque of the country there is a paid imam (prayer leader). Imams of the main mosques everywhere also act as preachers and deliver sermons on Fridays and lectures on special occasions. These prayer leaders usually belong to the lower working class with a rural background, though some come from the urban lower middle class. They graduate from religious studies institutions which are generally private and financially endowed or supported by religious institutions. Recently, some of them have been receiving grants from the government. Courses of instruction at these institutions are antiquated and are based on the syllabus created in the eighteenth century, which in turn is based on the literature belonging to the medieval period. Emphasis is on classical Arabic and in some cases on written Persian. Modern subjects and literature are completely shunned, with the result that the graduates of these institutions are out of touch with reality and the modern world.[153]

While this is so, the political influence of the ulema has increased significantly over the years. Several religious political parties have emerged. The three major ones are (1) the Jamaat-i-Islami, founded in 1941, which is now largely considered to be obscurantist; (2) the Jamiyat-ul-Ulama-i-Islam, founded in 1945, which is relatively moderate; and (3) the Jamiyat-ul-Ulama-i-Pakistan, founded in 1948, which is highly conservative. All these parties have exerted great pressure on the government for what they consider to be an Islamic state.[154]

A second major religious group is called the pirs or "holy men." Although not directly connected with a mosque, a pir is considered to have special spiritual powers, either because of his "demonstrated" charisma in the form of "miraculous" healing or other supernatural powers, or because he is the custodian of a shrine (mazar), either as a descendant of the saint for whom the shrine was built or as one of his disciples, or a descendant of a disciple. Although the pir is not required to have formal religious training, he must display great devotion and knowledge of the mystical experience to his followers. His followers, mostly villagers and tribesmen, reward him with gifts in cash or in kind. Nearly every rural family bears allegiance to one pir. It is estimated that the number of shrines in Pakistan totals over 10,000.[155]

Traditionally, there is a close affinity between the ulema and the pirs. The political parties of the country vie with each other to obtain the electoral support of the pirs. "Indeed, there is almost no political party that can survive without the support of the pirs. This is primarily because of their spiritual influence on the villagers, but also because in many instances the pirs are feudal landlords who employ a large number of disciples and followers."[156] In past national and provincial assemblies, the proportion of pirs has been quite high.[157]

Religious education is imparted primarily through the mosque and through sermons to the elders. The children are taught to recite the Qur'an in Arabic, a language they do not understand. The religious leader does, however, impart some knowledge of the beliefs and rituals of Islam to the young children. In Pakistan, Islam is followed merely on trust, without even understanding the words uttered in prayers. Such practices create and perpetuate an acquiescent attitude toward religious tradition, which is both uncritical and unproductive.[158]

In the earlier years of Pakistan, the state, in order not to alienate the support of the religious establishment, encouraged its participation in the constitution-making process and accepted a number of its suggestions and demands. These suggestions were incorporated in the Objectives Resolution, which became a guiding document for the subsequent constitutions of Pakistan. The state, however, rejected the ulema's demand for veto power in the legislative process. The ulema had demanded "the creation of a Board of ulama entrusted with authority to review all legislative Bills under consideration of the National or Provincial Assemblies in the light of the Qur'an and Sunnah."[159]

One of the state's major mistakes occurred when it initially agreed to include the sunna (i.e., the hadith literature) in the constitution as a source of law. The first constitution stated that "no law shall be enacted which is repugnant to the Injunctions of Islam as laid down in the Holy Qur'an and Sunnah, hereinafter referred to as Injunctions of Islam."[160] This meant that such socioreligious practices would continue which were derived from the hadith literature. Most of this literature, as we saw in the previous chapter, is spurious. This also meant that the religious establishment could invoke the sunna whenever any laws and social practices were changed to bring them into conformity with the needs of modern times. This mistake was apparently realized when the second constitution was formulated. Within a short time, however, the state gave in to the ulema's pressure and reincorporated the word sunna in the constitution.[161] The third constitution also retained sunna as a source of law and maintained, as before, that no law would be made contrary to the Qur'an and the sunna. Although the word "sunna" has always been used along with the Qur'an, its implication is the maintenance of the status quo.

The religious establishment carried out a coup when General Muhammad Zia-ul-Haq overthrew the elected government of Zulfiquar Ali Bhutto. General Zia not only had an understanding of Islam of the same level as the present-day religious leaders, but also had family ties with the Jamaat-i-Islami, a fanatical religious party.[162] In Zia's person, then, fundamentalist groups in Pakistan succeeded in gaining control of the state, a situation described as frightening by the political leaders who had worked for the creation of Pakistan.[163] The process of "Islamization" which ensued in Pakistan under Zia was therefore the work of religious groups, Zia being a part of those groups.[164]

The government launched its "Islamization" policy in June 1980, which was designed to impose the sharia law on the country, that is, the legal opinions and decisions that were formulated over a thousand years ago. Zia included representatives from religious parties in his cabinet and proceeded to promulgate laws that were undoubtedly their production.[165]

To establish an "Islamic state," Zia reconstituted the Islamic Ideological Council, comprising eminent personalities and so-called scholars of Islamic jurisprudence.[166] The council consisted of thirteen individuals, eight of whom were maulanas/muftis (one pir).[167] Following the thinking of the religious leaders, Zia declared that political parties were un-Islamic; he, however, believed monarchical rule to be Islamic. Following a tradition, he also declared: "Never trust the man who seeks office."[168]

Zia's Islamization program covered four areas: judicial reforms, the introduction of an Islamic penal code, new educational policy incorporating "Islamic tenets," and economic programs.[169] On June 3, 1980, Zia announced new measures designed to bring the legal code into conformity with the sharia law. Accordingly, a federal shariat court, consisting of religious leaders, was set up to replace the shariat benches that he had created earlier in the provincial high courts.[170] The measure is noteworthy, for it legitimizes the power of the ulema and gives them additional status in the society. This is precisely what the ulema had been agitating for so intensively in the past quarter of a century. Thus, an attempt was made to institutionalize theocracy by proxy in Pakistan. Traditional clothing was prescribed for the shari'a court jurists. Similarly, judges and civil servants were ordered to wear "Islamic dress," and women students were asked to wear the "traditional Muslim *burqa*," a covering over the dress from head to toe.[171] Of course, there is nothing "Islamic" about the dress except that it is a carryover from medieval times. It has serious psychological effects, however. The overall effect of such measures was that the society came to have a look of a large monastery.[172] Interestingly, no change was made in the military's dress, which continued to wear the efficient "Western" dress, which also gives a smart appearance.

Since lawyers did not have expertise in the sharia law, a sharia law faculty was created at Islamabad's Quaid-i-Azam University in 1979 to train them. A year later it was made a separate institution, the Islamic University. The hallmark of the measures to make laws in Pakistan "Islamic" was the enforcement of punishments as prescribed in the sharia law.[173] An educated woman's reaction was that the Sharia Ordinance had opened a Pandora's box. She pointed out the contradictions that existed among different schools of thought based on the traditions they followed.[174] Another woman, echoing the feelings of educated women, opposed the appointment of ulema as deputy attorneys-general and described the average mullah as an illiterate person.[175]

The government's new educational policy related primarily to the propagation and acceptance of the government's Islamization program among the people. Islamic studies was made compulsory for the bachelor's degree in all faculties.[176]

This study consists of knowing basic beliefs and rituals, prayers, and some aspects of Islamic history. The traditional schools of Islamic education were retained, and some secular subjects were made part of their curriculum. Their original curriculum was retained, however. This is an important point, as we will see later in this chapter. The dual system of education was therefore maintained.

In the economic sphere, the government made some changes of nomenclature so as to be able to call it an "Islamic system." Thus, for instance, the zakat system was introduced, which is a welfare system. Although the government made much of it, many people, while approving the basic concept of the zakat, question what real impact the system has had.[177] The issue really is one of taxation, and of its enforcement.

In 1980 the government instituted a committee of economists "to spell out 'an agenda for Islamic reform.'"[178] The committee's analysis and recommendations are revealing and interesting. In the *Report of the Committee on Islamization*, the authors "opted for a very gradual and deliberate process of introducing the Islamic [economic] system in Pakistan."[179] Its basic philosophy was that in Islam the state had a significant role to play in economic management because

social welfare requires not only a transfer of financial resources from the rich to the poor, but a diversion of real resources to the production of basic necessities of life. . . . the matter is too important to be left to the "invisible hand" of the market forces.

[The committee rejected] a strategy [that] was based on an explicit acceptance of income and wealth differentials, which were allowed to grow even further as a means of achieving rapid growth rates. . . . Islam, according to the committee, would not—as it cannot—use widening income differentials as a policy instrument to promote capital formulation and economic growth by virtue of its commitment to [justice and kindness]. It was the responsibility of the state to prevent the occurrence of a situation in which the initial cost of promoting growth was borne by the underprivileged segments of society.[180]

This was a radical departure from the past and in the spirit of the Qur'anic injunctions. The committee made a number of recommendations, of which the government accepted only some. As one leading analyst has said, "Quite a profound change would have occurred in the structure and growth patterns of Pakistan's economy had the government accepted the committee's recommendations in their entirety."[181] In their emphasis on economic growth with improved income distribution, the authors of the report made two concrete suggestions. One called for land redistribution in which ceilings on holdings would be applied to families rather than individuals. The second asked for the introduction of an inheritance tax equal to 30 percent of the deceased's wealth. The first recommendation was based on the fact that previous attempts at land reforms had not been successful; the second was meant to prevent the "intergenerational snowballing of wealth."[182]

The government did not accept these important recommendations apparently because the sharia does not say so! This conclusion is warranted because in July 1986 the Senate passed the Shariat Bill, which made the sunna and the Qur'an the supreme law and source of guidance for future legislation. The Shariat Bill also gave the Shariat Court the right to question any law it considered un-Islamic and to reject draft laws on fiscal dealings and family matters (including marriage, divorce, and inheritance).[183]

The authors of the report had strongly rejected the notion, widely prevalent in religious circles since the creation of Pakistan, that an interest-free economy and institution of zakat would result in an Islamic economic order. They described such measures as "undue obsession." Abolition of interest could well result in a "rise in the overall level of exploitation of the poor by the rich," they argued.[184] The committee pointed out that the purpose of the Islamic system of management was to achieve justice and kindness. This could be done through several means. The committee observed that Pakistan needed universal education, an improved quality of life through easy access to basic consumer goods, and a higher employment level. The committee acknowledged that these were the objectives of any economic system. This did not mean, the committee pointed out, that they could not also be the objectives of the Islamic economic system since they followed directly from Islam's own distinctive economic philosophy.[185]

Nevertheless, the government proceeded to introduce such measures as interest-free banking, zakat, and 'ushr (taxes to help the poor). The 'ushr is a levy on agricultural harvest. The zakat tax rate is 2.5 percent, whereas the 'ushr 5 or 10 percent, depending on certain conditions; the rates correspond to the rates set in classical Islamic law. These can be called cosmetic changes inasmuch as they refer more to labels than to anything else. Their overall effect is insignificant. Islamization measures introduced by the government for women have curtailed their access to the courts, education, and economic productivity.[186] The new measures have, in effect, upheld the conservative view of woman as property.[187]

As for the country's high birth rate, which is a serious problem and thwarts developmental efforts, the Islamization program made no effort to address the issue.[188] As Shahid Javed Burki points out, "without a major effort in this area, the country's population would stabilize at 377 million in the year 2035 at which point, having in the meantime overtaken the United States, [Russia], Japan, Brazil, and Indonesia, it would be the fifth most populous nation in the world."[189] In this respect, the ulema's views are revealing. The Council of Islamic Ideology, established in 1973, ruled in 1984 that artificial methods of birth control were un-Islamic.[190] It also ruled (and this is being cited here only to indicate how ludicrous is the thinking of the ulema, who happened to gain control of the state) that "men without beards were committing a crime against Islam."[191]

In 1949 Pakistan's leading political figures had hoped that, if the people were free to choose, they could be persuaded to opt for modern ways. They saw two ways of creating an ideological state. One, where the people in power impose a system through totalitarian methods, which was anathema to them. The second method was to trust the people and "have this much faith, that eventually the people, if guided rightly, would choose rightly."[192] This method was slower and involved risks. They opted for the second method with the hope that, with education, the people would choose a progressive rather than a reactionary interpretation.[193]

The people of Pakistan had chosen their state to be Islamic, and it was important that they pursue it, for it was "their way of saying that it shall be good."[194] The political leaders and intellectuals were aware, however, of the dangers the state faced from religious teachers. They put it thus:

There is definitely and emphatically the danger that the *mulla*, making the appeal emotional, will win the day. . . . There is the nightmare of Pakistan's going back to a rigid, backward, narrow, country. . . . For us, the intellectuals, the problem is that Pakistan shall not go back. That it shall not become simply an extension of Afghanistan. It is a nightmare for us. The danger of the *mulla's* coming to power is serious; it would be calamitous. This is the terror.[195]

RELIGIOUS EDUCATIONAL SYSTEM

Addressing the ulema, President Mohammad Ayub Khan once said: A great burden of responsibility rests on the shoulders of those whom God has endowed with the knowledge and understanding of our Faith."[196] That responsibility, he said, was "to liberate religion from the debris of wrong superstitions [*sic*] and prejudices and to make it keep pace with the march of time."[197] In order to assess the nature and grounds of knowledge of the ulema, as well as their capabilities, we need to examine the religious educational system of Pakistan. As for the ulema who got their education in pre-partition India, the religious educational system then was of the same nature.

One astonishing aspect of the religious educational system in Pakistan is that the syllabus followed is the one created in 1747 by Mulla Nizam al-Din.[198] This "comprehensive syllabus," according to the writer who carried out a survey of religious schools in Pakistan, has been followed in all Muslim religious schools of Indo-Pakistan for the last two hundred years. Table 5.1 presents the details of this syllabus, and Table 5.2 describes how the prescribed course of study is carried out. The most surprising fact to be gleaned from the syllabus is that the study of the Qur'an is excluded from it. In the last year of the study, two exegetical books are studied which form the basis of knowledge about the Qur'an; these exegetical books were written in 1316 and 1505.[199] In the twenty-one subjects covered by the syllabus, almost all the books studied belong to the

Table 5.1

Syllabus of Muslim Religious Schools
Prepared by Mulla Nizam al-Din, 1747

No.	Subject	Number of Books	Year of writing or the year author died
1.	Morphology	6	Not given for four books. Two written in 1414 and 1860.[a]
2.	Grammar	6	Not given for one book; the rest written in 1408, 1777,[a] 1224, 1447, and 1397.
3.	Eloquence and Rhetoric (allegorical expressions)	3	1397 and 1339.
4.	Science of Poetry (meter)	1	1229
5.	Logic	10	1414, before 1262, 1821,[a] 1345, 1708, 1795,[a] 1786,[a] 1731, 1690, and 1365.
6.	Philosophy	4	1210, 1438, 1652 and 1958.[a]
7.	Arabic	6	Not given for one. The rest: Literature 1814,[a] 1955,[a] 1123, 1009 and 846.
8.	Literature	1(includes 7 Arab poets)	Except poet Hamar-ul Radha (772), the rest belong to Jahilliah (age of ignorance).
9.	Science of Theology	5	1405, 1503, 1367, 1466, and 1500.
10.	History	3	Not given for one. Others: 1574 and 1346.
11.	Medicine	5	Not given for one. The rest: 1289, fifteenth century, 1036 and 1424.

Table 5.1 (continued)

No.	Subject	Number of Books	Year of writing or the year author died
12.	Astronomy	2	Not given for one; the other 1412.
13.	Engineering	2	1274 and 902.
14.	Debate	2	1672 and 1414.
15.	Jurisprudence	8	1755,[a] 1037, 1312, 1148, 1178, 1723, 1197, and 1677.
16.	Principles of Jurisprudence	6	1353, 1693, 1246, 1334, 1356, and twelfth century.
17.	Obligations or Duties	1	Died end of twelfth or middle of thirteenth century.
18.	Principles of *Hadis (Hadith)*	1	1449.
19.	*Hadis (Hadith)*	10	Not given for one. The rest: 869, 874, 892, 888, 918, 892, 932, 886, and 795.
20.	Principles of Exegesis	1	1762[a]
21.	Exegesis	4	1505, 1316, 1371, and 1352.

[a]Later additions.

Note: Names of authors and titles of books omitted for space considerations. The years have been kept in the same order as in the original source to coincide with the works cited there.

Source: Translated and adapted from Hafiz Nazar Ahmed, *Jaizah-ay Madaris-i 'Arabiyyah Islamyyah Maghribi Pakistan* (Survey of Arabic Islamic Schools of West Pakistan), (Lahore: Muslim Academy, 1972), pp. 587-93.

Table 5.2

Course Distribution of Religious Schools of Pakistan: Systematic Distribution of Books[a]

Class Year	Morphology and Grammar	Eloquence and Rhetoric	Logic and Philosophy	Literature	Biography of Prophet and History	Theology and Beliefs	*Jurisprudence* Principles of Jurisprudence	Debate	Medicine	Astronomy Engineering	*Exegesis* Principles of exegesis	*Hadis*[b] Principles of Hadis
1st	X		X									
2nd	X	X	X	X	X		X					
3rd	X	X	X	X	X		X					
4th		X	X		X	X	X	X				
5th					X	X	X				X	X
6th				X	X		X			X		
7th		X	X		X	X			X		X	
8th	Study of Hadis only (Ten Compendious books)											
9th	Only Qur'anic exegesis is taught.											

[a] Names of books have been omitted from this table; they are indicated by X mark.

[b] Hadis is Urdu rendition of hadith.

Note: In the last few years, recitation of some passages of the Qur'an is carried out.

Source: Translated and adapted from Hafiz Nazar Ahmed, *Jaiza-ey Madaris-i 'Arabiyyah Islamyyah Maghribi Pakistan (Survey of Arabic Islamic Schools of West Pakistan)* (Lahore: Muslim Academy, 1972), pp. 594-595.

medieval period. The writer who carried out the survey acknowledges that the information provided by the books is based on "ancient viewpoints."[200] Yet, the same writer, himself a product of a religious school, makes the unwarranted claim that the syllabus of religious schools is more comprehensive and "far-sighted" than the syllabi of government schools, colleges, and universities.[201]

Describing the manner of education in the religious schools, the writer states that these institutions do not provide chairs and tables. First, he says, to have tables and chairs is considered to be against the sunna and an imitation of the West; second, such a style is considered to be extravagant and against simplicity.[202] Students usually sit on the floor on a mat. When the teachers arrive in the classroom, the students rush to pick up the teachers' shoes and books as a sign of respect.[203]

As for women's religious education, there is no proper arrangement. Because women generally lack religious education, they suffer from "superstitions, ignorance, irreligiousness, and laughable traditions," according to the writer.[204]

At the time of the survey, there were 563 religious schools in Pakistan, with 34,384 students and 3,186 teachers.[205] The products of these institutions provide religious education and "intellectual leadership" to the bulk of the population and religious political parties.

ASSESSMENT OF THE DEVELOPMENT PLANS AND MODERNIZATION GOALS OF THE STATE

In the November 1988 elections of Pakistan, over fifty political parties vied in the contest to scoop the spoils of power. Over the years, politics in Pakistan has consisted of politicians "acting like children trying to grab the biggest handful they can from a bowl of sweets, and the army stepping in like a stern father to rap knuckles and take the sweets away."[206] In the Parliament that Zia instituted to continue his rule, "the successful candidates were there to make money, or were hereditary politicians from the big land-owning families who think it is their right to run the country and share the spoils with their friends. Plenty of money-making and spoils-sharing therefore went on."[207] Under such circumstances, the plight of an average Pakistani can be well imagined; to pacify and manipulate the population, the name of Islam is invoked time and again.

Pakistan's population is around 115 million. According to the 1981 census, 71.3 percent of the population lives in rural areas, and the literacy rate is 26.2 percent. The annual rate of growth in literacy from 1971 to 1981 has been about 0.5 percent. At this rate, without any further increase in population, it would take nearly 150 years before close to full literacy rate could be achieved. The literacy rate in urban areas is 47.12 percent and in rural areas 17.33 percent. The ratio of male and female literacy was 25.05 and 15.99 percent for the respective populations.[208]

The country's population has more than tripled in its 46 years history; in 1947 it was 32.5 million. According to the 1981 census, the labor force made up 27.6 percent of the total population; female labor force participation was only 2.1 percent. Thus, nearly half of the labor force is not only wasted, but it has other consequences that are not acknowledged or recognized by the policymakers. In Chapter 2 we saw the direct relationship between female employment and a significant drop in the fertility rate. Because of underemployment and unemployment, only 27.4 percent of the total employed labor force is wage employee, and roughly one-fourth of the employed labor force consists of unpaid family helpers found mostly in the rural areas.[209]

Pakistan is an agricultural country, but rural productivity remains very low. The yield per hectare of all the major crops is still far below their potential output.[210] How does one explain this? A major explanation would come from the socioeconomic structure of the society. Pakistani villages are characterized by landlordism. Landlords, most of whom are also former tribal chieftains, are not only economically dominant, but they also play a superordinate role in the social and political arena. Because of their dominant position, they determine the nature and rate of social change in the areas under their control. They typically work against social progress, and they ensure that they maintain their control and enhance their power. Such an economic and political structure is one of the causes of pervasive fatalism and dependence on God among the peasants of Pakistan. Surveyors have found that 100 percent of Pakistani peasants believe that fate is decided by God. Pakistani landlords characteristically surround themselves with religious aura, mystification, sainthood, and holiness. Rich landlords justify their entire existence as exploiters through charity, alms giving, and occasional acts of religious generosity.[211]

Under such circumstances, one can legitimately ask: What can development projects do? But this issue together with the whole question of prevalent religious practices and, most importantly, religious education—existing and desired—did not form an important component of the thinking process that went into the formulation of development plans for the country. The development plans were conceived merely in economic terms, and in those terms there were appreciable results. Thus, despite the fact that the first five-year plan (1955-1960) was not published until April 1957, it succeeded in increasing Pakistan's industrial assets three and a half times between 1955 and 1960.[212]

By 1963 Pakistan's industrial production was growing at 12 percent annually. Private industrial development in the second five-year plan (1960-1965) was taking place at such a rapid pace that targets set even in the revised Industrial Investment Schedules were sometimes exceeded by over 40 percent.[213] The long-term objectives of government policy were stated in what was called the Perspective Plan covering the period from 1965 to 1985. These consisted of "more than doubling the per capita income, full employment, universal literacy, . . . and a steady diminution in Pakistan's dependence on foreign assistance."[214]

By 1982 Pakistan's per capita income had increased to $380, making it possible to cross over from being a poor country to a middle-income one by the end of the decade when the per capita income is likely to cross the $410 dividing line.[215] However, the rest of the objectives remain as unfulfilled as they were in 1965.

Planners of the first five-year plan had strongly advocated land reforms. Later, the Planning Commission strongly recommended family planning and the Rural Public Works Program to energize the rural society.[216] However, after thirty years the situation is virtually unchanged. At the time of independence, in the territories that now form Pakistan, there were eighty landed families which together owned 3 million acres of land. When Ayub Khan carried out the first land reform in 1959 by limiting irrigated land to 500 acres and nonirrigated land to 1,000 acres for an individual, the pattern of rural life had not changed. In this reform only 2.3 million out of the 49 million acres of farmland were directly affected. By loosely interpreting the law, landed families effectively retained control over their lands and were allowed to transfer land on paper to their children, relatives, tenants, and servants.

When Bhutto carried out his land reforms in 1972, with a ceiling of 150 irrigated and 300 nonirrigated acres, holdings on land had already been divided by the above-mentioned ingenious methods to reduce the effects of the reforms. In this reform only 2.83 million acres were affected and only 512,886 acres were actually taken over by the government. When Zia-ul-Haq carried out his coup in 1977, many families owned over 5,000 acres of land, and families owning 1,000 acres were quite common. In his eleven-year rule Zial-ul-Haq carried out no land reforms. As a result, the pattern of rural society remains essentially the same as it was after Ayub Khan's reforms of 1959.[217]

Landed families in Pakistan amassed their huge landholdings during the colonial rule. "Loyal servants of the British Raj were rewarded handsomely with large tracts of land. Much of the landed aristocracy . . . owes its position to the loyalty of their ancestors to their British masters."[218] Significantly, Pakistan has potentially one of the richest agricultural sectors anywhere in the world; therefore, it ought to be one of the leading exporters of agricultural and dairy products.[219] Instead, in 1979 Pakistan had to import more than 2 million tons of food grains to give the population the minimum amount of food energy needed.[220] In 1983-1984 agricultural growth fell by 4.63 percent.[221]

Land productivity in the country remains low. This cannot really be attributed "to the lack of transfer of modern technology to the farmers," as one writer suggests.[222] Data available on Pakistan show that smaller farms produce more per acre than larger farms. In smaller farms, a greater percentage of the area is cultivated, and cropping intensity is also high; larger farms are managed inefficiently. Statistics show that on farms above 150 acres, only 34 percent of the area is cultivated; on farms below 12.5 acres, 87.6 percent of the area is cultivated with a cropping intensity of 118.3 percent; and on farms above 50 acres cropping intensity is 77.8 percent.[223]

Studies carried out between 1966 and 1969 show that gross income per acre on farms below 12.5 acres was Rs. 467.78 and on farms above 50 acres Rs. 134.35 (the rate of exchange then was Rs. 4.40 = $1). Income on farms larger than 150 acres is likely to be even lower.[224] Besides these vitally important economic reasons, other and equally important reasons justify a substantial reduction of landholdings in Pakistan. Most of the owners of large estates had not purchased their lands but were awarded to the ancestors of the present owners for their loyal services to the British. Another major reason for meaningful land reforms is the role played by the big landlords in the social and political life of the country. This class has always blocked progress and has a vested interest in the status quo. It has always sided with autocratic and reactionary regimes; it has backed every government, in or about to come in power. Before 1947, and almost until the end, most of the big landlords of Pakistan, as a class, had opposed Jinnah in his efforts to create Pakistan. They saw in the Pakistan movement a threat to their interests. They, therefore, formed an alliance called the Unionist party to thwart any attempt to create a just Islamic social order.[225]

Later, however, when it became apparent that the Pakistan movement had fired "the imagination of the people and could not be suppressed, they [the landlords] joined the Muslim League and assumed its leadership in their areas. The Muslim League was, therefore, smothered with these reactionary elements and the dreams of millions who had followed Jinnah to triumph were buried."[226] The chaotic conditions that have persistently bedeviled Pakistan's politics are essentially the work of this class. It was this very class that prevented "Bhutto from embarking on the course he had pledged himself to follow and effectively scotched any substantial move towards progress and change."[227] Zia had the backing of this class and the ulema when Bhutto was executed on a trumped-up charge.[228] In most of Pakistan's history, exploitation of the rural areas, where nearly 75 percent of the population lives, has been state-backed.[229]

Although Pakistan has made considerable economic progress since independence, it is in the area of social and economic planning that the country faces its most serious problems. Developmental planners have not given sufficient thought and attention to these two spheres. "Population increases have come very close to off-setting the gains of impressive economic growth in the sixties and the latter part of the seventies[, and eighties]."[230] The literacy rate in Pakistan is one of the lowest as compared to those of the other developing and developed countries. The school enrollment for 7 to 11 year olds is 98 percent in the developed countries, 68 percent in the developing, and only 23 percent in Pakistan; for children aged 12 to 18 years, enrollment is 64 percent in the developed countries, 39 percent in the developing, and only 9 percent in Pakistan; for 18 to 23 year olds, enrollment is 46 percent in the developed countries, 13 percent in other developing countries, and a minuscule 3 percent in Pakistan.[231] Data show that out of about 16 million school-aged children, only 51 percent can get education at the primary level, while the rest, over 7.5 million, cannot get any education. Of those enrolled at the primary level, 50 percent leave school without obtaining any education.[232]

The condition of higher education in the country is abysmal. Of the 26.2 percent of the population who are literate, 46 percent are at the primary level, 30 percent at the matric and intermediate, 3 percent at undergraduate, and only 1 percent at the graduate level.[233]

To increase the literacy rate, the fifth five year plan (1978-1983) launched a special program for the development of primary education. During this period 8,200 mosque schools were opened in the urban areas, with a corresponding increase in rural mosque schools. In the sixth five year plan (1983-1988), 4000 new primary schools and 40,000 mosque schools were projected to be opened to provide primary school facilities to nearly 5.5 million additional children.[234] Now, on the face of it, it seems a sensible approach to deal with the massive illiteracy of the country. However, if we remember the kind of education the religious teacher possesses, who ostensibly will be imparting education to the young children, the effort is likely to be counterproductive in the long run, for it would ensure the propagation of the same kind of ideas that have so far been prevalent in the society in different spheres of life. It is these ideas that have arrested growth in the society. The mosque schools can be productive provided there is a new breed of religious teachers who have studied the Qur'an and received modern education, and not the kind of education their syllabus provides. With such a system of education, in fact, the distinction between religious schools and secular schools breaks down. That would be the only way to ensure and make the claim credible that "there are no priests in Islam."

Analysis of Pakistan's development efforts shows that, in the 1960s, Ayub Khan's "deep commitment to improving Pakistan's economic performance had one important consequence: it provided the people of Pakistan with a more tangible objective to work for."[235] This was a radical departure from the conditions in which he had found the country when he assumed power. Until then, the religious teachers had dragged the country into what was essentially a sterile religious debate.[236] Ayub's "emphasis on economic development as the *raison d'etre* of his revolution seemed to change the nation's psyche."[237] The government's commitment to economic development and a generally supportive external environment that perceived the governmental policies as progressive had a dramatic effect on the country's economy.

The government's commitment to economic development in the 1960s had a powerful impact on the bureaucratic structure, which changed its own priorities. The performance of civil servants was to be measured in terms of their willingness to work for rapid national development, and not in terms of their ability to maintain law and order. With this new purpose in mind, Pakistan's civil service changed its style and transformed itself into a development service par excellence.[238]

Such was the response of the people to the government's emphasis on national development that during Ayub's "Decade of Development," agricultural "output increased at a rate unprecedented in Pakistan's history; by the end of the Ayub era, the country's output of foodgrain had more than doubled in just over eleven years."[239] In the 1980s, during Zia's regime, we see a contrast to the 1960s. Instead of focusing on developmental programs, the state through its "Islamization" programs dragged the country into facile religious controversies. The regime's preoccupation was with prayers. The president of the country announced how the system of prayers was to be organized in every village and urban district; it gives a good idea of the regime's priorities:

Only those persons are being appointed for this service of religion who have sound moral character and their piety is so exemplary that their words will have deep effect on the hearts of people. The procedure for this exercise *for the time being* [italics added] is based on persuasion and motivation and not on compulsion. But we are determined to succeed in establishing the system of prayer at all cost.[240]

While in the 1980s the country's gross national product increased at twice the rate of other low-income countries, the overall state of the economy was such that at "no time during the country's history—not even in the difficult period immediately following independence— . . . the economic institutional base was as weak as in the early eighties."[241] In international politics, images are an important component of interstate relations, especially with the West which is not impressed with religious slogans, and for good reason. For example, in the 1980s, "although Russian intervention in Afghanistan resulted in a serious reappraisal of Pakistan's strategic situation, it did not lead to a substantial increase in aid flows."[242] A Pakistan that is perceived to be progressive is most likely to receive technological assistance from the West, which can further enhance the developmental process. It can enhance, but the impetus and direction for development have to come from within the society, from its own consciousness.

CONCLUSION

In Pakistan, the way Islam has so far been taught, interpreted, understood, and practiced by the religious establishment, and as a consequence by the vast majority of the population, is almost completely at variance with what the Qur'an teaches. Astonishingly, reliance has been primarily on the hadith literature, which is the source of the sharia/sunna/traditions, and not the Qur'an itself. The result is that there is a very vague and distorted idea about what Islam means. The ideas on Islam are based essentially on a highly questionable collection of literature. The ideas generated by this literature occupy the consciousness of most of the people, and the ideas contained in this literature are mostly retrogressive, as evidenced by the present state of the society.

Modernist Muslim scholars have persistently argued and pointed out, for well over two centuries, that this is the main reason for the stagnation and decay of the society; that, for society to develop and advance, this situation will have to change. Policymakers have failed to grasp the essential point that, at root, modernism and progress are directly related to "the outcome of certain changes in the character of religious thought" itself.[243]

The evidence of history is that social transformations "have changed class relations, societal values, and social institutions."[244] Social transformations in the Islamic societies are directly dependent on the state of religious thought, for it regulates conduct in every sphere of life. Social transformations have created nations whose power and autonomy markedly surpassed their own pasts and "outstripped other countries in similar circumstances",[245] enabling countries "to break the chains of extreme dependency."[246] And social transformations do not take place on their own; the evidence of history is that in all the great social revolutions, the state has played a central role. In this process, the crucial element is the quality of leadership.[247]

It is extremely unlikely that the ulema will change their ways on their own; therefore, it is the state's responsibility to bring about that change. The only effective way to bring about that change is through an overhaul of the education system. As education becomes more general and the average Muslim is given the opportunity to study the Qur'an independently in a modern system of education, the theologian will progressively lose his importance.[248] And the study of the Qur'an cannot be left to the individual's initiative; it is too serious a matter to be handled in that manner. The modern system of education has demonstrated that, generally, individuals do not study even ordinary books unless they are made to study. The Qur'an is a very serious book and requires deep and intelligent study for the reader to grasp the message. Its *study* is crucial for a Muslim to understand what Islam really means and to dispel existing notions of Islam propagated by the religious functionaries.

Most surprising of all is that the state has yet to disclose to the people that Islam fully sanctions, and indeed requires, that people acquire material prosperity, as we saw in the previous chapter. It appears that a vast majority of those who have come to occupy state power have themselves not been aware of it. Otherwise, it would have been emphasized in the state's pronouncements regarding Islam and would have formed a key component of the state's policy and ideology. It is a mere tautology to make statements like "Islam is our ideology," or "Islamic ideology," without stating what it means. It should be expressed in tangible terms. An example has been given above; other examples can be cited. Most of the leading sections of the society exhibit a lack of understanding and commitment to even the most basic components of the ideology.

The forces behind the creation of Pakistan were both religious and economic. The state has, however, made little planned effort to translate the economic religious motives underlying the Pakistan movement into state policy.[249] So far, the state has not tapped this enormous productive force.

A dramatic and highly retrogressive change occurred in Pakistan in the mid-1970s when religious merchants captured state power through the coup carried out by General Zia on their behalf. The state then began emphasizing Islamic rituals and invoking "traditions" by giving names to it like sharia/sunna/hadith. This eleven-year history of the country at the hands of a fundamentalist regime, and what it was set about to do, can best be described and analyzed in the following terms:

Instead of society having conquered a new content for itself, it seems that the state only returned to its oldest form, to the shamelessly simple domination of the sabre and the cowl. . . .

The tradition of all the dead generations weighs like a nightmare on the brain of the living. And just when they seem engaged in revolutionizing themselves and things, . . . precisely in such periods of revolutionary crisis they anxiously conjure up the spirits of the past to their service and borrow from them names, battle cries and costumes in order to present the new scene of world history in this time-honoured disguise and this borrowed language.

. . . social revolution . . . cannot draw its poetry from the past, but only from the future. It cannot begin with itself before it has stripped off all superstition in regard to the past.[250]

Democratic political process—and life in general—got a fresh breath in Pakistan following the end of Zia's autocratic government in mid-1988. However, no real changes occurred in the nature of politics which remained agitational politics through and through. It is inconceivable that in such circumstances any meaningful developmental policies can be pursued in the country. The energies of the government in power are consumed in trying to stay in power or to deal with the chaos unleashed by the opposition groups. This indeed confirms our main conclusion that the problems of the country, be it domestic politics or economic and social conditions, are rooted in the ideological confusion that is pervasive in the country. This confusion manifests itself glaringly in the behavior of a vast majority of politicians who show no real concern about the problems that the country faces. The immediate need in the country is for the politicians to shift focus from themselves to the serious problems faced by the country.

This also confirms our conclusion that crucial to the development of the country is the reformation of the educational system. It cries for the abolition of the dichotomous system of education that is presently in vogue in the country. How conscientiously and successfully the reform of the educational system is carried out will determine not only the direction and pace of the modernization process, but also the solidity of the foundation on which lasting institutions can be built. The products of this reformed educational system would be capable of continuously providing the vision and the leadership to modernize and develop the country in a real sense.

6

THE RELIGIOPOLITICAL SYSTEM OF EGYPT AND MODERNIZATION

The first attempt to modernize Egypt began in the early nineteenth century but ended in a fiasco. Much of this movement toward modernization in the 1800s was based on international borrowing, and when Egypt was unable to pay its loans, the country was occupied by the British.[1] In the so-called modernization efforts, emphasis was on appearances. No major changes were made in the structures of the society; the society continued to function as it had in the preceding several centuries.

The movement to reform Egyptian society began in the late nineteenth century. Its leading figure was Jamal al-Din al-Afghani (1836-1897), who had lived in Egypt for eight years. His first call was to fight imperialism which had devastated Muslim countries; he advocated modernization of the country and adoption of Western science and technology.

It was not until 1952, however, that Egypt was able to end British occupation and become a sovereign independent state after seventy years of British rule. The coup of 1952 by Gamal Abdel Nasser marked the end of "two thousand years of slavery" by the Egyptians.[2] The new leaders faced a gigantic task. As Anwar Sadat phrased it in later years, "The problem was to get Egypt out of the Middle Ages, to turn it from a semi-feudal country into a modern, ordered, viable State."[3]

In this chapter our focus is on developments in Egypt after 1952, with special reference to the modernization efforts of the regimes. We will also examine an earlier part of Egyptian history, from around the turn of the century, which provided the intellectual basis for the developments that culminated in Egypt's independence and paved the way for subsequent modernization efforts.

STATE POLICIES REGARDING ISLAM, RELIGIOUS LEADERS' RESPONSES, AND STATE RESPONSES

Before 1952, the general pattern in Egypt was to bring the religious establishment under the control of the central government. This pattern continued after 1952, with the difference that the government was now "intent upon dominating all aspects of religion both 'official' and 'popular.'"[4] The extensive knowledge of the Muslim Brothers movement by the Free Officers prior to 1952 and its subsequent "disillusionment with it made the new regime especially sensitive both to the existence and the political possibilities of 'popular' Islam."[5] In the period prior to the seizure of power by the Free Officers, the ulema nourished the conservative spirit of the masses and backed the existing order.[6]

In that order, the condition of the Egyptian masses had worsened to such a degree after 1925 that it was close to subsistence level, while the population continued to increase. Although Egypt's major political party, the Wafd, "drew its strength from the land-owners and the Pasha class, it enjoyed the backing of the Egyptian masses whom it held, at least until 1942, in a kind of 'mass narcissism.'"[7] The party suffered from doctrinal vagueness and was seething with corruption and moral bankruptcy; its primary object was to stay in office.[8]

When Nasser and his fellow officers carried out the coup, their main purpose was to put an end to British imperial rule in Egypt. Beyond that, they had no clear plan of action.[9] Nasser thought that once the vanguard had performed its task, it would soon be followed by the masses marching to their goal.[10] Instead, chaos and persistent selfishness dominated.[11] There was a paucity of ideas. Nasser recalled that he once visited one of the universities and sat with professors to learn from their experience, but "not one of them presented a new idea."[12]

Nasser recognized that his country needed a social revolution in addition to the political revolution, but his understanding of a social revolution was only that of a vague Marxist prescription. He describes a social revolution as a movement "in which the classes of society would struggle against each other until justice for all countrymen has been gained and conditions have become stable."[13] That there are other methods of bringing about and sustaining a social revolution apparently did not cross his mind. It explains his preoccupation with the slogan "Arab socialism." It also indicates that a systematic analysis of the conditions existing in Egypt was not undertaken, or else it would have given pointers to the deep-seated causes.[14] Apart from their longstanding desire to free Egypt from British control, the revolutionaries did not have a coherent ideology to follow after they succeeded in gaining independence; this caused them great confusion and difficulties when they set about to govern Egypt.[15]

In Egypt an Islamic religious organization, Muslim Brothers, was established in 1928 by Hasan al-Banna. It was essentially a reaction to the prevalent socioeconomic and political conditions in Egypt, and it became a mass movement in the 1940s. By then Egyptian society had become deeply divided into two groups: the modernists and the traditionalists. The Muslim Brothers represented "a complete and full estrangement from western ideas, institutions and habits."[16] Its rallying call was the sharia; "it was to them not only the kernel of Islam itself but also a means of self-identification."[17] The leaders of this movement were the products of religious institutions; their ideas appealed to the mass of the population who were disillusioned with the prevalent socioeconomic order.

The Brotherhood had collaborated with the Free Officers in the overthrow of the monarchy and the ouster of the British. Nasser and his colleagues, however, were disdainful of the Brotherhood philosophy, believing that the Brotherhood's ideas of Islam were regressive and could not meet modern requirements.[18] The Free Officers, however, shared its hatred of the British occupation and exploitation of Egypt. Under the leadership of its founder, Dr. Hassan al-Banna (assassinated in 1949), it had sought complete removal of the British from Egypt.

Once Nasser and his colleagues were in power, the Brotherhood began to feel that their outlook was too secular. It also resented the state's interference in the affairs of al-Azhar University for allegedly political purposes.[19] In other words, the Brotherhood, considered itself to have a monopoly over Islam. The first confrontation between the government and the Brotherhood occurred on January 12, 1954, when members of the Brotherhood and student supporters of the Liberation Rally, the official political party, clashed. The state proclaimed the dissolution of the Brotherhood the next day. A state of emergency was declared on January 14, and 450 members of the Brotherhood, including its leaders, were arrested. In explaining the state's action against the Brotherhood, the Revolutionary Command Council (RCC) stated on January 15, 1954, that the leader of the Brotherhood, Dr. Hassan el-Hodeiby, had refused to support the revolution unless the sharia was implemented. According to the RCC, el-Hodeiby had presented unacceptable nominees to the cabinet after Nasser had agreed to accept three representatives of the Brotherhood. El-Hodeiby also demanded veto power for the Brotherhood in all legislative matters, a demand that was rejected by the RCC. He then instructed the Brotherhood to subvert Liberation Rally meetings and to organize paramilitary groups in the police, army, and student organizations.[20]

Bitter disagreements within the RCC surfaced in February 1954 over major issues. By July 8, the RCC restored the legitimacy of the Muslim Brotherhood. When the government concluded an agreement with the British on the Suez Canal on July 27, it provoked fierce enmity from the Brotherhood, which "denounced the government as 'heretics who do not comply with the teachings of the Qur'an.'"[21] This charge was made in a sermon at a mosque and provoked violent riots. On October 26, the Brotherhood attempted to assassinate Nasser when he was addressing a gathering in Alexandria. In Cairo the following day, mobs burned the central offices of the Brotherhood; on October 29, the government arrested the leader of the organization and banned the organization for the second time. On December 7, the government executed six leaders of the Brotherhood. The death sentence of the organization's leader, however, was commuted to life imprisonment.[22]

In Egypt, the ulema's opposition to the government dates back to 1809 when Muhammad Ali first attempted to curtail the power of the ulema. In that period, the ulema were members of the Egyptian elite and had wealth, power, and great influence on the masses. The power of the ulema gradually decreased in the course of the nineteenth century, along with the rise of an intellectual force that was secular in nature. "To these and other challenges the ulama reacted by becoming more rigidly traditionalists and conservative, opposing all change."[23]

Nasser and his colleagues "believed that the religious institutions could and should be adapted to promote the interests of a modern Egyptian nation-state."[24] To that end, Nasser maximized state control in different avenues of national life; all significant economic, social, and political institutions were placed under state control. Mosques, mosque officials (preachers, imams, muezzins), religious schools, religious foundations, and voluntary benevolent societies were also brought under state control.[25] Nasser wanted the religious institutions to espouse a version of Islam that would appeal to the masses as well as to the middle class.[26]

In the government's nationalization policy, the awqaf (religious endowments) were the first semiautonomous institutions brought under state control. The regime "felt that their reform was a pre-requisite to land reform, for through this system large areas of land had been set aside, the revenues from which were used to support mosques and religious institutions."[27]

In the judicial sphere, the sharia courts, which dealt with such matters as marriage, divorce, and inheritance, along with the courts of the minorities, were amalgamated into one "secular system" on January 1, 1956. However, the basis of the sharia courts, that is, the sharia itself, was retained as before. This is an important point, for it meant that society would continue to function on the basis of those rules and regulations that were incorporated in the sharia. Essentially, therefore, no change was effected in the content of law that is based on the hadith literature. Daniel Crecilius, however, argues that by preserving the sharia principles Egypt, though secular in part, remains an Islamic state and maintains the one vital link, sharia, that connects state and society to God.[28]

The argument is seriously flawed, however. It is too simplistic and dangerous a notion to argue that sharia is the link between state and society and God. There is a serious problem with the sources of the sharia which is based primarily on the hadith literature. We have observed the nature of the problem on several occasions in the previous two chapters.

In Egypt, as in Pakistan, the ulema invoked the sunna along with the Qur'an;

the source of the sunna, let us recall, is the hadith literature. In Egypt, when the Ministry of Awqaf (religious endowments) began preparing sermons for the mosques, a practice resorted to by the government as a reform measure of the religious establishment, the government's policies were espoused and backed up with quotations from the Qur'an and the sunna. The government asks the ulema to give formal legal opinions (fatwas) on such matters as birth control, land reform, nationalization, scientific research, foreign policy, and social affairs.[29]

The 1971 constitution of Egypt declared that "the principles of the Islamic Shari'a are a major source of legislation."[30] Although the word "principles" is used, dependence on the sharia means strong reliance on the opinions and rules and regulations contained in the sharia. Why can the principles not be derived from the Qur'an, which it clearly provides? The inclusion of the sharia in the constitution suggests (1) the strong hand of the ulema, (2) the fear of the ulema, (3) a moral shortcut, in that the necessary intellectual effort to rework out the principles and directions from the Qur'an is avoided; it is also strongly influenced by (2), and (4) ideological confusion.

When the permanent constitution was being prepared, the Preparatory Committee sought public opinion on the basic principles. The rector of al-Azhar, in a telegram to the chairman of the committee, asked that Islam be declared the official state religion.[31] This demand was similar to the one made by the ulema in Pakistan, as if such a declaration by itself would efface all the ills and problems of the Egyptian society.

Opinions varied on the issue of the sharia. Some members of the Preparatory Committee demanded "that the constitution prescribe the sharia as *the* principal source of legislation."[32] Echoing the opinions of the great mass of the Muslim ulama, Shaykh (Sheikh) Ali Sayyid Mansur of the Religious Institute at Assiut suggested that the Islamic sharia should be the source of Egypt's fundamental laws.[33] Whereas educated women demanded "that a new law of personal status be enacted, that the constitution contain (guarantees of) the freedom of the feminist movement, and that women be granted a fuller share of civil rights in keeping with their equality with men," the ulema's insistence was on the continuation of the sharia. Thus, the mufti of the republic, while agreeing with the demand for equalization, insisted that it "should be achieved within the framework of the provisions of the Islamic sharia."[34] Justice Hasan Muhammad was to the point when he said: "There is no need for inserting into the constitution any type of clause at all prescribing the sharia as a source of legislation. Such a clause would create unnecessary problems."[35] Dr. al-Utaifi attempted to make a distinction between sharia and Islamic fiqh (jurisprudence). For him sharia consisted of the Qur'an and the sunna,[36] forgetting that the source of the sunna and the sharia was basically the same—the hadith literature.

A further evidence of the ideological confusion is provided when the constitution describes the economic basis of Egypt to be "the socialist system" (Article 4),[37] as though the Qur'anic emphasis on equality and socioeconomic justice were not enough. The question really is one of intellectually and practically working out how equality and socioeconomic justice are to be achieved. The mere adoption of slogans like "socialist system" or "Arab socialism" is not the answer.

Article 19 deals with religious education and states: "Religious education is a primary subject in the general education curriculum." Ostensibly, religious education is to be of a very elementary nature. It is inconceivable, however, that Islam can be understood without studying the Qur'an. Why the primary source of Islam should not be studied in a systematic manner in the classroom in high school and beyond remains somewhat of a mystery. Its importance cannot be overemphasized, for in the preceding centuries, and up to the present times, the mass of the Muslim populations anywhere in the world has not studied the Qur'an. The emphasis has been on recitation alone, without thinking and analyzing what was being recited. Apparently, policymakers have not recognized how important and serious this matter is.

Bruce M. Borthwick concludes that since the constitution mentions religion in several places, "it definitely establishes religion as a part of the society and state," and he commends it as an "expression of the ideals and values of the leadership class that wrote it."[38] The issue is far more complex, however, and pious statements about religion do not mean much. We cannot help escape the conclusion, therefore, that when such references to religion (Islam) are made, advocates express and understand them primarily in terms of rituals and traditions. "What goes under the name of civics or social studies in American schools . . . takes place in Egypt in the courses on religion."[39] The religious texts presently used in the schools contain 72 percent of the material on political and social matters if "scriptural quotations" are left out.[40] While the source of these quotations is not clear, most of it is likely to be from the hadith literature.

To reform al-Azhar University, which was a bastion of conservative ulema, the government brought it under state control in 1961. Its curriculum was reformed (we will examine this issue in a later section), and four new departments were added—Medicine, Engineering, Agriculture, and Commerce. Of great significance to note here is the absence of all the disciplines of the social sciences. A girls college was also added with its own course of studies. At the same time, the government attacked the ulema through its media for being old fashioned and obscurantist; "They were also charged with being unable to deal with modern times . . . [and were, therefore,] turning people away from Islam."[41] The state has argued that, whereas Islam is a progressive religion, reactionary elements have arrested this quality. The state "believes that reformed Islam can promote national unity, economic development, political development and social change."[42]

How this reform is going to come about, the state does not seem to know. It has already accepted that "the sharia principles govern the nation," which is to say that the sharia or the hadith literature will continue to affect the thought processes or the psyche of the people. We have already observed what the state's idea of religious education is. It has also retained the personal status law as it has existed heretofore.

When Nasser and his colleagues seized power in 1952, they immediately stated that they wanted to modernize their society. Clearly, they felt that traditional societal practices (termed Islamic) were not in keeping with modern times. Yet they hesitated to reform these practices, and they continued to use Islam to legitimate their authority and to command the allegiance of all classes.[43] Although the regime, through "a law promulgated in 1960 but not implemented until after 1973," directed the Ministry of Awqaf (religious endowments) "to take charge of all the mosques in the country,"[44] it did not question and reform the content of the traditional religious education, which is the source of the traditional practices in vogue. A dichotomous system of education, secular and religious, was also maintained as before.

Egypt has been the hub of Sufi (mystic) orders for a long period of time. These orders have become so entrenched that in the popular religion in Egypt it is considered part of Islam. In order to check irrational and superstitious practices, the state discouraged many public rituals that the Sufi orders performed. However, the orders were allowed to operate under governmental control. In the early 1960s, the government also attempted to link these orders to the Socialist Union, the government political party. One consequence of government control has been the proliferation of orders that are not officially recognized and are not under government control.[45] It has been estimated that only 64 out of the 130 orders are officially recognized; 21 new orders have emerged since the revolution.[46]

In Egypt, the expression of Islam has centered primarily around the Muslim Brotherhood and the Sufi orders, with al-Azhar and other religious institutions providing religious education to the main elements of these groups. Religious leaders' responses to the state's policies regarding religion have come primarily from these groups. When the Society of the Muslim Brothers was banned in 1954, the members of the Revolutionary Command Council were apparently aware of the use that could be made of mystical Islam (Sufi orders) to combat the Brothers' opposition. They also sought to strengthen and widen its own base of support by stimulating and favoring the conceptions in popular Islam.[47]

In fact, the regime had started taking an active interest in the Sufi orders from March 1955 onward when Abd al-Hakim Amir, a leading member of the Revolutionary Command Council, was appointed to supervise the reform efforts that had originally started in 1947. Its leading figure was Ahmad al-Asawi. Seeing the potential usefulness of the mystical Islam for the regime, it proceeded to check the reform movement. The first manifestation of it came in 1957 when al-Asawi was forced to abdicate, and in his place Amir appointed his close friend, Muhammad Mahmud Ilwan, the head of the Sufi order al-Ilwaniyya al-Khalwatiyya. "Under Ilwan's supervision, an era of revival started for organized mysticism in Egypt," and it "was given a more prominent role at official religious celebrations, while more *mawalid* [birthday festivals of saints] were celebrated and on a larger scale than had been the case in the decade before the revolution."[48]

In 1961 when the state created its political party, the Arab Socialist Union, it deliberately encouraged its involvement in the organization of these celebrations, which were used to make propaganda for the regime. The Sufi orders, which were under the supervision of the Sufi Council headed by Ilwan, were increasingly used to distribute political and ideological propaganda. The Arab Socialist Union also became directly involved with the administration of the orders.[49]

The state thus aided and abetted the maintenance and creation of Sufi orders which, although they have existed for several centuries, have no basis whatsoever to exist in the first place when examined in the light of the Qur'an. The Sufi orders are totally un-Islamic and smack of paganism:

The shaikhs of the Sufi orders, who have come to be the spiritual guides of the people, have made religion a sport and a means of entertainment; the performance of their *zikrs*, . . . are only a confused mumbling of words . . . and the boisterous chanting of some of their special forms of petitions, or of portions of the Qur'an, on the occasion of the birthday festival . . . of some saint enlists more enthusiasm on the part of the people than [an understanding of Islam]. . . . miraculous powers are attributed to [the shaikhs], and they are considered to be a means of blessing, living or dead; and after their death, their tombs become objects of veneration, and their intercession with God is sought for, even for accomplishment of requests that are logically impossible.[50]

These practices have crept into Islam due to a number of causes, a major one of which is that religious leaders have themselves introduced them to strengthen their hold on the common people.[51] Many evil practices have resulted from the birthday celebrations of saints. The heads of the Sufi orders are venerated by the people, and blind submission to the leaders of these orders is inculcated. Many immoralities and irregularities are committed on the festivals of certain saints, like Ahmad al-Badawi at Tanta.[52]

Nasser himself, along with a number of high-ranking individuals, patronized a mystic, the shaykh (sheikh) Ahmad Ridwan, who was probably the best known and most venerated mystic in Egypt when he died in 1967.[53] A constant flow of visitors came to this shaykh. To facilitate this traffic, an asphalt road was constructed linking the mystic's village to the Luxor-Aswan Highway. A railway station also appeared near the village. The mystic is believed to have been Nasser's most important spiritual counselor.[54] The state played one Sufi order against another, and the orders against Muslim Brotherhood.[55] The state also used the Sufi orders in cultivating its relationship with other Arab states where similar mystic orders exist.[56]

Many leaders of Sufi orders attained political power, and, once in office, they used their influence, connections, and power to further the causes and power of their particular order with the object of making themselves even more powerful. This was not surprising given the state policy of reviving organized Islamic mysticism, which often caused the interests of the regime and the Sufi orders to coincide.[57]

Members of the Muslim Brotherhood had no difficulty in joining the Sufi orders since their basic philosophy was the same—anti-modernization, anti-Westernism, and imposition of the sharia, naively believing it to be a panacea for Egypt's multifaceted problems.[58] The orders, therefore, became a wider extension of the Brotherhood.

When Sadat became president in 1970, his liberal policies allowed greater latitude to religious leaders. The Shaykh (Sheikh) al-Azhar (rector of al-Azhar university), for instance, from time to time took positions in opposition to government policies, although, on the whole, he remained at the moderate modernist center of religious politics.[59] Sadat was also careful to get the support of the Shaykh al-Azhar when he visited Israel on a peace mission.[60]

The pressure of religious groups on the state was so great that, although a vast number of Brotherhood members had been imprisoned following their abortive coup attempt in 1965, the state had been periodically releasing them, a process completed by March 1975. The organization was subsequently permitted to publish its own magazine, although its request to organize as a religious organization was refused. The state, however, continued to experience stiff opposition from religious groups, many of which had been penetrated by members of the Brotherhood. In April 1974, an organization called the Islamic Liberation Organization attacked the Military Engineering College in Cairo with plans to assassinate Sadat who was delivering a speech nearby.[61] In this period of violent religious politics, a splinter group of the Brotherhood, Al Jama'at Taqfir wa al Hijra (the Organization of Penance and Migration) came to prominence when in 1977 it kidnapped and killed a former minister of awqaf. This organization advocates violence as a means of opposing and overthrowing governments that it considers un-Islamic; its leader even proclaimed himself caliph of Islam.[62] In October 1977 two more fanatical religious groups came into the limelight. The first was Jund Allah (Soldiers of God), whose 104 members were arrested by the government; in the second group, al-Jihad (the Religious Struggle), 80 arrests were made.[63] Following Egypt's peace treaty with Israel in April 1979, members of the Brotherhood were the first to object to the treaty. When riots broke out on the campuses of Asyut and Minya following the treaty, Sadat described the Muslim Brothers as a "state within a state."[64]

Earlier in 1973, Sadat had created a new post of deputy premier for religious affairs and had appointed a minister of awqaf. In addition, Coptic representation in the cabinet was increased from one ministerial post to two. Such measures indicated the importance the state accorded to religious issues and implied state efforts to reassert its control over religious matters.[65]

But such efforts, as in Nasser's period, merely treated the symptoms rather than the deep-seated causes that require long-term planning and remedies. Merely winning over or placating religious groups is not the answer. It cannot even buy "legitimacy" in its true sense, for winning over the loyalty of such groups means subscribing to their illegitimate ideas and professions about Islam. The cleavage between the modernists and the traditionalists cannot be resolved by such measures. And secularism is not the answer either, as many scholars continue to suggest.[66] The issue is primarily that of dealing with, not avoiding, the more serious religious questions, and the method and content of religious education. The biggest issue facing Egyptian society is that the majority of conservative religious leaders have thus far rejected any thought of reinterpreting doctrine or questioning tradition. They have successfully disciplined or ostracized from their body all the main reformers. To prevent any serious reform of al-Azhar or its traditions, the ulema declared that such efforts would mean an attack on Islam itself. Thus, the religious community was further alienated from the modernizing Egyptian elite. For their part, the modernizers of Egypt were forced to work their way around al-Azhar and religious questions.[67]

The issue of reform has remained contentious on several matters, but the biggest confrontation has been in the field of education. In Egypt, as in Pakistan, two opposing systems of education have existed. Since 1900 the modernists have tinkered with the government school system in order to introduce modern ideas without, however, touching the traditional religious system.[68] The reform of al-Azhar which occurred in June 1961 was essentially its reorganization. New administrative officers were appointed, four new departments—Business Administration, Engineering and Crafts, Agriculture and Medicine—were added, but in its religious orientations and curricula al-Azhar basically remained the same. As already noted, the social sciences do not even have a place in the al-Azhar system.

In the reorganization phase of al-Azhar, the state even assured the shaykhs that the "shariah law had not been abolished; the shariah system had simply been absorbed into the national system where shariah 'principles' would still be applied."[69] In the "reform" of al-Azhar, the battle that raged between the state and the religious groups was over structural reorganization rather than substantive issues.[70] The bitter, hostile, and later violent response of many religious leaders to the state was due to the end of al-Azhar's quasi-independent existence.[71] Al-Azhar was to continue as "the stronghold of religion"; a primary consideration in its reorganization was to make the graduates of this institution job-worthy.[72] The law of June 1961 which sought to "reform" the institution did not address serious questions relative to the content of the religious education. On this account, there is a ring of hollowness to the principles of the law which stipulated:

1. To maintain al-Azhar's position as the largest and oldest Muslim university in East or West.
2. To maintain its position as the stronghold of religion and Arabism from which Islam will be renewed in its true substance to all levels and every locality in society.
3. To graduate scholars who have a knowledge of religious science, but also practical knowledge and experience, so that religion will no longer be their only craft or profession.
4. To destroy all barriers between al-Azhar and other universities, so that Azhar graduates may enjoy equal opportunity in the spheres of knowledge and work.
5. To give a common amount of knowledge and experience to all Azharis so that they may be intellectually and psychologically equal to all other sons of the Fatherland.
6. To standardize school and university certificates in all United Arab Republic universities and schools.[73]

Because serious questions relating to religious issues have not been addressed and resolved, Egyptian society is characterized by a sharp cleavage between secularists and traditionalists. Nearly half of Egypt's population is under 20 years of age. Many of them are flocking to religious educational institutions and oppose all Western modes of behavior.[74] This group of people rejects modern civilization and is clamoring for seriously mistaken and misunderstood "Islamic norms." Religious leaders and their cohorts have thus caused one of the most serious crises in the history of the Egyptian state.[75] They have paralyzed state power and have succeeded in thoroughly confusing political leaders and the mass of Egyptian society because of the prevalent ideological confusion in the society. Religious groups, many of them militant, not only challenge state authority, but also physically attack members of the state administration. They mobilize vast sectors of the population against the state, undermining public order; they represent a serious division in the body politic.[76]

A hasty and seriously flawed conclusion in this dilemma which the country faces would be to suggest "a secular formula of identity."[77] The real solution is to arm the population with the correct information about what Islam teaches. This would require compulsory and independent study of the Qur'an for Muslims at the high school level and beyond; this would also require doing away with a host of subjects that are included in the so-called religious sciences. It would necessarily be a long-term solution. Secular institutions can then be expected to function successfully.

Paradoxically, both Nasser and Sadat exhorted the separation of religion and politics, yet both sought support from religious groups to legitimize their policies. This seems simple enough, but its consequences for the polity were very serious. It legitimated not only the existence and propagation of religious groups, but, what was even more serious, it conveyed the message to the masses that the religious orientations and ideas of these groups were sound and, therefore, worthy of emulating. The prevalent ideas in the society about Islam, therefore, basically remained unchanged.

In this section we have covered the state's responses to some of the main ideas of the religious establishment. Therefore, we will not discuss them separately as we did in the last chapter.

MODERNIST INTELLECTUALS' VIEWS OF RELIGIOUS MATTERS AND PRACTICES

The forerunner of modernist thought in Egypt was Muhammad Abduh, a pupil of Jamal al-Din al-Afghani whom he met in 1872. Abduh (1849-1905) was a theologian, reformer, political activist, and grand mufti of Egypt around the turn of the century. Initially, Abduh had collaborated with the rebels in the Urabi uprising against the Khedive (the hereditary viceroy under the Ottoman empire), who was supported by the British troops that had occupied Egypt in the summer of 1882.[78] When the revolt failed, Abduh was exiled for over three years. On his return, he became convinced of the futility of such efforts to change Egypt. He perceived that the problem facing Egypt and other Muslim countries was not the material power of the West but the decay of the intellectual and social spheres of Muslim societies as compared to the West.[79] He, therefore, attempted to revise some of the orthodox conceptions of Islam which he felt were not in keeping with modern times. He vehemently rejected the centuries-old orthodox conception that the doctrine and law of Islam had been formulated for all times to come by the medieval interpreters. His most revolutionary idea was his espousal of the right of every generation to go back to the original sources and interpret them according to its own light. He also called into question the orthodox view of what these sources were. He believed the Qur'an to be the only real primary source. As for the sunna (tradition of the Prophet), he considered only a minute number of hadiths, mostly concerning the life of the Prophet, as genuine. For the traditional third source of the doctrine, the consensus of the community, the unanimity which Abduh would accept was that of universal reason which, after the Qur'an, he believed to be the main source of doctrine.[80]

Abduh held the ulema responsible for the sorry state of Muslim societies; they had totally neglected the modern sciences. "They continue[d] to busy themselves with what might have been suitable for a time that is long gone by, not realizing the fact that we are living in a new world."[81] They had failed to study and learn from the Western societies. He pointed out that the wealth and power of Western societies was due to their progress in the sciences, including the social sciences, and education. He called it the first duty of the government to spread education and the sciences in the country.[82]

While Abduh advocated the revision of the sharia and the reformulation of the Islamic doctrine, his thought contained ambiguities, reservations, and contradictions that partisans were to exploit later and invoke his authority. Abduh had earlier stated: "Representative government and legislation by representatives chosen by the people are entirely in harmony with the spirit and practice of Islam from the very beginning."[83] Later, however, he assigned a special role to the ulema who, along with the leaders, were to decide "all judicial, administrative, and political affairs, including the revision of the Shariah, which they will determine 'according to the principles of divine law concerning the promotion of the beneficial and the avoidance of evil,' and in harmony with the conditions of time and locality."[84] Some of the ambiguities and contradictions in his thought were later exploited by the Muslim Brotherhood who revived some of the slogans and ideas of his leading disciple, Muhammad Rashid Rida, and gave them a totally different meaning.[85] While Abduh was a strong believer in human reason, he surprisingly gave a higher status to the ulema for the exercise of this faculty, a position that was not only unreasonable but also exploited by the later ulema.

Notwithstanding some of the shortcomings in Abduh's thought on ontological grounds, his analysis and strong criticism of the prevalent ideas and practices about Islam in the Egyptian society were sound. He reproached the Muslims for having falsified the teachings of Islam. In addition, he reproached the ulema for their unhealthy anxiety to observe in the minutest details rituals like ablution and fasting or for making religion a profession for lucrative ends. The popular conceptions of Islam, he pointed out, were religious in name only. He also pointed out that false innovations were introduced in Muslim customs in later times. The ulema, he argued, occupied themselves with nothing else except commentaries and supercommentaries that they understood badly and explained even more badly.[86]

At the same time, Abduh took to task intelligent people for not attempting to reform the society. "They seem, he said, to wait till the reform comes to them."[87] He emphasized the role of education in the reform, and he called for, first of all, the reform of education which would pave the way for other reforms. He forcefully argued that

those who imagine that in merely transplanting to their country the ideas and customs of European peoples they will in a short time achieve the same degree of civilization, deceive themselves grossly. They take as their point of departure what is in reality the [result] of a long evolution. . . . [With the] blind imitation of the West . . . we shall only arrive at a superficial and scarcely durable transformation, which will suppress our morals, our customs and ruin all our personality.[88]

Abduh made it clear to the religious leaders that their so-called orthodox attitude was actually going against the real Islam, which was a thoroughly rationalist religion; that the Muslims had fallen so low because they had strayed from their true religion.[89]

Under the impact of Abduh's thought, two schools of thought developed in Egypt. Some have maintained that the concessions he made to modern thought were dangerous and unnecessary, and that no rethinking of doctrine or law was necessary, while others have developed his emphasis on the legitimacy of social change into a virtual division between religion and society, each with its own norms.[90]

Qasim Amin (1865-1908), a pupil of Abduh, was initially cautious in his discussion of Islam and society; later, however, he strongly criticized the idea that in the past Islam had achieved a perfect civilization. He pointed out that the sciences had developed after the Islamic civilization had reached its high point, and it was through the sciences that human civilization developed further. He also drew attention to the fact that the bygone Islamic civilization had lacked political maturity.[91] The political system that developed in Islamic societies was based on despotism which, as his contemporary, Lutfi al-Sayyid, pointed out, bred the vices of servitude, for despotism long continued destroys individuals as well as societies. It prevents the full growth of individuals and makes them less than human.[92] Amin pointedly attacked the notion that civilization can be developed by clinging to the past. Perfection, he argued, could not be found in the past, even the Islamic past. It could only be found, if at all, in the distant future. He dispelled the notion that, whereas the West was materially better than the Muslims, the Muslims were morally better.[93]

Another modernist writer of Egypt, Muhammad Rashid Rida (1865-1935), examined the issue of the backwardness of Muslim societies. Earlier, he had joined a mystic order, Naqshbandi (which is still in existence in Egypt and some other Muslim countries), only to abandon it after a revolting experience.[94] In examining the state of Muslim countries, he concluded that Muslims were backward because they had lost the truth of their religion, a situation that was encouraged by despotic politic leaders. Islamic civilization was created "by the Qur'an and the moral precepts enshrined in it, and can be re-created if Muslims return to the Qur'an."[95]

Rashid Rida dispelled the prevalent notion, widespread even today, that modern civilization is the result of technical advance. Technical skill, he argued, "is potentially universal, and its acquisition depends on certain moral habits and intellectual principles . . . ; and such habits and principles are in fact contained in Islam."[96]

Rashid Rida's thought, however, contains ambiguities and is beset with serious problems. Although he wants to reform Islamic law, he accepts the four schools of law that developed in Muslim societies, which are based primarily on the hadith literature; he wanted "a gradual approximation and amalgamation by them."[97] In deciding matters for which there is no clear text or its authenticity is doubtful, he maintains that it should be decided by human reason but be "guided by the principle of interest, interpreted in the light of the general principles laid down in the Qur'an and hadith."[98] Reliance on hadith is noteworthy. He also accords a special status to the ulema who are "the guardians and interpreters of the law."[99] This is to endow them, in effect, with a special faculty and implies the acceptance of the so-called Islamic subjects as a necessary condition to understand Islam, which is not true. His position on Islam is, therefore, virtually the same as that of the orthodox ulema.[100] Nevertheless, throughout his writings, Rashid Rida maintained that "the fundamental fault . . . which underlies the present degeneracy is that Islam has been suffered to drift away from its early simplicity . . . . Thus the decisive characteristics of Islam . . . have disappeared."[101] Like his master, Abduh, Rashid Rida exhorts Muslims to devote their means for the establishment of schools which he calls the most excellent of all good works. He considered the founding of schools to be better than the founding of mosques, for the prayer of an ignorant man in a mosque has no value, whereas through schools ignorance can be removed. He criticized the prevalent governmental system of education for failing to provide adequate religious training.[102]

A famous writer of Egypt, Taha Husayn, explains that the traditional way of thinking in Egypt is threaded through and through with fatalism and determinism. The people accept socioeconomic miseries as "an expression of the divine will" and disregard any social, economic, and political causes.[103] The society's religious life is conditioned by two groups—the Sufi shaykhs "who derive their authority from the divine grace that rests upon them, and the ulama, who derive their authority from their knowledge of the religious law."[104]

The intellectual elite that developed in Egypt in the 1920s and 1930s possessed a worldview and self-view that was both modernist and conservative.[105] It has continued to prevail in later generations. This approach to the world has essentially been contradictory. The intellectual elite felt that only an intellectual avant-garde, which was aware of the reasons for Europe's superiority and its own society's backwardness, and which knew the people's general will, could lead Egypt to the path of development. Strong conservative elements in the educated elite also wanted to lead Egypt into an era of progress, but by preserving the existing social order and without causing a significant social trauma. These conservative elements did not want the masses, or the lower classes, to participate actively in the process of modernization. They wanted the masses, who were dominated by religious elements and irrational impulses, to "remain passive and be led 'unawares' to the progressive society of the future. For their active participation would involve a change in their social status, and this would inevitably lead to social chaos and mass anarchism."[106]

Muhammad Husayn Haykal and his colleagues were representative of this approach. Haykal visualized Egypt developing along the lines of Europe. "He assumed that as Egypt modernized and progressed, religion in general—and Islam in particular—would disappear. He sought to separate Islam from social life, and to establish a secular, humanist and rationalist system of belief that would guarantee freedom of thought and of scientific inquiry."[107]   The intellectuals of the interwar period, however, underwent a crisis of thought in the confused intellectual milieu, the legacy of which still prevails in Egypt. The intellectuals replaced their Western orientation with a traditional Islamic orientation as the central foundation of their subsequent intellectual development. By doing so, the intellectuals opened the floodgates to popular, pseudoscientific Islamic literature that functioned entirely as an apologia for seventh-century Islam.   The intellectuals are fully responsible for this negative development. They were carried away by the emotional glorification of a vague Islam without being aware of its serious consequences. They ultimately led the society to a state of disorientation. They sacrificed rationalism and rejected Western cultural orientation without being able to produce viable Muslim-inspired alternatives. The result was sterile apologetics and ideological confusion.[108]

Such an approach has had grave consequences for Egyptian society.   The intellectuals' ideological orientations were no doubt conditioned by a reaction to the political situation existing in Egypt in which an alien power was dominating it.   Western colonialism's impact on Egypt was of the same nature as in other Muslim countries, an impact that so disoriented the societies that they have not yet fully recovered from it psychologically. The reactions that colonialism set in motion culminated in a negative response by most of the intellectuals and the masses.   Sufficient recognition and awareness has yet to develop that such a response is self-destructive and that massive intellectual efforts are required to set the societies on the correct course.

Western colonialism created a resentment among the masses, whose results were essentially negative at the political as well as at the social level.   The colonial interregnum has had a profound psychological impact on Muslims, severely damaging their ability to rethink their heritage objectively in order to create an Islamic future. Instead of keeping a rational distance from his heritage of the past, the average Muslim was pushed to cling to that past.   Even Muslim scholars cannot say with impunity today what certain Muslim scholars could say in the seventeenth or eighteenth centuries.   Although Muslim conservatism has been strong for centuries, colonial rule gave it a new psychological basis and a rationale.[109]

The situation has been further compounded and reinforced by (1) the system of education that developed under colonial rule and has been maintained since independence, and (2) the content of "Islamic Studies in the West and its influence both on the vision of the West of Islam and on Islamic studies in the Muslim countries."[110]   Islamic Studies as it has developed in the West is not "devoted to the substance of the Qur'anic teaching," and is polemical in nature, which further feeds and reinforces anti-Western attitudes in Muslim societies.[111]

It provides additional fuel for fire to conservatives and helps them in gaining and maintaining legitimacy in their societies. In addition, since Western Islamic Studies is not grounded in the Qur'an, its conclusions are as superficial as those of the conservatives in Muslim countries. Furthermore, "Muslims who come to Western centers and pursue Islamic studies go back trained as orientalists!," which is to say that their scholarship is also sterile.[112] The primary responsibility for such a state of affairs, however, rests on the political and intellectual leaders of Muslim countries who, barring some outstanding exceptions, have not fully realized the seriousness and implications of the issues involved. It was the ideological confusion of Egypt's intellectuals which "laid the groundwork for the extreme reactionary era that emerged after the Second World War, in which 'the whole ideological sphere was dominated by a romantic, vague, [and] inconsistent . . . Muslim orientation.'"[113] The ideological vacuum that was left by the Egyptian intellectuals was filled by the totally confused and superficial ideology of the Muslim Brothers, and subsequently by other religious groups.[114]

Even amidst such an intellectual climate, there emerged a modernist writer like Khalid Muhammad Khalid who challenged the religious establishment in no uncertain terms. His book *Min Huna Nabda* [From here we start], which was initially banned from publication with the connivance of the ulema, on the grounds that it was a communistic and anti-Islamic book, is a stinging critique of the religious situation in Egypt (published in 1950).[115] Khalid said that the aim of the book was "to remove from religion the scum and dross of interpretation attached to it and to confute the claims of the exploiting tyrants of society."[116] Although Khalid was somewhat carried away with the slogan of socialism, what he really meant was to end the blatant exploitation and misery of the masses. However, he mistakenly thought that Egypt's renaissance would occur through economic measures, and he referred to them when he said that "the document of advancement and progress upon which the real renaissance of Egypt must be recorded is still blank."[117]

Khalid attacked the ulema for propagating the idea that Islam revolved around such conceptions as punishments and alms-giving. He argued that Islam had exhorted social justice and equality, that "Islam had never regarded charity as a possible means for the advancement of nations; that in making charity a lawful economic system, [its] advocates only open the door for all people to go a-begging."[118] He pointed out that one of Egypt's biggest social problems was the population explosion, which he described as "a continuous deluge of human flesh." As he put it, "people never stop to think whether or not their prospective descendents . . . [the] helpless victims[,] will have any opportunities in life."[119]

The invisible hand behind this "deluge of human flesh," Khalid tried to show, was none other than the traditions falsely attributed to the Prophet.[120] Narration of such traditions was a regular feature of sermons in the mosques. Khalid described the sermon books as "those wretched . . . books, a page of which is sufficient to exterminate whole people."[121]

STATE RESPONSES TO MODERNIST INTELLECTUALS' VIEWS OF RELIGIOUS MATTERS AND PRACTICES

In Egypt, modernist writers have oscillated between modernism and conservatism, with the result that no clear synthesis of thought has developed. This duality is reflected in the thinking and writings of some of the leading intellectuals:

Such leading modernists as Taha Husayn, Muhammad Husayn Haykal, and Mahmud Abbas al-Aqqad, were, by the 1930s, already in hasty retreat from their earlier positions of secular liberalism and the adoption of European culture. Their reverential studies of the early . . . Islamic Community smacked of frantic and solicitous apologia for their earlier rationalist-secular attacks upon religion and its cultural heritage. A romantic proclivity for the epic quality of early Islam now became a major characteristic of their writings.[122]

This has in turn affected the thinking of the political leadership ever since Egypt became independent in 1952. The Charter of 1962 declared Egypt's intention to move away from total reliance on the West. While this is understandable to a certain degree, its declaration that "the real solutions to the problems of one people cannot be imported from the experience of another"[123] was short-sighted and dangerous. For it meant a wholesale rejection of the experience of the West, from which valuable insights and lessons can be learned. Nasser's regime, recognizing the emotional appeal of Islam among the masses, "solicited from the ulama formal legal opinions (*fatwas*) on the entire range of its activities, including birth control, land reform, nationalization, scientific research, foreign policy, and social affairs."[124] It also sought to sell socialist ideology on the basis of Islam.

The regime seemed to have thought that by invoking socialism as a state policy, the state would have the power to nationalize various institutions of the country, thereby promoting development and modernization of the society. Interestingly, in the Egyptian case, the state made religion an important factor in the politics of the nation, in which Islam was introduced into the political debate not by the ulema but by the state itself.[125] To be sure, the state was aware that Islam could "become a political vehicle for religious groups," and therefore, it carefully monitored religious discussion. In its politicization of Islam, however, the state has taken a seemingly paradoxical approach toward Islam. Both Nasser and Sadat were correct in denying the so-called Islamic religious groups and religious leaders a political role. They rightly feared that religious politics could destroy the Egyptian society and give political power to fundamentalist groups whose programs had already been rejected by the Revolution. Yet the state consciously used Islam to legitimize its foreign and domestic programs and repeatedly called on Islamic religious leaders to provide cultural, moral, and spiritual leadership to the country.[126]

The state, in effect, was attempting a shortcut in handling a deep-seated problem that can be remedied only through profound creative thought and effort, careful planning, and a strong commitment to reform the society. The foremost issue is that a systematic and comprehensive modern interpretation of Islam is required. Thus far, the modern interpretation of Islam "has been an ad hoc activity centered on certain specially singled out issues, without an explicit methodology."[127] The essence of the problem has been that Muslims, generally speaking, lack the psychological and, consequently, the scholarly equipment to reinterpret Islam for the modern age. The traditionalist is basically unwilling to undertake this task because for him it would be a sinful and harmful innovation. As for the fundamentalist, he refrains from undertaking this task, for he fears that it would explode some of his most cherished theses. The fundamentalist is essentially "a literalist and far more impervious to reason than the traditionalist conservative. . . . the fundamentalist . . . is intellectually extremely superficial, emotionally fanatic, and educationally threadbare."[128]

Under such circumstances, the state's reliance on the ulema was itself a superficial attempt to reform the society. At best, it could only maintain the status quo, if indeed that, for the society could very well degenerate further. It is vitally important to note here "that whatever modern interpretation of Islam has occurred, it has occurred at the hands of modern educated thinkers," which at once shows how false the impression is that the ulema possess any special expertise in Islamic religious matters.[129] It also shows how important it is that in the modern system of education in Muslim countries the study of the Qur'an be an integral part of the education so that it no longer remains a fortuitous matter for modern educated Muslim thinkers to emerge.

Throughout the Nasser and Sadat regimes, the state continued to emphasize that there was no place for religion in politics. Thus, in August 1979, while addressing the religious leaders, Sadat warned them not to involve themselves in politics or to use Islam for their own narrow political purposes. He told them that religion and politics should be kept separate, and he criticized the Muslim Brotherhood for its activities.[130] The confused thinking in official circles is also reflected in the state's support "to the officially recognized Sufi orders, while simultaneously attacking the excesses of ecstatic Sufi practices."[131] It could be argued here that the state was merely being politically wise not to alienate the support of religious groups, that there was pressure from domestic as well as international conservative religious groups and regimes, and therefore the approach taken by the regime was sound.[132] Now, there is some merit in this argument; it is also, of course, fairly obvious that the state cannot reform and restructure the society overnight. But that is not the issue here. The real point is that we do not see the state taking such measures that could be seen as reforming the society in the long run. In other words, the state was not moving beyond the status quo. In addition, those who came to occupy state power, even though they were modernist in their outlook to begin with, were confused by the sheer magnitude of the opposition and the onslaught of the religious groups.

This situation also happened because the intellectuals had failed to realize the seriousness of the religious issue and its implications for the society, and had failed to address the core issue surrounding Islam—how to remove the highly distorted ideas that have come to be associated with Islam, and how to make it so well understood that the correct interpretation occupies the consciousness of the people. It is necessarily a long-term solution, and the only viable one.[133] But it is an issue that requires more attention than any other issue, for it directly affects all other issues.

Both the state and the intellectuals have failed to address the issue in a systematic manner. Nasser, though emphasizing secular nationalism, seemed more interested in political adventurism and in using popular Islam as a legitimating force for state's policies, thereby giving sanction and support to the ideas prevalent in popular Islam.[134] They gained further legitimacy and strength following Egypt's defeat in the 1967 war with Israel. Thus, a great opportunity for the state to lay down and implement a framework of reform in the intellectual sphere was lost. This is so because the Egyptian society in the aftermath of the 1952 revolution was in a raw form, so to speak, and was entering into a formative phase in its development.[135] And this happened because the state and the intellectuals were themselves not clear as to what the real problem was and how to correct it.

Thus, when Sadat came to power, the religious groups and the popular notions of Islam were well entrenched, which he well recognized. He, therefore, "took, the calculated risk of condoning a revival of the activities of the Islamic groups, hoping thereby to be able to marshall their support for his regime and to counter antagonistic Nasserist and leftist influence among students and workers."[136] He also managed to secure a tacit pledge from the religious leaders to limit the scope of their activities and the means of pursuing them.[137] In the bargain, Sadat had "to accommodate the Brothers through the highly publicized amendment to the Constitution in April 1980 stipulating that 'Islam is the religion of the State' and the principles of Islamic Sharia 'the main source of legislation.'"[138] "Neither Nasser nor Sadat ever really addressed themselves seriously to the challenge"[139] and to the grave problems and their repercussions embedded in the popular notions of Islam. This is rather surprising, considering that both of them had rural roots and therefore had first-hand knowledge of the prevalent religious ideas and practices. Their attitude to the whole question of how prevalent ideas about Islam affected the society and in what ways, therefore, seems frivolous,[140] and displays a lack of intellectual incisiveness on the part of Egyptian elites. It does, however, show that the ruling circles were themselves not clear in their thinking about Islam. This is understandable, for they, like the masses, were heavily conditioned by the existing ideas of religious teachers in a dichotomous system of education, secular and religious. They were thus unable to formulate policies that could arrest the traditional Islamic ethos among the masses.[141] Therefore, both factors—the religious groups and leaders and the popular notions of Islam—became powerful obstacles in the process of modernization.

RELIGIOUS EDUCATION AND THE EDUCATIONAL SYSTEM

Religious education in Egypt has centered around the al-Azhar for the past several centuries; it has generally been considered an institution of higher learning in Islamic studies, and its graduates have traditionally provided intellectual leadership to both the masses and the elites.

It was the shaykh and mufti Muhammad Abduh who first recognized that the educational system at al-Azhar required reform. Such has been the influence of al-Azhar on other institutions, particularly the mosques, that Abduh felt that its reform "would be tantamount to reforming the entire body of Islam."[142] However, the other ulema offered such fierce opposition that he was prevented from carrying out the reforms he had thought of. An English journalist visiting Abduh in 1905, the year of his death, reported him saying:

Here I am, all alone. . . . Not one of the professors will help me; not one of those who teach benevolence will come to my aid. I want to teach something useful in this university, as a change from these decayed old commentaries which have become empty of all meaning, and more harmful even than your old books written in the Middle Ages. (Muhammad Abduh said this and pointed to the heap of bulky tomes leaning against the wall of the room.)[143]

Abduh described the education he had received at al-Azhar as "filth" and remarked that he "had spent ten years sweeping the filth of the Azhar out of [his] mind," and even then he had not "finished cleaning up."[144]

Al-Azhar continued to function as an exclusive religious institution of learning until 1961 when the state finally succeeded in making it a state university with some other faculties created in it, apparently to make it a general university to accommodate thousands of students whom the other state universities could not absorb.[145] In any case, al-Azhar scholars have not responded well to the challenges confronting the traditionally interpreted, understood, and accepted, conceptions of Islam. Their responses have been rather vague. Moreover, they have lacked "the audacity of thought and the originality of approach that are the necessary premises of any Islamic revival and of a renaissance of the real values which [would] constitute an answer to the challenge of the outside world."[146]

The law of 1961 which opened four new colleges at al-Azhar—Agriculture, Business Administration, Engineering, and Medicine—preserved the essential character of the institution and was rather apologetic in its approach to reform the institution.[147] In the national education system, although religious education was emphasized up to the high school level, the state lacked a bold approach to religious education. Noteworthy is the omission of the study of the Qur'an in a comprehensive and systematic manner, although the curriculum includes the reading of the Qur'an at the primary level.[148] Islamic religious education of a general nature is spread in the school years in the following manner: (1) preparatory grade—from first through third year; (2) elementary grade—from third year through six; and (3) high school—years 1 and 2.[149]

Analysis of the national education system through an examination of the contents of the textbooks is quite revealing regarding the direction the society is taking and its prospects for reform and progress. Egyptian leaders emphasized topics of development and Arab socialism in their statements in the 1960s. The books and curricula from this period were marked by two distinguishable layers: external and internal. The external layer, where religious educational goals, chapter headings and such like matters are stated, gives the impression of a great estrangement from the traditionally interpreted and understood conceptions regarding Islam. This impression is misleading, however, for an examination of the texts shows little resemblance between the internal and the external layer. Although at places religious arguments are presented to justify the reforms necessitated by modernization, "the general social conception of the authors, as well as their stand on sensitive social topics, such as the status of women and family planning, is fundamentalist Islamic."[150]

Study of the curricula and textbooks for social education, from which one would expect important contribution to the country's modernization process, reveals that the perspective on social issues is much the same as that of the books of religious instruction, which is thoroughly fundamentalist.[151]

Religious education imparted in schools is predicated on the traditional idea that religious law or the sharia covers every aspect of a person's private or public life. Various traditions are explained on the basis of the hadith literature. Preparatory school textbooks contain chapters that survey the Qur'an, the sunna, and religious law. High school textbooks provide more in-depth treatment of the history of the Qur'an, the relation between it and the sunna, and some other matters,[152] but the actual study of the Qur'an is not part of the curriculum. Egyptian authors of these books make wide use of the hadith sections to discuss social and national issues.[153]

Educational textbooks provide a good indication of the values imparted and encouraged among the students. Changes in value orientations are contingent on whether or not a particular educational system inculcates and encourages the critical faculties of its students; the contents of the textbooks provide the clues.

The solution of Egypt's demographic problem, which represents one of the greatest obstacles in the country's quest for modernization, is closely linked to a change in the traditional outlook. In books that deal with Islamic religious education, the issue of family planning is never raised at all.[154]

Discussions of women's social status in the textbooks reveal two main approaches: (1) The condition of the Arab woman is compared with that of her counterpart in the pre-Islamic period in order to show the contribution of Islam in raising her status, but comparison with the modern Western woman is avoided altogether; (2) no criticism is made of such sharia laws that discriminate against women and that are based primarily on the hadith literature or the opinions of the early Muslim legists. As for textbooks relating to national social education, they do not come to grips with the traditional image of women or suggest any fundamental change of values in this area.[155] A change of values is also required in the traditional approach to labor, which looks contemptuously at those who are engaged in manual or technical vocations. The ideas of liberty, equality, and democracy are treated superficially in the textbooks. Thus, slavery is uncritically accepted, and hadiths are quoted as to how slaves should be treated. In addition, the question of why a class of servants should exist in the society is glossed over. Similarly, the concept of citizens' rights is not even mentioned.[156]

In the reform of al-Azhar through the law of 1961, new faculties were created to make the graduates of this university more marketable. Sadat also echoed this objective in the 1960s when he said that through his travels abroad he knew that other nations which sent their students for study at al-Azhar wanted them to learn more than religion so that they could be of use in their homelands.[157] The new faculties created may well make the graduates of this university more marketable because of their specialization in the new fields. This is not, however, our concern here. Rather, we must examine the content of the religious education imparted at this institution, for those who receive religious education at al-Azhar become religious leaders to the masses through the mosques where they eventually preach and occupy a special position. Those who pursue religious education beyond the elementary level are also generally recognized as scholars by the state and the society. An almost similar "reform" of al-Azhar was carried out through Law No. 49 of November 1930 which established three new faculties: Islamic Law, Muslim Theology, and Arabic language.[158] The reform of 1961 was a very superficial one, for "the religious sciences [were] generally . . . left untouched so as not to stir up undue trouble."[159]

The curriculum of the religious subjects which has been followed at al-Azhar since the eighteenth century can be classified into two main categories—the transmitted or the religious sciences, and the linguistic and rational sciences.[160] The material that is taught in the so-called religious sciences is based on the works of writers most of whom belong to antiquity. The ideas that are passed from generation to generation through religious subjects, therefore, belong to that era. The principal religious works that have been taught at al-Azhar, beginning in the eighteenth century (the record of which is available), show the following picture. Although some of the works may have been dropped in recent years, the instruction is grounded primarily in these works. In other religious institutions and mosques, the teaching has been the same as that of al-Azhar, although by no means as comprehensive. In such institutions the teaching has consisted mainly of prophetic traditions, Qur'anic exegesis, jurisprudence (four schools), and grammar.[161]

In the advanced courses taught at al-Azhar, the subjects that have traditionally been taught are shown in Table 6.1. The names of authors and the titles of works have been omitted for space considerations, and only the years of the authors' death are given to indicate the period.

Surprisingly, the study of the Qur'an, which requires the use of human intelligence and reason, is omitted. Instead, emphasis is on such subjects and their contents that are largely irrelevant to grasping the teachings of the Qur'an. Instruction imparted through the above subjects and their contents is thoroughly confusing and disorienting.   Its living example is the existing state of the society. The effects of such instruction are not limited to Egypt; they are spread to neighboring Arab, African, and other countries who send their students to al-Azhar for "higher education" in Islamic studies.   The Muslim Culture and Missions Department of this institution also sends its teachers abroad.[162]

The educational background of the religious teachers who impart religious instruction in different forms is revealing, as shown in Table 6.2. Seventy percent of the imams (religious teachers) in governmental and private mosques have no educational qualifications whatsoever, and 79 percent of the religious teachers in private mosques that particularly abound in the rural areas have no educational qualifications at all. Table 6.3 presents the educational qualifications of muezzins (those who make calls for prayers in the mosques).   Both governmental and private mosques utilize the services of Qur'an reciters, most of whom are unpaid volunteers.   In 1962, 83 percent of them were unpaid volunteers, and 96 percent had no educational qualifications.[163] Great emphasis is placed on the recitation of the Qur'an, which in itself is regarded to be a very pious act.   This also encourages emphasis on literal interpretation of verses instead of understanding them in the overall context of the Qur'an and keeping in mind the historical situation.

Although the state "sought some genuine reforms in religious organization and practice, . . . this goal has been clearly secondary and progress toward it rather limited."[164] Instead of attempting a genuine reformation of religious ideas and practices, the state merely used Islam "to buttress nationalism, socialism and the one-party 'popular democracy'" in the Nasser era.[165] Apart from some administrative changes, no significant reform in the religious sphere has yet been undertaken in Egypt. To illustrate by merely one example, ideas of fatalism have

Table 6.1

Syllabi of Advanced Religious Courses at al-Azhar University

Subjects	Years of the Works
Kira'at (knowledge of the correct delivery to be followed in the recitation of the Qur'an)	1398
Tafsir (Qur'anic exegesis)	1459, 1505, 1143, 1286, 1569, 1574.
Hadith (prophetic traditions)	870, 1517, 1520,1451, 1448, 875, 1277, 886, 892, 888, 915, 1276, 1487, 1149, 1278, 1565, 1520, 1694, end of 10th century, 1389, 1252, 1258, 1278, 1623, 1505, 1659, 1623, 1505, 869, 1357, 1576, 892, 1565, 1605, 1623, 1517, 1710, 1149, 1605, 1658, 892.
Mustalah al-Hadith *(the technical terminology of the traditions)*	1448, 1605, 1710, 1299, 1366.
Fiqh (jurisprudence) (1) Hanafi	1451, 1552, 1562, 1778,1562, 1595, 1677, 1480, 1549, 1677, 1197, 1457, 1036, 1296, 1415, 1406.
(2) Shafi'i	1106, 1569, 1520, 1278, 1565, 1565, 1466, 1433, 1349, 1520, 1505, 1523, 1111, 1440.
(3) Maliki	795, 1710, 998, 1535, 1655, 1365, 1535, 1546, 1687, 1689, 1694, 1532, 1584, 1710, 1426, 1397.
(4) Hanbali	1623, 1735, 1223, 1283, 1560, 1560, 1361.
Usul al-Fiqh (principles of jurisprudence)	1085, 1460, 1566, 1370, 1460, 1248, 1355, 1310, 1427, 1677, 1562, 1346, 1398, 1533, 1285, 1457, 1474, 1431, 1480.

Table 6.1 (continued)

Subjects	Years of the Works
Fara'id (the laws of inheritance)	1512, 1520, 1512.
Tauhid or *Kalam* (theology)	1486, 1652, 1631, 1668, 1142, 1389, 1355, 1413, 1286, 1348, 1173, 1605.
Tasawwuf (mysticism)	1717, 1565, 993, 1309, 1240, 1111, 996, 1119, 1235, 1300, 1234, 1038, 1279, 993.
Nahw (syntax)	1323, 1273, 1360, 1367, 1398, 1499, 1360, 1564, 1360, 1248, 1492, 1122.
Sarf (morphology)	13th century, 14th century, 1257, 1390, 1248, 1287, 1520, 1273.
Balaghah (rhetoric)	1338, 1390, 1229, 1413, 1534, 1505, 1412, 1483, 1598, 1143.
Lughah (lexicography)	1002, 1414, 1320, 1368, 1505, 904, 1038, 889, 1355, 1483, 1537, 1474.
Arud and *Kafiyah* (prosody and rhyme)	1229, 13th century, 1454, 1228, 1520, 1424, 1359.
Mantik (logic)	1534, 1767, 1264, 1520, 1430, 1359, 1486, 1389, 1640, 1276, 1364, 1389, 1283, 1364.
Mikat wa Hai'ah (calculation of the calendar, times of prayer, etc., and astronomy)	1527, 1446, 1406, 1221, 1412, 1658, 1710, 1595.
Hikmah (philosophy)	1264, 1475, 1276, 1037.
Adab al-Bahth (the art of controversy and discussion)	1355, 1413, 1494, 1537, 1737, 1413, 1291, 1436, 1494, 1560.

Note: The works dealing with arithmetic and algebra have been omitted. The years of the works have been kept in the same order as in the cited source to correspond with the titles given there.

Source: J. Heyworth-Dunne, *An Introduction to the History of Education in Modern Egypt* (1939; reprinted, London: Frank Cass and Co., 1968), pp. 45-65.

Table 6.2

Educational Qualifications of Imams

Type of mosque	High[a]		Intermediate[b]		Below Intermediate		None		Total	
	No.	%	No.	%	No.	%	No.	%	No.	%
Governmental	1,108	52	367	17	226	10	446	21	12,147	100
Private	227	2	716	6	1,630	13	9,710	79	12,283	100
All mosques	1,335	9	1,083	8	1,856	13	10,156	70	14,430	100

[a]University degree or diploma from an institute secondary school.
[b]Secondary school certificate.

Source: Morroe Berger, *Islam in Egypt Today* (Cambridge: Cambridge University Press, 1970), p. 41.

Table 6.3

Educational Qualifications of Muezzins

Type of mosque	High[a]		Intermediate[b]		Below Intermediate		None		Total	
	No.	%	No.	%	No.	%	No.	%	No.	%
Governmental	14	0.6	45	2	171	8	1,993	90	2,223	100
Private	—	—	21	0.2	173	1.5	11,0680	98	11,262	100
All mosques	14	0.1	66	0.5	344	2.5	13,0616	97	13,485	100

Source: Morroe Berger, *Islam in Egypt Today* (Cambridge: Cambridge University Press, 1970), p. 41.

been noted at the highest level of political leadership in Egypt. In the aftermath of Egypt's defeat in the 1967 war with Israel, the president of the country "took refuge in a popular saying that he recalled to the nation: Precaution is useless against fate."[166] Thus, God was made responsible, in effect, for Egypt's shortcomings.

The Society of the Muslim Brothers raised the issue of the general state of the educational system as early as 1935. The society sent delegations to the Ministry of Education and the prime minister and met with members of Parliament "to publicize the need for reintroducing religion in the schools of Egypt as a necessary prelude to the reconstruction of the schools on a truly national and Islamic basis."[167] In 1938 the then education minister, Muhammad Husayn Haykal, proposed to the rector of al-Azhar that secular and religious education be combined. The leader of the Brotherhood, al-Banna, forcefully argued that secular education

alongside the traditional Azhar-type education had created formidable conflicts between the two groups, a situation dangerous for a nation seeking "rebirth", since the greatest need was "unity of culture." . . . "Religious people" are misguided in thinking that they will be done with the evils of secularism by ignoring it; secularism will be conquered only by mastery of the fields of "science and learning."

Banna therefore suggested that education should be neither purely Islamic nor purely secular . . . , but should harmoniously blend religious character and moral training with scientific training.[168]

What would be the content of the religious education? Here the approach taken by Banna, other leaders of the Society, and the subsequent intellectual and political leadership has been most uninspired. Their idea of religious education has been of the same kind as has traditionally been taught at al-Azhar. Most surprisingly, the study of the Qur'an, according to Banna, "would depend on the student's specialization; a student in arts and Islamic studies in higher learning would be required to know the whole of it."[169] Thus, the only source that can effectively combat distorted ideas about Islam, and is the only way of understanding Islam, was excluded from study by the general student body, even in the realm of thought of the Muslim intellectuals of Egypt. As we have noted earlier, the study of the Qur'an even at al-Azhar is not a main field of study. Instead, emphasis is on the so-called religious sciences, most of which are based on the hadith literature or writings from the medieval period. In the state school system, as we observed earlier, religious education is very elementary, and the study of the Qur'an is excluded.

To coordinate and facilitate planning, the state created various administrative and coordinating structures like the Supreme Council for National Planning and the National Planning Commission, and in 1960 the Institute of National Planning with research and training facilities was established. Although a comprehensive plan was published in 1960 for the next ten years, only vague projections were made for 1965-1970. In addition, internal conflicts within and without the social core group and the accordance of high priorities to the military establishment due to external considerations prevented internal reform and attention to national education. Subsequent developments have not made any significant positive changes in these fundamental aspects of national life. The educational field also suffered because of poor planning in the 1950s and 1960s.[170]

By far the most serious mistake was made at the highest political level in the person of President Nasser who, ruling in an autocratic manner, preoccupied himself with external affairs and image-making instead of paying attention to the serious problems confronting Egypt in the socioeconomic and educational arenas. Egypt suffered not only from bad planning, but also, as one study concluded, "from the administration habits of the total government."[171] Following the 1960 plan, in which some of the targets were achieved, the state made no new plans. Despite the general awareness that education requires complete transformation, the goals of the third educational plan (1970-1975) remained the same as those of the previous plans. Although the goals ranged from universalization of primary education to vocational, technical, and scientific training, and other aspects of education, the achievements were not impressive. Even at the primary level the rate of growth decreased appreciably each year in the 1960s. More disturbingly, "the rate of increase in the number of girls enrolled in this period slowed even more appreciably."[172] Contrary to the claims made that 80 percent of children enter the first grade as compared to 45 percent before the revolution, it has been estimated that "only about 55 percent of all children between the ages of six and twelve are actually enrolled in school."[173] To eradicate illiteracy, the state seems to have been quite content to provide primary education to a greater number of children.

Because the objectives have been set so low, the achievements have been even lower. Most of those who do graduate from rural schools lapse back into illiteracy within a few years. And primary education cannot really be expected to produce the kind of orientations that are so vital for modernization.[174] Add to this the orientations that are passed on by religious teachers and parents (most of whom have had no real education), and we have a vicious circle. The state itself made it difficult for children to move beyond the preparatory stage. The first five-year plan (1960-1965), for example, stipulated that only 43 percent of those who pass the preparatory school certificate examination can be admitted to secondary schools. The examination itself is such a difficult challenge that a significant percentage of all students fail.[175] As for the low standards of secondary education, these schools do not give an education as understood in the West. They establish bad habits such as memorization. Students are not encouraged to think for themselves or to express their opinions.[176]

One study has shown that 44 percent of secondary school graduates showed dissatisfaction with the kind of education they received; 82 percent of these graduates did not like the kinds of jobs they were performing. In addition, there is widespread distaste for technical occupations in the Egyptian society. As for the teachers, they are poorly paid and have no interest in their profession. The curricula of public schools do not address the country's problems in any objective manner. Instead, emphasis is on propaganda and myths. Traditional cultural attitudes predominate the society. The state, through its own propaganda, has encouraged such attitudes; its emphasis has been on Arab nationalism.

Traditional attitudes in the Middle East as a whole are so strong that very few opportunities exist for girls to acquire any education at all. On average there is one girls' school for every three or four boys' schools. In Egypt 80 percent of the females and 60 percent of males are illiterate. This grave crisis in the educational arena is attributable to such factors as inadequate planning and financing, the neglect of rural education, rapid population growth, low living standards, and high dependency burdens. If these factors continue, universal enrollments in the first grade will not be achieved for eighty-six years.[177] To make matters worse, the curricula have still not been adapted to developmental needs.[178] The development of a meaningful and progressive higher education is a far cry. Based only on the state of education in Egypt and the attention it has received from the state so far, one reaches the inescapable conclusion that modernization will remain an elusive and almost chimeric concept for the foreseeable future.

ASSESSMENT OF THE DEVELOPMENT PLANS AND MODERNIZATION GOALS OF THE STATE

When Nasser and his colleagues carried out the coup of 1952, they were inspired by the idea of a self-respecting and modern Egypt. The Egyptian society had been stagnant for centuries. Therefore, theirs was a great opportunity to arrest the further decay of the society and to reorient its bearings.

The revolutionary regime was well aware of the abuses of the big landlords and the poverty of the people. The developmental approach the state took from the beginning was, however, rather haphazard and ill planned. Egypt's massive socioeconomic problem—overpopulation—was largely ignored, and family planning did not form an integral part of development planning.[179] Although the state focused on industrial development, creating work for 350,000 in the period 1952-1963, population grew by 650,000 in a single year.[180] This lackluster approach by the state to such a major social issue was in keeping with the thinking of the traditional spokesmen of al-Azhar and other religious leaders, particularly of the Society of Muslim Brotherhood, who showed no real concern about the economic implications of overpopulation.[181]

Although the state's industrial investments in the first five-year plan exceeded the target rate, investment in agriculture lagged behind the planned target. Industrialization certainly has a place in the development process, but it must be carried out with agricultural development and in directions that are economically feasible.[182] In 1964 and 1965 there was critical shortage of food supplies and consumer goods. Constructive civilian projects that could have been undertaken were sacrificed for the growing military establishment. In 1965-1966 Egypt's military budget was $506 million, whereas the average annual investment during the first five-year plan was $686 million. The military budget exceeded 10 percent of total national income ($4 billion).[183] Nasser's preoccupation with external affairs and image-making led to the neglect of domestic problems. In the three-year war in Yemen, Egypt spent at least $30 million a year in hard currency. Tunisia's Habib Bourguiba identified Egypt's real problem when in 1965 he stated in Morocco that if certain African leaders busied themselves more with their countries instead of their revolutionary or leftist complexes, or occupying themselves with imperialism or neocolonialism, their countries would benefit from it. The United States also frequently advised Nasser that his foreign adventures were major stumbling blocks to continuing American aid.[184]

The state's operative doctrine in the Nasser era, which lasted until 1971, was socialism, and along with that it emphasized pan-Arabism. To bring about what Nasser perceived to be a socialist society, the state resorted to nationalization of industrial and commercial enterprises. The nationalization measures increased after July 1961 when the first victim was the cotton trade. On July 20, 1961, all banks and insurance companies, as well as 400 big enterprises were brought under state control. In August 1963 Nasser nationalized all trade which hit an estimated 450,000 tradesmen. The nationalization measures stifled private enterprise which the state found it difficult to replace.[185]

The state had carried out land reforms soon after the military regime was in power, limiting landholding above 200 feddans (1 feddan equals approximately one acre) to 2,000 proprietors. After implementation of the 1961 law, the upper limit was reduced to 100 feddans, which only 5,000 proprietors could own. Although the government propaganda for nine years spoke about social reforms, the gains were small and the land reform was only a drop in the ocean.[186] Productive efficiency or the productivity of labor is an effective way of raising living standards in the long run. In Egypt the productivity of labor in the first five-year plan was dangerously low; for agriculture and industry, the increase in productivity was of the same size as in the 1950s.[187]

Agricultural policies and agrarian change are a litmus test of elite will and intentions in the development process of the developing countries.[188] In the transfer of resources from the agricultural sector to the industrial sector, the crucial question revolves around how such strategies are implemented. In a vast majority of the cases, implementation is not only wasteful, but also agriculture is undermined without promoting industrial growth. Rural populations are kept in poverty and therefore cannot generate sufficient demand for the new industries that become costly and inefficient and are unable to absorb surplus labor from the countryside. The rural workers who migrate to the cities add to the unemployment situation in the cities. The overstaffed bureaucracies and public enterprises become yet another dead weight on the economy. National savings rates inevitably suffer because the state must satisfy the demands of these urban constituencies. In such situations, the state resorts to the costly venture of importing capital instead of bringing about the politically formidable tasks of socioeconomic and agricultural reforms. In time this pattern grows into a vicious circle. It is this pattern rather than an international division of labor imposed by the core which is at the heart of external dependency. It sustains the low level of wages in the developing countries, which is "the most important factor in the maintenance of the unequal exchange between the core and the periphery."[189]

The above situation is glaringly noticeable in Egypt, where industrialization has been accompanied by growing food imports, even though most of the labor force is engaged in farming. Rising population has exacerbated the situation.[190] In the period 1945-1964, the United States provided $943.1 million and the communist block $1,441 million in aid to Egypt.[191] By 1963 Egypt had become the largest per capita consumer of American food aid in the world. Since Egypt's peace treaty with Israel, it has been the second highest recipient of American aid.[192] Egypt's external dependency intensified as a result of poor economic planning and performance during the Nasser era. The seeds for this growth in dependency were planted in the early 1960s at the height of Nasser's socialism.[193] Egypt's case demonstrates that the elites, not societies, cast themselves into the arms of the core, primarily because of poor developmental planning and lack of will by the elites.[194] It also suggests that in such situations the elites are themselves not seriously interested and committed to the development of their societies.

The real cause of underdevelopment is not the transfer of surplus appropriated by the core from the periphery but rather the effects of structures at the periphery that prevent the creation and productive investment of the surplus at the periphery.[195] To prevent dependency, effective structural changes are required which contribute to savings and growth in the agrarian sector. This is by no means an easy task because rural populations in the underdeveloped countries are notorious for their recalcitrance and resiliency to patterns of influence and power.[196] Nasser's Egypt had not only accepted low-level economic performance but also abetted it through the regime's policies.[197] Table 6.4 gives a good picture of Egypt's external dependence. Investments in Egypt have always come from foreign credits swinging from Western to Eastern and then back to the Western bloc in high drama. Although the religious establishment heaps abuse on foreign nations, it does not give any thought to why Egypt is not even able to feed itself. Instead, it shamelessly accepts the

Table 6.4

Special Indicators of Egypt's External Dependence, 1950-1980

Indicator	Monarchy		Nasser Era			Sadat Era		
	1950	1955	1960	1965	1970	1976	1978	1980
1. Cotton Exports/Total Exports	85%	78%	71%	56%	45%	26%	19%	4%
2. Visible Trade Deficit/GNP	4.1%	4.4%	.5%	3.8%	4.7%	13%	26%	10%
3. Foreign Loans/GI(1952)	26%	23%	11%	33%	38%	85%	108%	71%
4. External Debt:£E million	—	—	—	247	1,340	4,970	10,500	11,200
5. External Debt/GNP	—	—	—	1.8%	42%	49%	107%	85%
6. Debt Service Ratio	—	—	—	22%	25%	44.3%	65.5%	53%
7. Imported Arms: US$ million	—	336	170	810	1,070	2,690	2,000	1,500
8. Imported Wheat: kgs. per capita	24.3	30	44.5	71.6	39	88.6	103	129
9. Wheat Aid: kgs. per capita	—	—	13	27	6	24	37.6	35.7
10. Worker Remittances: £E million	—	—	8	29	84	612	1,730	2,860

Note: The figures include undisbursed credits; serials (4—6) refer only to nonmilitary debt. The ratio in (6) is that of servicing to value of *visible* exports. The entries in (7) are cumulative totals of disbursed and undisbursed military credits for the intervening time period. Wheat aid in (9) is almost exclusively from the U.S., except in 1970, when it comes from other sources.

Source: John Waterbury, *The Egypt of Nasser and Sadat: The Political Economy of Two Regimes* (Princeton, N.J.: Princeton University Press, 1983), p. 30.

prevalent conditions and propagates and instills such ideas that have brought ruination to the country. Every person in Egypt receives an average of over 100 kilograms of imported wheat per year, or about 70 percent of the total consumption. "Egypt's jugular vein runs through Iowa, Nebraska, and the Dakotas."[198]

Economic development and the lessening of dependency are contingent on the state's ability to generate domestic savings for investment in development projects. External borrowing is the most critical element of dependency and tends to perpetuate itself when the state avoids the hard questions of domestic resource mobilization and extraction.[199] By resorting to heavy deficit financing, the state also avoids facing and resolving deep-seated societal problems that cause external borrowing to occur in the first place. It translates into unwillingness or a lack of political will on the part of the elites and an unawareness of the root causes of the society's ills, which lie in the thought processes of the individuals forming the society.

In the mid-1970s Egypt moved from a socialist economic policy to an economic liberalization policy, which was now the state's new approach to development. It is represented in the equation "Arab capital + Western technology + abundant Egyptian resources = development and progress."[200] The economic liberalization policy aimed at importing advanced technology and attracting capital for economic development. In this open-door policy, and in the absence of any overall strategy for development, all types of projects were permitted. Centralized planning was virtually abandoned; the only stipulation in this frenzied economic activity was that the state would make decisions on a case-by-case basis. In the agricultural sector the emphasis was on high technology and capital.[201]

Not surprisingly, this economic policy turned out to be a disaster. It literally led to deindustrialization of Egypt; industrial activity as a percentage of economic activity shrank. While Arabs rushed into tourism and luxury constructions, Egyptians shifted their activities to the free zones to escape socialist laws and into servicing of the expanding international trade. Little industrial activity was even contemplated. The consumer goods sector experienced rapid expansion, which was financed through deficits. The extent of the national debt was astounding. By 1975-1976, the trade deficit was around 20 percent of the gross domestic product (GDP). The foreign debt equalled or exceeded the GDP. Debt service alone was 10 percent of the GDP. This policy increased the poverty of the poor and made the rich richer.[202]

During the period 1973-1976 Egypt received loans worth over $9.1 billion from twenty-one countries and international organizations. Most of these loans were of the worst type—short-term credits. These loans did not cover Egypt's military debt, which is estimated to have been two-thirds of the nonmilitary debt. A significant portion of the nonmilitary loans was general finance.[203] The sociopsychological effects of these loans on the Egyptian society can be well imagined. Its net effect was that the society would continue to operate on the same value systems, norms, and work ethics as before.[204] Under the Law for Arab and Foreign Investment, an investment of $1,134 million was made in the Egyptian economy. The most remarkable facet of this investment was that investment in food production, which is the most serious issue facing Egyptians, was a mere 1 percent of the total investments.

The country's development efforts have been heavily marred by its rapid population growth. In 1977 its population was 40 million concentrated in 3.7 percent of the surface; in 1976 its population density was 664 persons per kilometer, almost of the same magnitude as in Bangladesh or Java. The cultivated area was even smaller, constituting 2.4 percent of the total (23,928 km). The workforce participation rate has remained low over the years, averaging around 30 percent, which means that for every employed person there are three dependents; the workforce is also heavily gender-biased.[205] The number of females who are active in the workforce has registered an increase of only 1 percent since 1947. It is estimated that Egypt's population (45 million in 1984) will jump to between 62 and 74 million in the year 2000 and may be as high as 139 million in 2030.[206] Egypt's population is expanding at the rate of 3 percent per annum; there is, therefore, a great need to complement the "development approach" with a strong family planning approach.[207]

The real problem in the Egyptian development efforts has been that, while its leaders have not been unaware of the economic problems facing the country, they have tended to seek their solution in the political sphere, and in a haphazard manner. National policy formulation has not been part of a coherent strategy but has tended to be dictated by real and perceived threats to the regime. Since 1952, the Egyptian government has often searched for

solutions to real problems by stepping outside their parameters. There is the phenomenon of flight from responsibility of the kind—"imperialism is responsible for our backwardness, but imperialism is the weapon of the super-powers whom we cannot combat, therefore we must suffer our backwardness indefinitely." A variant of this outlook gave rise . . . to Egypt's active pursuit of Arab unity on Egyptian terms . . . [:] "Egyptian leadership must be acknowledged in all collective Arab efforts." This outlook is at the heart of Egypt's enracinated impulse toward defensive imperialism. Its correlate is the assumption that Egypt cannot tend to its own affairs until the region is put in a supportive mood. A third type of "flight forward" is to treat knotty problems as insoluble and end-run them.[208]

Egyptian elites have tended to divorce economics from politics. For them the "real" problems have existed in the political sphere, rather than in the economic field: "Domestic and international politics are seen as the determinant elements; the economy and the organization of the means of production are subordinate. Political will sets the course of the nation; economics flows therefrom."[209]

The state apparatus—the civil service and public sector—is legendary for outright corruption. While this was so in "socialist" Egypt, it became even worse following the open-door policy. High-ranking officials have been involved in kickbacks, embezzlements, black market operations, and the like. A study in 1978 found that "454 high-ranking bureaucrats had sentences pending against them that had never been imposed."[210] Nasser's son-in-law, who was advisor to Sadat on Arab affairs and director of the Arab Military Organization, was for years believed to have been receiving large kickbacks.[211] The will to transform Egyptian society from a backward, almost stagnant state to a modern society has never been a class phenomenon; it has been limited to a few persons in the top leadership. Scholars observe that Egypt, like other countries of the Middle East, underwent a managerial revolution before the industrial revolution could take place, and "that Egypt's leaders [have] confused the proliferation of technical and managerial cadres with modernization itself."[212]

By depending heavily on foreign loans, the state has postponed structural reforms that alone can move it toward real independence.[213] Through such policies the state has encouraged apathy and dependence on the dole among the masses. Another major feature of the country's external dependency is the state's encouragement of its most skilled and productive labor force to work abroad to earn foreign exchange. Through their earnings the state has been able to maintain a favorable balance-of-payments situation. At the same time, the state robs the country of a sizable portion of its most skilled and enterprising labor force.[214] Out of a total labor force of slightly over 10 million active workers in the country, over 1 million Egyptians are working abroad. Although this is temporarily alleviating the country's massive unemployment problem, it is not a real solution. It is another indication of the state's inability or reluctance to address and solve a pressing domestic economic issue. The situation is analogous to that of Pakistan where nearly 2 million highly skilled and enterprising Pakistanis are working abroad and the state is merely content with "boasting" that the migrant workers provide more foreign exchange than the total exports of the country. In both cases, the basic societal problems remain unresolved, and the state seems content and resigned to the situation.

As in the case of an overall development strategy, Egypt has no coherent overall strategy for encouraging exports.[215] The country has concentrated on one major item for export—cotton; in 1978 cotton and cotton textiles provided nearly 40 percent of total commodity exports. The World Bank estimated that in the mid-1980s another single commodity—crude petroleum—accounted for nearly 50 percent of commodity export earnings. To make matters worse, "Egypt's exports are seriously handicapped by the erosion of the exportable surplus owing to rising domestic consumption, the nature and effects of bilateral trade, problems of institutional change and marketing in agricultural products, and low factor productivity and poor quality in manufacturing."[216]

Because of the country's massive poverty, the state has had to subsidize the prices of essential commodities, which in 1982 amounted to $2,466 million. The subsidy on bread alone equalled one year's revenue from the Suez Canal plus some $350 million.[217] Since power was transferred to Mubarak in 1981, no perceptible change has been noticeable in the state's overall approach to the country's problems from previous years. As far as planning in Egypt is concerned, it is remarkable that after 1965 the country had no multiyear plan until one was announced in 1983.[218]

Nearly one-third of the Egyptian workforce is on the public payroll—3.2 million people out of a workforce of 10 million. The armed forces, which were over 1 million in 1973, are not included in this figure. In 1980 Egypt's civil service consisted of 2.1 million people; from 1962 to 1972 the civil service grew by 7.5 percent per annum, while the workforce increased by 2.2 percent. For mere survival, they have to depend on two jobs, sometimes both on the public payroll. The average workday for these civil servants varies "between one-and-a-half and three hours. . . . Along with the moonlighting, petty corruption in such circumstances is unavoidable."[219]

CONCLUSION

When Egypt achieved its independence in a real sense following the coup of 1952, its leaders aspired to make it a self-respecting modern state. They were not clear, however, as to how to achieve this objective. Their policies, actions, and statements in the following decades have shown very confused thinking. To be fair to these leaders, however, it must be stated here that the problems they inherited were of gigantic proportions. These were further compounded by the lack of a clear direction from the Egyptian intellectuals in the preceding several decades, going back, in fact, to more than a century ago when Muhammad Ali first attempted to modernize Egyptian society.

Aware of Islam's appeal among the masses, the state has merely used it as a tool to legitimize its policies and to seek legitimacy for the government. It has sanctioned and encouraged such blatantly un-Islamic and illegitimate practices as the Sufi orders; it has used such groups as a source of support against the Muslim Brotherhood. The larger and more pressing issue—the reform of the traditional practices and orientations that are labeled Islamic—has not been touched by the state and has been treated as if it does not even exist. Its effect is so deep, however, that it affects such matters as manual and technical professions which are looked down upon. Indeed, it affects all aspects of life as religious leaders and many Muslim scholars never tire of stating, to the point of boasting, without realizing the ill-effects it generates. Although the Egyptian modernist intellectuals have, to a considerable extent, censured the prevalent Islamic orientations, attitudes, and practices in the society, they have not yet worked out a system of religious thought that would be applicable to the present times. Their thought has oscillated between modernism and traditionalism, with no clear direction for further development.

With regard to the religious leaders, given their intellectual background, orientations, and attitudes, they cannot be expected to bring about such changes in the prevalent religious thought and practices that would move the society out of its centuries-old stagnation. The biggest problem in this area is the prevalent dichotomous system of education. Until this structure of education is demolished and religious education, that is, the study of the Qur'an, becomes part of general education, no real changes in the structure and direction of the society can be foreseen. The state has been content with haphazard efforts to increase literacy in the population; the state's objectives in the educational sphere, on which the whole structure of the society rests, have been very limited. Not surprisingly, therefore, the results have also been very limited. In sum, "the transformation of the society from a state of underdevelopment to a state of development must begin with change in the very substructures that give rise to the prevailing mentality."[220] In Egypt, as in other Muslim countries, a major problem has been that for the elites

"appropriate" development does not involve transforming the existing social structures or changing the prevailing mentality and culture. On the contrary, it attempts to contain the effects of transfer of selected western technology. Social, cultural, and political innovations are rejected . . . . This way, the process of development becomes restrictive, selective, adaptive, partial, slow, and compartmentalized. Essentially, this version of development promotes conditions of dependency, social class disparities, repression, elitism, and alienation. The whole society, in fact, is relegated to historical marginality.[221]

The state has attempted to develop the country economically without any comprehensive plan or strategy. Initially, land reforms were carried out as an isolated measure. Here, too, the basic conditions have remained the same as before, notwithstanding the fact that some lands were given to the peasants. In agricultural products Egypt remains heavily dependent on aid from foreign countries.

Religious circles in Egypt have continuously argued that in Islam religion and state are one united system. Their idea of this unity is to politicize Islam and to use it as a powerful weapon to attack the establishment and to keep it thoroughly confused and always on the defensive. They are able to achieve this because of widespread distorted ideas about Islam which are not only naive but un-Islamic. For the society to be able to develop in any meaningful way, it is crucial to address this issue, and the only way toward this end is through a reformed and modern system of education. As things are, it will be a long process and a long time before Egyptian society can be modernized. The beginnings of that process have yet to be made. Islam has been understood and used in Egypt as a sport at both the popular and official level, and the arena for it has been both domestic and international politics.[222]

Nearly a century ago, Muhammad Abduh observed that Egyptian society, like other Muslim societies, had stagnated because it lacked "almost all the virtues emphasized in Islam;"[223] even the work ethic which has been emphasized in the Qur'an, has been neglected by Muslims for centuries. Instead, most people use "the concept of depending on God as an excuse for their slothfulness."[224] This is as true today as it was in Abduh's day. The real problem, as Abduh observed, has been that through misinterpretation and abuse the tenets of the Qur'an have been distorted. Instead of understanding the Qur'an, an overwhelming majority of Muslims' ideas of Islam are rooted primarily in the so-called traditions that are alien to the Qur'an.[225] These traditions represent a formidable obstacle to modernization. Egypt, in the words of Abduh, waits until reform comes to it.

7

THE RELIGIOPOLITICAL
SYSTEM OF TURKEY
AND MODERNIZATION

Turkey's case is somewhat different from the case in Pakistan and Egypt. It is similar to the extent that its population is overwhelmingly Muslim; it is different in that ever since its inception as a modern republic, Turkey has followed secularism as its main doctrine.   It sought and implemented separation of religion and state as a state policy. Because of this difference, it offers an interesting comparison with the other two countries and other Muslim countries in general.

Turkey's study is also interesting and important because it has had the longest period of independent existence among Muslim countries in recent history. It has now been independent for seventy years.   Indeed, if we consider the period of the Ottoman empire, the area that now forms Turkey has remained sovereign for over six centuries. After the First World War, the Turkish mainland was occupied by foreign troops for a brief period, but Mustafa Kemal Atatürk "was able to force the evacuation of foreign troops from the Turkish mainland, to negotiate an honorable settlement," and to maintain Turkey's sovereignty and independence.[1]

Allied troops occupied Turkish territory following the Mudros Armistice signed on October 30, 1918, between the Allies and the Istanbul government. On August 10, 1920, the Allies signed the Treaty of Sevres with the Istanbul government, which was meant to destroy Turkey's independence.   Thereafter the Allies were engaged in a running battle by the nationalists who were led by Mustafa Kemal.   Following the defeat of the Allies, the Armistice of Mudania was signed on October 11, 1922.   On July 24, 1923, the Treaty of Lausanne was signed between Turkey and the Allies in which Turkey received almost everything determined by the National Pact (January 12, 1920), which was the result of the two congresses held earlier on July 23 and September 4, 1919, chaired by Mustafa Kemal.[2] Our focus in this study, then, will be on the period from 1923 onward when the Ottoman empire was no more and Turkey emerged as an independent nation.

STATE POSITION AND POLICIES REGARDING
ISLAM AND RELIGIOUS LEADERS' RESPONSES

For centuries, the Ottoman rulers had ruled the territories under their control through the institution of sultan-caliph. It was an autocratic institution in both the temporal and religious spheres, with the ruler acting traditionally as the religious leader of the Muslims, even though the existence of the caliph was not a necessary condition of worship and public welfare.[3] For religious opinions and decisions he depended on the advice of the ulema. Thus, both rulers and ulema enjoyed immense power, and both often manipulated each other. Since "the caliph's power was always based on armed force, even when it was invisible and did not have to be used, . . . free expression of opinion was not possible."[4] Since free thought in politics was impossible, no real study of politics had been carried out by Muslim thinkers under these conditions.[5] This had a spillover effect in other areas of life where thought remained suppressed.

Given the onslaught of the Allies against the Ottoman territories and their division, initially Kemal Atatürk did not propose the abolition of the caliphate for political reasons. Atatürk's decision to subsequently abolish the caliphate was sound, for it was a religious office that constantly meddled in the affairs of the state. Through this office, religion had become a political instrument in the hands of the rulers who manipulated it as they wished. Atatürk was therefore correct in seeking and establishing the principle of separation of religion and state.

I must however qualify Atatürk's idea of the separation of religion and state with an all-important caveat. The separation, essential as it was, should not have meant the relegation of religion to an obscure corner. This was vitally important because the *study* of Islam, that is, the Qur'an, and of socioreligious ideas prevalent in Muslim territories (which later became independent Muslim countries) under Ottoman rule, had not been carried out in the 641 years of Ottoman empire which came to an end only in 1923. As we observed earlier, exercise of all thought in this period was suppressed. The situation in other Muslim countries was similar and became worse when they fell under colonial rule. There, too, the study of Islam in a systematic manner was not carried out, for Islam was totally brushed aside and made simply a private affair that was limited to the observance of rituals only.

In this context, Donald Eugene Smith makes an all-important point when he observes that a society that is predominantly Muslim must pursue Islamic ideals; if it does not, it is liable to lead to complacency or corruption. The reason for this being that if any other ideals are adopted, no matter how similar they might be to the Islamic ideals, there will be a lack of understanding and commitment to those ideals, for the intellectual bases of those ideals will not be understood. This will be so because the adopted ideals, in this case the Western ideals, come from a similar, yet different, religious tradition. Therefore, unless one subscribes to that tradition, one is not likely to be sincere and firm in one's commitment to those ideals. It follows, therefore, that the only viable option for a Muslim society is to understand and implement the Islamic ideals. This can come about only when one has studied Islam. It involves great intellectual effort and cannot be achieved through a shortcut. As Smith puts it:

Slowly . . . the outside world is beginning to discern the importance of transcendent ideals, and to realize that it is better to have ideals, even when not lived up to, than to repudiate them outright. It is important that practice be good. It is equally important that, when practice lapses, good ideals be acknowledged so that there be something to which one can appeal.[6]

An ideal Islamic state "is a state which Muslims consider to be good."[7] A Muslim's idea of goodness is conditioned preeminently by the fact that he or she is a Muslim, and it is the acceptance of Islam (i.e., the Qur'an) as the source of knowledge concerning good and evil which makes a person Muslim. Islam, therefore, is "the form of his apprehension. Crucial, then, in his striving for the good society, is the interpretation of Islam. And this has, precisely, become the crucial intellectual and spiritual question of the Muslim world."[8]

Western democracy, laudable as it is, cannot be transposed to another society, particularly Islamic, merely through a democratic form of government:

Western democracy is in an extremely meaningful sense Christian . . . democracy has both a political and an ethical element: it cannot exist without the concurrence of both a governmental form and a popular ideal. This ideal, the ethical aspect, is no fortuitous ingredient: it must have content, and must have solid basis for continuing support. A democrat must believe not only in the democratic structure of the state; he must believe also in the fundamental significance and value of the other persons in his society.[9]

The ethical element in an Islamic society or an Islamic democracy must come from Islam.[10] Only then does it become viable, and only then can there be a commitment to it, for it will contain within itself the elements of loyalty and accountability. For this to be operative in any meaningful way, however, the first requirement is great intellectual effort to rework out the entire structure of religious thought in Islam. Only then is it possible to eliminate the gross distortions that, through the centuries, have been made a major part of Islam. This is vitally important, for it affects the thought processes of Muslims in every aspect of life. Indeed, the study of Turkey shows us that in the absence of such an undertaking, and the mere adoption of Western democracy, how such a society has fared in the modern world. It shows us whether secularism, in the absence of the nonresolution of ideological confusion in the population, by itself has made or is in the process of making the country modern and progressive.

When the Turkish National Assembly abolished the caliphate in 1924, Mustafa Kemal Atatürk explained that it was abolished because it had ruined the Turkish people. The caliphate was essentially political. The very effort to make it purely spiritual had proved this for it had become the rallying point of discontented elements.[11] Notwithstanding the fact that abuses of an extremely serious nature had taken place in the preceding several centuries of caliphal rule, religious circles throughout the Muslim world were in an uproar at its abolition.[12] It was a reflection of how stagnant Muslim thought in general had remained for an entire historical era.

Spearheading the Turkish revolution, Atatürk almost singlehandedly carried out a number of social reforms that were concerned with the religious and, consequently, every aspect of life in Turkey:

a. Polygamy, [which until then had been illegitimately] declared legal in Islam, was prohibited (1925) and civil marriage was made compulsory (1926); women were given full suffrage and equal rights with men to hold office (1934).

b. The Eastern head-dress, the fez, was forbidden and replaced by European hats and caps (1925).

c. Religious orders and societies were suppressed and members of the clergy [Muslim] forced to wear a uniform dress prescribed by the state (1925).

d. A new legal code, based on European models, replaced the old code which was based for the most part on the Islamic Shari'a (1926).

e. The Turkish state was declared officially secular (1928).

f. The Arabic script was made illegal and replaced by the Latin script (1928). [Atatürk's reasons were that very few people understood the Arabic language, and the Turkish language, widely spoken, had remained undeveloped.]

g. The Gregorian (rather than the Muslim Hijra) calendar was officially adopted (1926); replacing the Muslim Friday, Sunday was made the official weekly holiday (1935). [Atatürk had Turkey's commercial interests in mind for doing so.][13]

Atatürk's victory over the Allies had won him unparalleled prestige both at home and abroad. The Turkish people followed him in what he asked them to do, albeit not without some opposition; for all practical purposes, the state was Atatürk. Yet he was cautious in bringing about the reforms. Explaining to a crowd of men and women why he had introduced the hat, he said: "We have to resemble the civilized world in our costume also."[14] For the same reason women were asked to remove their veils. The overall purpose of such measures was to break the power of the fanaticism of Islamic conservatism which had become the hallmark of a Muslim society.[15] The sweeping nature of the reforms suggests how exasperated Atatürk felt at the state of the society. He felt that such measures were necessary to change the people's psychology. Atatürk understood human nature well. He saw that the changes he envisioned would require a sharp, even painful, break with past habits and a strenuous effort to initiate new ways. "Basic change, he realized, must be felt simultaneously by all the Turks . . . [and] changes had to penetrate into private life."[16]

Atatürk deemphasized militarism and sought to build a civil society. Through the centuries, his predecessors had come to regard success in the battlefield as a sign of perfection. Consequently, cultural attainment lagged.[17] It was to this end, to create a modern and viable civil society, that Atatürk undertook the reforms that have been mentioned earlier. It was the refusal of the ulema to rethink the sharia law in the preceding Ottoman rule "which ultimately resulted in the secularism of Mustafa Kemal, the Atatürk."[18] Although separation of religion and state became a state policy and principle, he never indulged in religious persecution.[19] There was no "liquidation" of religion. If Islam had lost any of its influence over the people, it was because of the superficiality and incompetence of the religious teachers. The single aim of the Kemalists was to secularize the political life. Most of the people had never learned to distinguish between religion and politics. Their failure to grasp this idea was another reason why the nonpolitical caliphate was abolished after it had been tried for sixteen months. It was necessary and inevitable that the state assume the functions of education and public works, many of which were previously performed by the religious functionaries and supported by the pious foundations (religious foundations).[20]

Atatürk was to the point when he told the nation in his mammoth and historic speech: "We . . . recognize that it is indispensable in order to secure the revival of the Islamic Faith, to disengage it from the condition of being a political instrument, which it has been for centuries through habit."[21] Countering the propaganda of his adversaries that he and his colleagues were using the law for Restoration of Order and the Courts of Independence as tools of dictatorship, he informed the Grand National Assembly that exceptional measures, which nevertheless were legal, were required for the nation's social development.[22] He also informed the house that it was necessary to abolish the fez, which sat on people's heads as a sign of ignorance, fanaticism, and hatred of progress and civilization.[23] So strong was the tradition of wearing the fez that it had become synonymous with Islam; failure to wear it was considered apostasy.[24]

The state, through Atatürk, abolished all sects and titles such as sheikh, dervish, junger, tschelebi, occultist, magician, and mausoleum guard,[25] some of which had acquired religious prestige and sanction. For the mass of the people, Islam had come to mean occultism, belief in superstitions, and, at best, preoccupation with prayers and mindless following of traditions. Atatürk convincingly argued that a civilized nation could not let itself be led by people like sheikhs, dedes, seids, tschelebis, babas and emirs; a people were not civilized if they let their destiny be decided by chiromancers, magicians, dice-throwers, and amulet sellers. If he had let this continue, Atatürk said, he would have committed the greatest blunder in the cause of progress and reawakening. It was for this reason that he carried out the reforms.[26]

The state encountered strong opposition from reactionary and rebellious elements who had formed the Republican Progressive party. The party appealed to the masses on the basis of religious promises.[27] Invoking "respect for religious ideas and dogmas," the party appealed to the people for the reestablishment of the caliphate and religious law. The party wanted to protect the medressas, the tekkes, the pious institutions, the softahs, the sheikhs, and their disciples. The party charged that by abolishing the caliphate the Kemalists had ruined Islam and that the people would be made unbelievers. The party advised the people that the assimilation with the Occident meant the destruction of Islamic history and civilization.[28]

Atatürk pointed out that the party attempted to provoke the religious fanaticism of the nation and advocated that it respected "religious thoughts and religious doctrines."[29] He then raised a fundamental question regarding the politicization of religion and its effects on society. The question and the answer given by Atatürk completely vindicate his position and the call for the separation of religion and state:

Was not this principle [respect for religious thoughts and religious doctrines] the standard of all those who pursued personal aims whilst they allured and deceived the ignorant, fanatical and superstitious people? Has not the Turkish nation for centuries been dragged into endless suffering and into the pestilential swamps of obscurity under this banner, rescue only being possible through great sacrifices?[30]

Atatürk and his colleagues were not only courageous, bold, and farsighted in the reforms they had undertaken, but they were also sincere in their efforts to reform the society.[31] Their theory of change and the movement they launched were designed "to change customs and institutions, conduct and interests, by fiat."[32] They were convinced that there was not enough time to wait for the culmination of the slow process of evolution; people must use their energy and will to force every material element of life through modern molds and modern patterns.[33] As one observer who saw the developments unfolding in Turkey reported, under the inspiration and insistence of Atatürk, the idea that progress was created by human efforts was generally accepted. Through this buoyant, youthful doctrine, progress was seen being made—progress that was the result of the attitude implicit in reformism.[34]

The drastic action which the state, through Atatürk, undertook to separate religion from politics was fully justified in the conditions which then existed in Turkey, even though in Islam there is no independent organization, like the church hierarchy, to regulate religious affairs. It is the state's responsibility to regulate these affairs for the purposes of both education and administration. This does not mean at all, however, that religion be politicized or have a political office, as had come to be established in the Ottoman empire. That Atatürk's action was fully justified is illustrated through the actions of the Ottoman sultan who was at the same time holding the title of caliph, or religious head of the entire Muslim community. He had actually conspired to accept slavery for Turks. His actions also show how dubious religious traditions and customs had gripped and paralyzed the minds of the people. The Turkish people and the army had no suspicion at all of the padishah-caliph's treachery. Because of the close relationship between religion and tradition for centuries, they remained loyal to the throne. Under the influence of this tradition, the security of the caliphate and the sultanate was far more important for them than their own safety. It was too impossible an idea for them that the country could possibly be saved without a caliph or a padishah. Those who thought otherwise, Atatürk observed, would immediately have been branded as people without faith and patriotism.[35]

Contrary to what some writers have stated, that Atatürk was irreligious, he well understood many of the essential teachings of Islam. His struggle for Turkey's independence and the honorable settlement of Turkey's claims emanated from this understanding. He called it "the religious and national duty" of Turkish leaders to keep Turkey independent and sovereign.[36] Nearly a fortnight after the revolutionary leaders' rupture with the government had begun, on September 25, 1919, Abdul Kerim Pasha, who at one point acted as an intermediary between the sultan and the revolutionary movement led by Atatürk, implored Atatürk to maintain the office of the "Sublime Sovereign" in these terms:

The Good God who guides our destiny will undoubtedly show the leaders the best way to save the nation and the country. . . . It is sure that His decisions are sublime and that their manifestations are near at hand. His hand is over all others. Thanks to His Divine benevolence, my beloved Soul, everything will turn out well in the end. . . . [37]

Atatürk, who continuously emphasized in his speeches that it was the nation's will that would ultimately decide the fate of the country and that this will represented the Divine Will, replied:

We implore the most Gracious and most Merciful God to reveal His sublime manifestations, which are so near at hand, for the salvation of our unhappy and noble nation. . . . Undoubtedly, my most venerable Pasha, "the Hand of God is over all others," but it is none the less a fact that those who try to find a way to solve this question [Turkey's independence] and overcome all the difficulties that encompass it must have a fixed aim. . . .

The nation will act according to the Divine Will and, as you have said, its desires will come to a happy issue.[38]

Atatürk was well aware of the importance of Islamic teaching for Muslims; we know this directly from him. However, religious rivalries, privileges, and outdated religious ideas had so devastated the country that he was eventually compelled to opt for secularism. By choosing to do so, however, and although his motives were sincere in making Turkey a modern, progressive country, he was sidestepping a major and serious issue facing Turkey which was the root cause of the decay of the Ottoman Empire—the reconstruction of religious thought in Islam. Secularism would ensure that this would not take place, for in the Islamic context it is the state's responsibility to regulate the community's religious affairs, including religious education. That in the past the state apparatus had grossly misused this responsibility should have meant greater efforts to rectify the problem rather than avoiding it.

Let us return to the point that Atatürk was aware of the necessity of religious teaching for Muslims. In July 1919 the idea of the American mandate over the Ottoman territories was circulated so as to preserve the empire, which Atatürk rejected. Several proposals were suggested which encompassed the mandate. Among others, they included (1) the extension of public education and (2) the guarantee of freedom in education and religion.[39] Atatürk replied that the development and extension of public education under the mandate would mean the establishment of American schools in every part of the country. How, he asked, could this proposition be brought into agreement with Ottoman and Islamic teaching? The second proposal, he replied, was important to a certain extent, but it could not be of any particular significance if the privileges of the patriarchates still existed.[40]

When the revolution was a success, Turkey's sovereignty established, and the state declared to be secular, the question of Islamic religious education became a private affair, which is to say that the prevalent Islamic religious ideas in the society continued to operate as heretofore. Appalling as this condition was, with the "'disestablishment' of Islam" in the society, a vacuum was created in the society with the passage of time.[41] Thus, a writer who observed Turkey in the mid-1940s reported:

. . . it would be incorrect to imagine that the decline of Islam and of Islamic art has everywhere resulted in a liberation, a breaking of fetters. On the contrary, it has often left a wide gap, almost a vacuum, which nothing can at present be found to fill. . . . An entire generation, otherwise well-equipped, is in danger of being brought up with little or no *moral* training at all; not because the teachers have neglected to instil it, but because they have nothing to instil. . . . A Director of Education in a provincial town asked me some months ago whether the British Council could not be persuaded to set up a number of British schools in Turkey for the sole purpose of demonstrating the best method of character-training.[42]

The state, under the reins of the Kemalist elite, acted under the illusion that cultural change could be imposed from above through the force of law.[43] Although some of the reforms of the Kemalists in the religious sphere were extremely necessary and urgent, and therefore fully justified, the reformers did not probe deeper to discover what was wrong with the prevalent Islamic religious ideas that had so decayed the Turkish society, and how to correct the situation. This was by no means an easy task and could only have been possible in the long run, primarily through reforms in the educational system, which could provide the atmosphere and the setting in which necessary reforms could be consciously understood by the masses, effected, and sustained. By failing to undertake this task, the Kemalists' reforms essentially remained flawed. The Kemalists' aspiration to westernize Turkey, a Turkey where men and women had equal rights, wore modern dress, danced and dined in the Western way, and were versed in Western philosophy and art, had little meaning in the value structure of the countryside. The state, through its secular policies and programs of westernization, had threatened the "value system of a traditional Islamic society without providing, at the same time, a new ideological framework which could have mass appeal."[44]

Although Atatürk's success in the struggle for Turkey's independence and sovereignty had given him extraordinary stature and prestige, his adherence to the policy of secularism was by no means without opposition, especially in the countryside. This opposition, or the responses of religious leaders and circles, then and subsequently, will be discussed separately when we take up the state's responses to religious leaders' and functionaries' views regarding Islam.

How grossly flawed the state's approach and policy toward secularism was is tellingly captured by John Grant who traveled the length and breadth of Turkey in the mid-1930s. Near the old town of Ankara, in the vicinity of a street-school, he reports:

A pretty little girl whom I was trying to photograph, what with the excitement of seeing the schoolmaster and with protesting against the taking of the photograph, dropped her copper water bowl.

Picking it up hurriedly, she wiped it up with the end of her head-scarf.

"May Allah forgive thee," she innocently lisped, "there are the verses of the Qur'an inscribed in this bowl, and the Holy Inscription had touched the ground—fallen even where my feet are."

That little remark, more than anything else throughout my wanderings into the modernist Turkey, convinced me that Islam has a very deep root in the hearts of the real Turkish people, nor can, indeed, be divorced from their minds. . . . [45]

MODERNIST INTELLECTUALS' VIEWS OF
RELIGIOUS MATTERS AND STATE RESPONSES

By far the most influential Turkish scholar from the beginning of the twentieth century until the creation of Turkey as a republic was Ziya Gökalp (1876-1924). His writings, beginning in 1911, had a powerful impact on developments in Turkey. The first period of his writings, from 1911 to 1918, culminated in many of his ideas being materialized when Atatürk established a nationalist regime in Anatolia. During this period Gokälp began discussing Turkey's fundamental problems and how to resolve them, an undertaking that he continued in the second period of his writings, from 1922 to 1924.[46] The main theme that runs through his writings was the question of how the Turks should adopt Western civilization and how this effort should be harmonized with the Turkish and Islamic traditions of the people. Gökalp was not the first Turk to raise this question, but his uniqueness was in the fact that he discussed this question in a coherent intellectual framework and drew some conclusions that served as formulas for a cultural policy.[47]

Atatürk was conversant with Gökalp's ideas, some of which he shared, and his drastic reforms show the influence of Gökalp's ideas. Indeed, Gökalp was on the constitution committee that prepared Turkey's constitution in 1924; he was the architect of the constitutional clauses specifying secularism and freedom of conscience and thinking. He argued for westernism, democracy, political and economic national independence, and secularism. Not all of his ideas, however, were followed by the republic, and some of his ideas in later years were forgotten or distorted.[48]

As long ago as the eighteenth century, there were signs that Turkey would have to adapt itself to the requirements of modern civilization, which meant changes in the political, economic, social, and cultural and intellectual spheres. None of these came about, however, Later, the Tanzimat (meaning reorderings or reorganization) edicts of 1839 and 1856 recognized that changes were required in the Turkish society, which meant that old institutions had to give way to new ones. Two factors, however, prevented the satisfactory application of this idea: despotic rule would have had to give way to democratic rule, which the men of the Tanzimat were apparently unwilling to do; and second, inherent in a medieval society's contact with the European expansionist economy and politics were economic and political consequences.[49] Because of the difficulties arising from these two factors, mainly for the Ottoman rulers themselves, they did not pursue their program of modernization sincerely, nor did they understand the nature and scope of the social transformation that modernization required. This led to mere imitation. A major consequence of this approach was the creation of dichotomies in almost every sphere of life. It resulted in two sets of ideas, two sets of institutions, and two opposing loyalties (one to the old and the other to the new), which stood side by side.[50]

This was the situation Gökalp faced and sought to address. He believed this anomalous situation was the result of "a lack of adjustment between civilization and culture".[51] Civilization, he argued, is based on traditions that are created by different ethnic groups and transmitted from one to another. Culture "is composed of the 'mores' of a particular nation and, consequently, is unique and *sui generis.* "[52] Civilization and culture, he pointed out, were not antithetical but instead complementary and essential to each other. To be useful, however, civilization must become part of the culture. If it does not, a given society not only lacks coherence, but also is bereft of a major component of social reality. Elements of civilization assume meaning and function in a society only when they become part of culture; otherwise, civilization merely becomes imitation and lacks any foundation. That appears to have been the case in Turkey and other Muslim countries "where civilization had come to be a mere skeleton corroding and annihilating all cultural flesh and blood of the social body" because it was not assimilated.[53]

Gökalp's ideas and writings were concerned primarily with the concept of nation, with the intent that Turkey must become a nation in the modern sense or on the European model. He rejected the theocratic conception of nationality and saw secularism and democracy as the twin principles through which modern nations had emerged. He seems to have taken, however, a too literal and too rigid a conception of secularism, not recognizing that such a formulation was basically opposed to the Islamic conception of state. He also mistakenly thought that culture was independent of religion or religious ideas. To this end, he even sought to grope for Turkish culture in the pre-Islamic period of Turkey, and he resorted to dubious history to prove that Turkish culture fulfilled the requirements of modern civilization.[54]

Despite some inconsistencies and shortcomings in his thought, the conclusions he reached were so new and bold that Gökälp's contemporaries were fascinated.[55] He argued that there was no incompatibility between Western civilization and Islam; he rejected the idea that Islam was a civilization or that Western civilization was synonymous with Christianity.[56] The attributes commonly associated with Islam and Turks, like asceticism, fatalism, seclusion of women and their low status, and polygamy, he pointed out, were wrongly so attributed. Their origins lay in the ancient Arab and Persian culture, and were subsequently wrongly incorporated in the sharia.[57] He attacked the Islamists for insisting on the restoration or the return to sharia. The religious teachers, he pointed out, had failed to distinguish between universally valid truths in Islam from those aspects that were relevant to a particular time and space. They identified Islam with ritual and sharia rules and stood against everything new. They wanted to maintain their rigidity in the face of progress and contemporary conditions, and therefore they clashed violently with the needs of the people and the present times. This was the basis of the Westernists' idea that Islam and contemporary civilization were incompatible. But the Westernists were wrong because they did not take care to proceed in a cultural framework.[58]

Gökalp had called on the Turkish elites to reach civilization through the cultivation of culture.[59] Paradoxically, however, through his advocacy of secularism, which the Kemalists fully embraced, the most important component of the culture, Islam, was left out as if it did not exist. Cultivation of the culture should have meant to address this issue; the only effective way to which was that the *study* of the Qur'an became a vigorous national activity through the reform of the educational system. This was essential because in the preceding centuries of Ottoman rule it had not been done, the evidence of which is the existence of such practices, traditions, and customs which, when confronted with the Qur'an, do violence to it. Islam, as Gökalp was well aware, had only been understood in the preceding several centuries in Turkey and elsewhere in terms of some rituals and rules. Under these conditions, resort to secularism as a state policy was, therefore, a capital mistake.[60]

Gökalp argued that in an organized society religious mores needed to be separated from political or cultural mores because religious mores tend to bequeath a charismatic power and value to the institutions to which they are related. He believed that in organic societies religious mores still exist, but they are confined to those ideals and sentiments that are spiritual and sacred; they do not extend to secular institutions—a conclusion that is seriously flawed.[61]

Gökalp's advocacy of separation of religion and state was a radical departure from the existing organizational basis of Muslim societies and was basically sound. However, he seemed to compartmentalize the different spheres of a society in too rigid a fashion, forgetting that the prevalent religious mores have a direct impact on other mores, be they cultural, economic, or political. The separation of religion from politics was, by itself, not enough, important though it was. What was of crucial importance was the content of the religious mores. Since over the centuries these mores had been corrupted and the corrupted religious mores assimilated in the society, the first requirement was to put this right, which meant confronting the issue. It was here that the advocacy of secularism was at fault, for it meant that the prevalent distorted, indeed, antithetical ideas to Islam would continue to operate in the psyche of the people, even though the state had removed some abuses and malpractices in the religious sphere. Even for these measures to be effective, it was imperative that the people recognize and believe, on their own, that many prevalent religious ideas and practices had been corrupted through the ages and therefore needed to be reformed. This was the state's responsibility to bring about; by enforcing secularism at this stage, the state virtually shunned this responsibility and left the people groping in the dark by making Islam "an entirely private affair."[62] While, officially, profound changes had taken place in the religious sphere, in reality there was not much change. In 1937 women in the countryside, for instance, "still stuck to the convention that a decent woman has to cover her hair."[63] While many people could still get religious education through the traditional religious schools, they were imparted the same education as before. The practice would continue in the future because there was nobody to correct the situation.

Curiously, while Gökalp spoke glowingly that there were no priests in Islam, he made religious knowledge a prerogative of some people through the concept of the division of labor.[64] Here he was following the traditional approach to religious knowledge and had in mind the various branches or subjects that had emerged in Islamic religious education, most of which are irrelevant in understanding what the Qur'an teaches. On this point the Qur'an itself states in several places: "And we have made the Qur'an easy to understand, so is there anyone who will think [and understand?]" (54:17, 32 and elsewhere).

Contrary to what the Qur'an says, Gökalp wanted "specialists in religion" to impart religious knowledge.[65] Gökalp, like other Muslim religious teachers who have continued to advocate a special class of "religious people," quotes a Qur'anic verse to further substantiate his argument. But the verse, from the earlier period of the revelation, was applicable to the special circumstances existing then, as is apparent from the verse itself: "The believers should not all go out to fight. Of every troop of them, a party only should go forth, that they (who are left behind) may gain sound knowledge in religion, and that they may warn their folk when they return to them, so that they may beware. (9:122). But Gökalp completely ignores that and says: "From the beginning there were persons charged with the duty of the dissemination of religion; such were Muftis, teachers, shaikhs, imams, khatibs, preachers, and pilgrimage guides."[66]

Gokälp also ignores the fact that one major factor causing distortions and corruptions to appear in Islamic religious ideas and practices was that a class of people had arrogated to themselves an authority over religious matters. Subsequently, this authority was corruptly legitimized by rulers for their own personal motives.

From the reasoning that he followed, it was easy for Gökalp to conclude that secularism ought to be the state policy. A class of people could still carry out the task of religious education, as had been the practice until then. But it was a major mistake, for it would ensure the dissemination and propagation of such erroneous religious ideas and practices as was the case before. In other words, secularism served as a mechanism to freeze these ideas and practices as they were, even though the intention of the state was otherwise, as is apparent from some of the needed social reforms that it undertook.

In a recent study, Taha Parla has argued that Gökalp had given realistic weight to Islamic tradition in his tripartite synthesis of Turkism—Islamism—Modernism.[67] The problem was that some Kemalists misunderstood Gökalp as an advocate of religious conservatism, while the radicals on the right considered him an uncritical advocate of westernism. The Kemalists, therefore, eliminated the second term in Gökalp's tripartite synthesis of Turkism—Islamism—Modernism, and the radicals refused to allow the third term. "Consequently, the Kemalists denied the debt they owed to Gökalp for their own laicism, albeit learned from him, although he had tried hard to couple it with the modernization of religion in a secular direction as an ethical system."[68]

Indeed, credit is due to Gökalp for his advocacy of laicism in a system of government that had had centuries of tradition of ecclesiastical control and influence. Beyond that, however, if we keep in mind the gross distortions, indeed outright deviations, that had become part and parcel of Islamic religious thought, the "modernization of religion" could not have occurred in a secular society, as I have argued above.

Similarly, it is not enough that an ethical system should exist, say, through proclamation. Moreover, as Fazlur Rahman has pointed out, Muslims have never worked out an ethics of the Qur'an. The result is a profound misunderstanding of what the Qur'an teaches. It is important that people grasp the rationale and logic behind an ethical system which, for Muslims, means the study of the Qur'an in a systematic manner and without any intermediary. Indeed, a Muslim cannot know what Islam is all about unless he or she has studied the Qur'an. In the Islamic context, advocacy and practice of secularism militates against this vitally important aspect. Indeed, the fact that Islamists of then and now are engaged in a wholesale rejection of the modern way of life (granting that not everything in the modern way of life is sound or good) is clear proof that their knowledge of Islam is not rooted in the Qur'an and, therefore, amounts to being un-Islamic, as I have shown in Chapters 4, 5, and 6. Moreover, since the ideas contained in their "knowledge" are presented as Islamic, they are accepted by the general population who, through the centuries, have been conditioned to view religious knowledge as the prerogative of religious teachers. Its consequences for the individual and the society are serious and dangerous, for, to repeat the words of a court of inquiry instituted in Pakistan in 1953 (Chapter 5), if "you can persuade the masses that something they are asked to do is religiously right or enjoined by religion, you can set them to any course of action." This finding alone shows the relevance of religious education, that is, the study of the Qur'an in combination with modern education.

This approach to modernization, in the Islamic context, is not only the only viable one, but its potentials are unlimited. It also opens a whole new array of possibilities in the evolutionary process of modernization itself, in the distant future.[69] It is in this intellectual climate that "a fruitful scientific investigation of Islam" and, proceeding from there, meaningful religious reform in Islam can take place.[70] The enshrinement of secularism in the republic's constitution as a state policy arrested this possibility.[71] Paradoxically, In his later years Gökalp had also emphasized the importance of Islam as a character-building factor and attached great importance to religious education for the youth.[72] By accepting and advocating secularism, however, he was also accepting the traditional approach, method, and curriculum of religious education that could continue privately in a secular environment through private institutions.[73] In such an environment reform of religious thought would be exceedingly difficult, if at all possible.

Gökalp saw the harmful effects of mixing religion with politics and argued that theocracy and clericalism must be eliminated from political life and that complete sovereignty must be accorded to the state. He felt that the state's legislative powers should not be limited by canon law, and that laws should not be considered as unchangeable.[74]

Gökalp did not seek an end to the dichotomous secular and religious educational systems, for he only advocated that the main religious colleges (*medrese*) should be merged with the Theological Faculty of Constantinople University.[75] The abolition of religious colleges, which Atatürk undertook following Gökalp's advice, did not end the dualism of secular and religious education, for religious education continued independently and with the same content as before. The dualism could only have been eliminated through fusion, and not isolation of one from the other, as had been the case already. Atatürk had perceived that the traditional religious education was a major obstacle in making Turkey a modern and progressive country. Where I think he erred was that he did not recognize that religious education, through primarily the study of the Qur'an, could be fused with secular education and a balance achieved.

The perception behind Atatürk's abolition of the Theological Faculty at Constantinople University in 1933, like the abolition of religious schools, was sound insofar as it sought to remedy the negative part of the problem. Yet it was a partial and limited perception, for it did not see the possible positive elements hidden behind the apparent problem, which could open new possibilities and directions, backed up with untapped sources of energy and motivation. Its realization would have required first-hand knowledge of the source of Islam, that is, the Qur'an, by everyone in a modern intellectual environment.

The difficult task was the creation of this environment, which could only have occurred in the long run, given the negative influence and practices of the preceding several centuries. It is in this environment, in which the teachings of the Qur'an are intelligently internalized, that the fixation on the symbolic practices and ceremonies would be removed. This could lead to their reformation following reformation of religious thought and, consequently, thought in general, for the purpose behind them would then be well understood.[76] The new intellectual environment would provide the needed strength to carry out the reforms. It essentially means a higher stage of mental development, which can happen only when the Qur'an is understood in its totality, and when isolated or individual verses are not made the focus of attention. Emphasizing individual or isolated verses can lead to meanings that are completely at variance with the spirit of the Qur'an. The new intellectual environment would also serve as a powerful antidote to fanaticism, which is an outgrowth of ignorance wherever it occurs.

In Muslim societies there has been a fixation on symbolic practices and ceremonies. A mistaken belief has developed that what is required of a Muslim is to follow the symbolic practices and ceremonies, even though the rest of the Qur'anic doctrine is blatantly violated or disregarded, or not even studied. No effort is made to understand the purpose behind the symbolic practices, with the result that magical results are expected from them. The idea and purpose behind these symbolic practices and ceremonies has been understood in only a very limited sense, whereas the major teachings of the Qur'an have largely been neglected and not understood, because they have not been studied (or pondered on as the Qur'an puts it).

This approach would also have gradually led to the elimination of the dichotomy between, what Gökalp has called, the popular civilization and official civilization, or the historical bifurcation between the people and the government or the elites.[77] This duality of civilization has developed in Muslim societies primarily through the way religion has been used and the place it has been given in the society. It has primarily been used to emphasize symbolic practices. By confining Islamic religious education to the private sphere, it has not been allowed to enter the intellectual pursuits of Muslim societies. Thus, the elites, primarily conditioned by secular education, have held a different worldview, or culture, than the masses, who have been conditioned by the popular and unstudied ideas and practices attributed to Islam.

In both cases, the groups' ideas and practices are not grounded in the source of Islam, which leads them to vastly different directions in culture and civilization. To end this duality, both groups must be grounded in the source of Islam and at the same time receive modern education. In such a situation, it would no longer be the case, as Gökalp thought, that the elites alone "possess civilization" which they need to take to the people, and at the same time "receive education in national culture" from the people.[78] Short of this approach, the respective groups' conception of "civilization" and "national culture" would also remain seriously flawed; indeed, the bifurcation would also remain. It was this bifurcation between the elites and the masses which made it difficult for the Kemalists to carry out their "reform from above."[79] Secularism did not break this bifurcation, which was the intention of both Gökalp and the Kemalists. Rather, it reinforced it because the popular culture or popular civilization which was based on the traditional values, and the tenets and practices of orthodoxy, which for centuries were mistakenly and unhesitatingly identified with Islam,[80] were given a splendid opportunity, through secularism, to thrive in isolation.

In his study of Gökalp's works, Parla has argued that

when Gökalp introduced Westernism as the third element of his tripartite synthesis of Turkism, Islamism, and Modernism, he meant, beyond the scientific and technological accomplishments of Western capitalism, a particular brand of social-political thought, positivistic in methodology, and thus scientific, and idealistic in epistemology, and underlying moral philosophy. The social-political theory and model of society and polity that characterized this school of thought was solidaristic corporatism, which rejected the liberal and the Marxist model.[81]

The corporatist model was an improvement on the liberal model, which was "unintendedly atomistic and consequently disruptive of the equilibrium and survival of the social organism." Borrowing the Marxist critique of liberal capitalist society as inherently anarchic, the model substituted corporation for the class, thereby providing harmony to society and "refuting the Marxist critique in the end."[82] In his tripartite synthesis, Gökalp was looking on Islamism as an effective basis for solidarism and as the source for moral guidance, which would serve as an effective check on the fascistic variant of corporatism.[83]

Gökalp's introduction of Islamism in his approach to corporatism in the Islamic context is not only sound, but also the only viable one. It also has the potential for improving the corporatist model itself, the condition for which would be a reworking out of Islamic religious thought and ethics, and first reaching the parameters of the existing corporatist model. In fact, it becomes an important basis for rejecting secularism (as commonly understood) which, paradoxically, Gökalp advocated and the state implemented as a leading principle of state policy.

The tripartite synthesis that Gökalp sought is therefore likely to remain chimeric in a secular setting. Gökalp's confusion as to how to arrive at this synthesis, and Atatürk and his colleagues' rejection of this possibility, are embedded in the preceding history of Turkey, in which the reign of Sultan Abdul-Hamid (1876-1908) provided the climax and the anticlimax. It is this period which provides us the clue to the seeming paradox we have referred to earlier:

The Hamidian regime [1876-1908] did not foresee that a policy of political suppression would breed a generation manifesting intellectual characteristics antithetical to the dominant features of the regime's ideology. Under the noses of the zealous "men of religion," a whole generation of "materialists" sprang up. Their view of life contrasted strangely with the most characteristic feature of the mentality of the time—superstition.

By establishing the omnipotence of his . . . state, Abdül-Hamid imperiled . . . religion. There came into existence a cleavage in the minds of the intellectuals between the two. Thenceforth, the Hamidian [religion and state] seemed a nightmare to the sincere intellectual. *He was cut off irrevocably from trust in the possibility of a marriage between the two*. That is why the intellectual [in Turkey] cannot understand how the idea of an Islamic State could be an attractive ideal to many Muslims. He has an ineradicable antipathy for such an ideal as the legacy of the Hamidian period.[84]

Religious hypocrisy had reached new heights in the preceding fifty years or so of Atatürk's revolution. In the words of Musa Kazim (1858-1919), a leading religious leader of the post-Hamidian era,

the celebrities of corruption used to indulge in worshipping in order to cover up their sins, and used to have their prayer rugs follow them wherever they went, even to their offices. . . . In order to become a favourite of the Palace and Government, one had to enroll in the flocks of the religious orders.[85]

In this section we have focused on the thought of Ziya Gökalp and its impact on Turkey prior to and since the Turkish revolution. We have discussed this thought at some length because "through his works, and indirectly through his many students and disciples who came between the two world wars to fill important posts in the Kemalist party and bureaucracy, in academia and in the press, Gökalp continued to exert immense influence on the political and intellectual life of inter-war and post-war Turkey."[86] Moreover, in twentieth-century Turkey, his effort to build a coherent political theory for an Islamic society has not yet been duplicated.[87] He was a mentor of many Kemalists, including Atatürk himself; his "ideas were like Gogol's 'Overcoat,' from which all the rest issued and within which all the rest sought intellectual moulding."[88] Yet, the official Kemalist leadership has shown somewhat of an ambivalent attitude toward him, mainly because of the controversies that developed over his thought. Between his death in 1924 and Atatürk's death in 1938, no transcription of his works appeared in the Latin alphabet which was officially adopted in 1928. The apparent reason seems to be that the Kemalists had already rejected the second term of his tripartite synthesis of Turkism—Islamism—Modernism. His voluminous works remained scattered in unsystematic publications until 1973, when the Ministry of Education began to collect them.[89]

Another important modernist writer of Turkey was Namik Kemal (1840-1888) whose ideas had a strong impact on Gökalp and whom Atatürk described as the father of his emotions.[90] Kemal drew the attention of his countrymen to the concept of patriotism or nationalism. Although his thought suffers from inconsistencies and confusion, he introduced in Turkey the important doctrine of natural rights and the sovereignty of the people, which had never found a place in the sharia[91] and the bankrupt philosophical thought in Islamic territories. He also advocated a constitutional form of government and argued that since constitutional systems had already been developed and tested in the West, there was no need to invent a new one.[92] The most serious flaw in his thought was that he wanted to uphold the sharia even though he acknowledged that its provisions could be altered in accordance with the requirements of the time.[93] He also wanted to uphold Islamic jurisprudence, which was the legal foundation of the sharia.[94]

Although Kemal rejected the idea of secularism in an Islamic state,[95] he did not explain how a successful fusion of religion and state could be brought about in an Islamic state, or what it really meant or entailed. Beyond his call for a constitutional government and the doctrine of sovereignty of the people, therefore, he essentially accepted and advocated the status quo. As is apparent from the constitutional controversies that ensued throughout 1876 (a constitution was promulgated on December 23, 1876), the problem was that Kemal and others who were engaged in the constitutional discussions were, on the whole, operating within the traditionally accepted parameters of Islamic religious thought.[96] Upon founding the republic, although the Kemalists courageously went beyond these parameters in practical terms, traditional religious thought was left intact, and in isolation. Therefore, it could affect people's consciousness in the same way as before. We will examine this aspect in the next section.

STATE RESPONSES TO RELIGIOUS LEADERS' VIEWS AND DEMANDS REGARDING ISLAM

After the republic had been formed, the sympathies of the dervish brotherhoods, which had become an integral part of the Ottoman society, remained suspect for the new order that Atatürk and his colleagues sought to establish. The dervish orders had thrived on religious foundations that were endowed with landed property in perpetuity; thus they acquired vast economic means and power.[97]

By the nineteenth century, when the Ottoman empire had been in a state of decline and political power had slipped from the hands of the sultan and the central government, two-thirds to three-fourths of the land was held in the form of religious endowments. A majority of these foundations (up to 75 percent) were semifamilial whose chief beneficiaries were the founder and his posterity to the extinction of his line, at which time it could revert to the poor. Semifamilial evkaf (singular *vakif* is a Turkish rendering of Arabic *waqf*, meaning religious endowment) was prebendary, that is, the founder appointed himself and his posterity to various posts in the institution. The founder appointed himself to the position of a sheikh if he created a dervish convent, a professor if he founded a theological college, and an administrator of the foundation, whether it was a mosque, soup kitchen, inn, hospital, or any other institution which was created. Through the last office, the founder and his posterity exercised absolute control over the foundation and its revenues.[98]

Beginning in 1839, when the Tanzimat or reforms were introduced, the government instituted a number of measures to bring the religious endowments under state control to receive revenues that were then deposited in the Imperial Awqaf (religious endowments) Treasury. However, the independently administered estates in mortmain were not brought under state control for any purposes.[99] They were still independent when the Turkish revolution occurred. Moreover, all religious endowments, whether or not they were in mortmain, continued to run their medreses (medieval colleges where law and theology were taught predominantly) and mektebs (primary schools). Although the Ottoman government's policy in the nineteenth century was to appropriate the revenues of the dervish orders, the "orders continued to survive into the early twentieth century, dispossessed of their revenue."[100]

The dervish brotherhoods did not take well to the government reforms. The

Kurdish revolt of 1925 was a reaction to the government's secularist stance. After the revolt was suppressed by the state, Atatürk in his speech at Kastamonu on August 30, 1925, said:

Gentlemen and fellow countrymen, know that the Turkish Republic cannot be a nation of sheikhs, dervishes and mystics. The truest path is the path of the civilization. . . . I could never admit in the civilized Turkish community the existence of a primitive people who seek happiness and prosperity by putting their faith in such and such sheikh, a man opposed to the sparkling light of civilization which encompasses all science and knowledge. In any case the tekyes [religious orders] must be closed. We will obtain strength from civilization, science, and knowledge—and act accordingly. We do not recognize anything else. The essential aim of the tekyes is to keep the people in ignorance, and make them act as if they were insane. The people, however, have chosen to be neither silly nor insane.[101]

Immediately thereafter, on September 2, 1925, the Grand National Assembly passed Public Law No. 677, which outlawed the dervish orders, religious houses (tekkehs and zawiyehs), and all religious orders. People were prohibited from living as members of any orders or from wearing costumes or bearing titles of any orders. All mosques that were attached to religious houses and mausolea (turbehs) were closed. The office of the custodian of all such establishments was abolished.[102]

On March 3, 1924, the state, through Public Law No. 429 had already established a Presidency for Religious Affairs "for the dispatch of all cases and concerns for the Exalted Islamic Faith which relate to dogma and ritual, and for the administration of religious foundations."[103] The state had thus washed its hands of any concern with the question of Islamic religious education. As far as the state was concerned, the issue did not exist, or even matter. To justify secularism and to provide a seemingly rationalist basis for it, Kemalist nationalism, à la Gökalpism, in order to "discover" national culture, made the mystic literature, heterodox sects, heretical movements, and similar activities objects of special interest. In the songs, tales, myths, and dances, which were previously considered un-Islamic, people "discovered" expressions that were considered true to the spirit of modern secular culture.[104] The new Turkish historiography described the Turks, who until then had been identified with Islam, as the products of all the great religions and to have successively passed through Shamanism, Buddhism, Judaism, Christianity, Manichaeism, and Islam. Disregarding the Islamist view of Turkish history, the new historiography declared the Islamic period to be only an episode in the national and civilizational aspects of Turkish history which was portrayed as extending from China to Central Europe. In this international character of Turkish history, the Turkish people were portrayed as thoroughly secular. Within the context of religious history, they had merely been followers.[105] In this new view of history, it was then a short step for Atatürk to proclaim and propagate the idea that the Turk did not belong to any particular religion.[106]

The secularist view of the Kemalists was articulate and clear in its negative aspects, but it lacked a positive doctrine. This lack of a doctrinal basis made the Kemalist secularism hollow and open to attacks by the Islamists.[107] It disregarded the fact that in the preceding 621 years of Turkish history, Turkish national culture was heavily conditioned by the prevalent conceptions and customs that had come to be attributed to Islam and occupied people's consciousness. A radical transformation in people's consciousness was undoubtedly needed. To be effective, however, it was essential that it be sought and achieved by disseminating the correct picture of Islam through education. Otherwise, not only was disorientation the likely result, but also people's consciousness would continue to be occupied by the distorted ideas and practices attributed to Islam. Atatürk was correct in rejecting the established order, but two factors prevented the transformation of religious structures, values, ideas and practices, which directly affected the social and cultural spheres and which in turn affected all modernization efforts: (1) the dogmatic opposition of religious circles, and (2) Atatürk and his colleagues were not clear about the appropriate methodology which could have led to the transformation.

Kemal Atatürk had first-hand knowledge of Islam's appeal to the masses and its mobilization force. The same mobilization force that he witnessed in the Turkish war of independence could have been utilized in the quest for modernization. What was required was the study of the Islamic doctrine, that is, the Qur'an, to dispel the wrong ideas and practices that had come to be associated with Islam. Atatürk had effectively politicized and galvanized the masses through his appeal to Islam. In 1920, in a speech in Adana, he addressed the crowd as the Muslims of Adana, religious brothers of Adana, the leaders of the jihad armies of the ummah (Muslim community) of Muhammad.[108] Interestingly, this speech was not included in the three-volume work of Atatürk's speeches which was later published.[109]

Although the sultan's government opposed the nationalists in their struggle for independence through the fetva (authoritative religious decision) given by the chief of the religious leaders (who was under the direct control of the sultan), the ulema played a major role in the war of independence. Religious leaders organized many cells of the Society for the Defense of Rights. The resistance movement in various towns was also backed by the ulema through various fetvas, reminding the Muslims of their obligation to fight. Their calls for jihad effectively mobilized the masses in the liberation effort.[110] During the two decisive congresses of Erzurum and Sivas, arranged by Atatürk in the early stages of the struggle, a number of leading religious leaders participated. Twenty-three out of the 56 delegates at Erzurum were either directly or indirectly connected with the medreses.

When the First Grand National Assembly was convened in 1920, religion was at the forefront. In convening the Assembly, Atatürk had pointed out that it would take place on a Friday so that the delegates could participate in the Friday prayers and then enter the Assembly building. To emphasize the religious significance of the day, he said that the Qur'an would be recited in mosques throughout the country. At the time of the First National Assembly opening, out of 437 delegates, 116 had a religious background. Of the delegates who finally took their seats in this Assembly, 73 out of 361, or 20 percent, were clerics. Their percentage "dropped to 7 in the Second Assembly of 1923, to 4 in the Third Assembly of 1927, to 3 in the Fourth and Fifth Assemblies of 1931 and 1935, to 2 in the Sixth Assembly of 1939, and finally, to 1 percent in the Seventh Assembly of 1943."[111]

The entire basis of legitimacy of Atatürk's cause was Islam. When the Seyhu'l-Islam (chief religious leader) of the Istanbul government denounced the revolutionaries as rebels and called on the Muslim population to kill pronationalist forces in the name of religion, the counter-fetva of the religious leaders of Ankara, which was endorsed by 156 religious leaders from various Anatolian towns, effectively discredited the religious authority of the Seyhu'l-Islam and provided unflinching support of the masses to Atatürk. The counter-fetva was ingeniously worded to argue that the sultan-caliph had become a prisoner of foreign countries, and, therefore, it was the duty of Muslims to liberate him from captivity. The tax commissions that were formed during the war to collect revenues for the nationalist army were run by the clerics.[112]

The mobilization effort in the liberation struggle was impressive, and it was based entirely on religion. The Kemalists did not realize the importance of the mobilization aspect of modernization[113] without which modernization efforts would remain seriously handicapped. Mobilization of the people for modernization can be likened to mobilization for war. In each case, the effort is likely to be doomed to failure if the masses do not fully believe in the motivation for mobilization. The prevalent conceptions of Islam no doubt ran counter to the demands of modernization, and Atatürk correctly saw this as the biggest obstacle in making Turkey a modern, progressive country. For modernization efforts to succeed, the foremost task was to change these conceptions, which could be effective only if the people came to believe in the new conceptions on their own, through education. It meant going back to the original source of Islam, that is, the Qur'an, in an intelligent manner, keeping the historical conditions of the time well in mind. It required a new approach to education, in which the study of the Qur'an was carried out concurrently with modern education. This was a difficult and, necessarily, a long-term task. But this was the only viable approach, and its results lasting, in an evolutionary process. Clearly, the Kemalists did not see this, or were prevented from seeing this by the prior history of their country in which religion had played a very negative role; they had witnessed it.[114]

The Kemalist approach did not go unchallenged, although the traditionalists had no better approach to offer than to continue as before, which Atatürk did not allow.[115]   But the underlying issue of reform of religious thought remained unattended. Through secularism, the state glossed over the most fundamental issue of the society which had caused the progressive decay of the society through the centuries. The state defined its attitude toward religion as laicism. The Republican People's party (RPP), the founding party of the republic, declared in its Statutes of September 9, 1923, that one of the most important principles to which it adhered was to separate religion from worldly matters. The same principle was reiterated in the party's statutes of 1927 and 1931. When the principle of laicism was introduced into the Turkish constitution in 1937, the Ministry of the Interior explained it thus: "We say that . . . religions should stay in consciences and places of worship and should not be mixed with material life and worldly concerns."[116]

The issue of religion came to the surface in secular Turkey in the mid-1940s, when the single-party rule of the Kemalists gave way to a multiparty system. Religion now entered politics again. The new political environment provided an opportunity to air religious grievances through political parties. To be sure, religious leaders and groups had nothing new to offer except to reinstate religion in its old form, which the Kemalists had good reasons to reject in 1923. But the republic's approach to religion had virtually left the society in suspension. The republic was unable to replace even the most elementary functions which the Islamic religion, with all the distortions and misconceptions that had crept into it, provided to the individuals. These functions related to self-identity, regulation of psychological tensions, a system of thought and belief that made it possible to handle one's encounter with daily life, and a host of other functions. The new republic was unable to replace such functions with any new ideology. Turkish nationalism was the only aspect of Kemalism that all classes embraced. Other doctrines that were espoused appealed only to the graduates of the secularized schools. Neither Kemalism nor its associated doctrines could replace Islam in the lives of the masses.[117]

The state did not grasp the larger issues involved in the religious question. As a consequence, a number of religious outbreaks took place during the 1920s and 1930s. The 1925 rebellion in east Turkey was led by a tribal chief and leader of the Nakshibendi sect. Thereafter, the state responded with a heavy hand at the barest indication of any attempt to revive the old religious order. In 1925 the government hanged one individual for his resistance to the changing of headgear.   A leader of a fundamentalist group who criticized the government's reforms was persecuted by the state.[118] When Atatürk's successor Ismet Inonu decided to allow opposition parties to participate in the 1946 election, the opposition parties established effective channels of communication with the mass of the peasantry through rural notables. Between 1945 and 1950, twenty-four political parties were formed, out of which at least eight had explicit references to Islamic themes.[119]   The most important religious party in this period was the Nation party which stressed the need for religious reform. It called for greater emphasis on Islamic values and greater respect for Islamic institutions. It also sought to end state control of religious organizations and to include courses on religion in the primary and secondary school curricula.[120]

None of these parties, however, played any significant role in the elections. Even the Nation Party could send only one deputy to the National Assembly. Voter appeal was strong to none of these parties, for the parties could offer nothing more than a promise to create a more relaxed atmosphere. The Democratic party which unseated the Republican People's party (which had been in control of the government since the revolution) did, however, make religion one of the issues in its party program. However, its appeal was not limited to the question of religion alone; it promised the peasants not only religious freedom, but also better economic and living conditions, and facilities.[121]

The Republic People's party was aware of the appeal of religion to the masses and did take measures to enhance its popularity on that basis. During the Seventh General Congress of the party in 1947, delegates criticized the RPP governments for neglecting the religious training of clerics as well as for not providing religious education to the youth. The government's secularization policies were blamed for the alleged lack of public morality.[122] Among the proposals submitted to the Congress on religious matters were the following, some of which are revealing, for they suggest basically the same approach to Islam as was the case in the Ottoman empire:

1. The tombs of saints and other holy men should be reopened.
2. An elective course on religion for one hour a week, to be given to students with a written approval from their parents, should be included in the primary and secondary curricula.
3. The party program should . . . include a statement of the RPP's decision to permit elective courses on religion in the primary schools.
4. The program of the Ministry of Education should state that elective religious courses are part of the primary school curriculum.
5. Higher schools of religion should be opened.
6. Prayer Leader and Preacher Schools should be reopened.[123]

RELIGIOUS EDUCATION AND THE EDUCATIONAL SYSTEM

The state acted on the proposals mentioned in the previous section, which indicates that virtually no change had taken place in the state of religious thought in the country since the collapse of the Ottoman empire. It also indicates that secularism helped freeze religious thought in the state it was in at the time Turkey became a republic.[124] The Ministry of Education prepared a program of religious courses to be attended in private by the graduates of primary schools for which textbooks were approved. In 1949 elective religious courses were formally introduced into the primary school curriculum for two hours a week. The courses were to be taught by qualified teachers certified by the Ministry of Education. The Ministry also announced a plan in 1947 to establish private religious seminaries for graduates of middle schools, with a five-year program of studies; for lycee graduates, two-year courses on religion were to be made available. In 1948 the government established Prayer Leader and Preacher courses in ten cities; in 1949, a higher institute of religion was established in the University of Ankara. In 1948, for the first time since the republic was established, foreign exchange was made available for the pilgrimage to Mecca. "Religion" made a full comeback in 1949 when the so-called sacred tombs were reopened, which had been closed since 1925.[125]

Prime Minister Adnan Menderes, in his presentation of the Democratic party's government in 1950, indicated that secularism had been unsuccessful in Turkey and, therefore, could be changed. One of the new government's first measures was to lift the ban on ezan (the call to prayer) in Arabic. The measure was unanimously passed by the Assembly. A month later, the government permitted the broadcasting of Qur'anic readings over the state radio. The state ruled that all primary school students were required to attend classes on religion unless their parents specifically asked for an exemption. The state also established Prayer Leader and Preacher Schools in seven cities in 1951, and their number was increased to 16 in 1954-1955. In the same year, the state increased the budget of the Presidency of Religious Affairs from 3 million to 8 million Turkish liras. In a decade of Democratic party rule, the budget had increased to nearly 40 million by 1960.

In the new government's tenure of office, an unprecedented increase occurred in the following: publication of religious books and pamphlets; pilgrimage to Mecca; visits to local shrines; wearing of religious garb in public; mosque attendance; and construction of new mosques or repair of old ones. During the Democratic party's ten year rule, 15,000 mosques, or approximately 1,500 mosques a year were constructed. Even more significant was that during this decade the number of religious organizations (e.g., organizations for the construction of mosques or for the teaching of Qur'anic courses) mushroomed at an unprecedented scale. Whereas in 1949 the total number of religious organizations was 95, in 1951 it grew to 251, and by 1960 it had reached the figure of 5,104.[126]

This shows that, beside the extraordinary growth of religious organizations, religious education fell into private hands more completely, which was the case in the previous history of the Ottoman empire. Thus, no change took place in the content and method of religious education. This education continued to be imparted by the so-called men of religion, who were carrying forward the learning and legacy of al-Azhar. We have already examined the situation at al-Azhar in the previous chapter. By politicizing religion, the government was seeking to divert public attention from economic problems and extensive violations of civil liberties.[127]   By politicizing religion too, both the government and the opposition parties were at the same time diverting the nation's energies, both   inside   and   outside   the   Assembly,   into   endeavors   that   were counterproductive.   In sum, the state's responses to the religious circles' views regarding Islam (barring some of Atatürk's courageous and appropriate reforms) have been uninspired and reek of confusion.   As a consequence, Islam in Turkey, as in Pakistan and in Egypt, remains unreformed. Its negative impact on the population can be well imagined when we realize that, as late as 1964, almost two-thirds of the Turkish population was illiterate.[128]

Atatürk had repeatedly stressed that "his purpose was 'to purify' Islam and to open the gate for a reformist Islamic thought," so that the society would be liberated from the hold of a distorted Islam, making it possible for a new type of free individual to emerge.[129] Without doubt Atatürk's intent was sincere, and his analysis of the problem was sound. However, what he sought and what was required could only be brought about in a modern intellectual environment. By confining Islam to the private sphere, that requirement was not met.   The intellectual construct of the separation of religion and politics was also sound except that it was too literally understood and adopted, disregarding the peculiar environment in which Islam was kept in the preceding several centuries, both in the Ottoman empire and elsewhere.   Even in secular Turkey, the reality was that religion was a datum of life. Turkish intellectuals were aware of the power ramifications inherent in the religious question but remained insensitive to the issue.[130]

The Turkish Parliament began a debate in 1947 to decide whether to establish religious educational institutions that could train "more enlightened men of religion."[131] Thus, policymakers thought religious education required some kind of special expertise which, as we have seen in Chapter 4, is a seriously mistaken idea that has continued to be propagated and believed in, in the last several centuries of Muslim history.   The Assembly raised the issue that the lack of religious education was undermining national morality and that the youth was ignorant of religious principles.   When the military junta toppled the Menderes regime in 1960 for what it considered to be the excessive exploitation of religion, it argued that there could be no compulsion in matters of faith. The new constitution adopted in 1961 proclaimed through Article 19 that everyone was to be free in his or her religious belief.[132]

Now, in a country where over 98 percent of the population declares itself to be Muslim, religious belief is not the issue.   The issue is that of religious education, its content and method. It is of vital importance because studies have confirmed the pervasiveness of Islam in everyday life.[133]   In the rural areas where the social structure remains undifferentiated, land is unequally distributed, and where extended families and tribal structures are the rule of the day, "religion is 'an opium which the local rural strata make the people swallow' so as to maintain the status quo."[134]

In provincial towns there has been a notable increase in the number of religious organizations. "One of the most important indicators of community involvement in religious activity is the increase in honorary courses of Qur'anic recitation . . . ; these courses are financially supported by the community after obtaining permission from the Directorate of Religious Affairs to establish them. In 1951 there were 237 such courses; by 1968 the figure had grown to 2,510."[135] The highest degree of community involvement in recitation courses is in "the core provinces of the Ottoman Empire, the provinces where the empire first took shape and therefore the most traditional in nature."[136] These are *recitation* courses that show mere reverence for the Qur'anic verses rather than an intelligent understanding of the Qur'anic teaching. In 1958,

Nuretin Topcu, a traditionalist Turkish intellectual, pointed out that the reputation of these courses among their audience . . . was that of classes which "sowed a few items of mythological information in young brains" . . . . This information was seen as a "thin and useless propaganda course" which "had been placed in the same slot as music and physical education." Topcu stressed the need to make religious knowledge of wider interest and philosophically better grounded. This same wish emerged from a survey on lycee courses of religion in 1969.[137]

Although recently the demand for religious education has increased, it is still viewed in Turkey, as in Pakistan and Egypt, as a separate and independent field of study. Thus, all classes in Turkey "now demand that religious education should be placed on the same footing as 'laic' curricula."[138] Although this may bring uniformity to religious education in the different provinces of the country, the differentiation between the secular lycees (high schools) and the Imam Hatip (Prayer Leader and Teacher) schools has created a cleavage in the educational system in Turkey. The Imam Hatip schools offer rural clientele the opportunity of high school graduation. The curriculum of these schools is also attractive to families who want to keep their children within the traditional culture. Interestingly, educational authorities have sought to prevent access to university education for students of these schools, but without success.[139]

Table 7.1 explains different levels of religious schools and the number of students receiving religious education for the period 1951-1978. For all practical purposes, the graduates of these schools provide religious education to the polity. Since their curricula are based on subjects that have traditionally been taught in religious schools of Muslim countries in the last several centuries, religious thought and ideas preeminently belong to medieval times, when a particular direction was given to religious thought. A survey carried out among the workers of a textile factory in Izmir in 1978 confirms this situation. The survey found that an overwhelming majority of the people interviewed believed "that praying together was the most important aspect of Islam."[140] It also found that religious education was considered to be the best way to train good citizens,

Table 7.1

Religious Education in Turkey, 1951-1978

	1951-52	1955-56	1960-61	1965-66	1970-71	1974-75	1976-77	1977-78
Orta Level[a] Imam-Hatip								
No. of schools	7	16	19	30	72	101	248	334
No. of students	876	2,181	3,377	11,832	42,600	24,091[b]	86,053	108,309
Lycee Level Imam-Hatip								
No. of schools		7	17	19	39	72	72	103
No. of students		254	1,171	1,648	6,708	24,809	25,688	26,177
Yüksek Islam Enstitüsü[c]								
No. of schools			1	3	5	1,856 (1973-74)		
No. of students			165	846	2,024			
Ankara University Faculty of Theology								
No. of students	79	83	230	447	518	515		
Qur'an-Teacher Courses								
No. of courses	170	235	643	1,083	1,298			
No. of students	11,568	12,235	27,677	53,482	56,169 (1968-69)			

[a]Middle level, three years after the primary education of five years.

[b]Some Imam-Hatib [Prayer Leader and Preacher] schools have been gradually closed, in others all the classes were converted to classical middle schools."

[c]High Islamic Institute, college level but not university.

Source: Walter F. Weiker, *The Modernization of Turkey: From Atatürk to the Present Day* (New York: Holmes and Meier, 1981), p. 109.

but the dominant attitude regarding religious education was that of prayers.[141]

In the country's approach to education, the lise (lycee) or the high school is "regarded as a selective institution for the few rather than as a universal secondary school for all."[142] In other words, the state has set very low aims in providing education to its citizens. Basically the objective has been to provide a modicum of education to the masses so as to make them barely literate. We have seen the same approach in the case of Pakistan and Egypt. Only 40 percent of the orta (middle school) graduates enter the lises. A survey conducted in 1962-1963 found that most student look down on vocational or commercial-type education, considering such education to be "more appropriate for the less competent orta graduate."[143] The lises have been thoroughly secular since 1924 when religion was altogether eliminated from the curriculum.[144]

The overall educational situation in Turkey "reveals few indications of any coherent policy."[145] For example, although the number of students enrolled in schools increased substantially in the period ending 1960, the increases obscure serious weaknesses. The expansion was not the result of any systematic planning. The expansion did not keep pace with the country's rapidly growing population, and expansion outstripped expenditures.[146] The report of the Turkish National Commission on Education is revealing. In 1961 it pointed out that

the schools of Turkey "are unable to prepare children adequately for life," and that, "socially, culturally and economically," education was "not functional." More specifically, the report noted that the quality of teaching, the teachers, and the physical facilities would have to be greatly improved if Turkey was to attain the level of development and Westernization to which it aspired.[147]

Since the state has not followed a coherent educational policy, in Turkey, as in Pakistan and Egypt, two separate educational systems have been in operation: a traditional Islamic education and a European-type education. This situation has serious consequences. The traditional religious education system is not only based on the curricula established in the medieval ages, but it also does not employ the teaching methods and approaches used in the modern schools.[148] It has given religious education the appearance of a highly specialized discipline, which it is not, nor is it supposed to be. The two educational systems have actually created two distinct social classes, opposed to each other. The clerical class, which has lost power to modernists, is basically trying hard to recover some of its power in the educational sphere.[149]

By 1970 Turkey's literacy rate was only 38.1 percent, but even this low rate is misleading, for often a person who is able to scrawl his name is considered literate.[150] Moreover, although the given literacy rate in Turkey is considerably higher than that of Pakistan and Egypt, Turkey's lead on this score is offset by the time scale of modernization, which is nearly thirty years more than the other

two countries.[151]   Great variations of literacy exist in the different regions of
Turkey. While the province of Istanbul has a literacy rate of 73.4 percent, the
province of Hakkari has a rate of only 11.5 percent. Since 1955, only sixteen
of the sixty-seven provinces in Turkey have shown an increase in literacy, and
the increase has been rather insignificant.[152]

Thus far, the state's endeavors in the education field have focused on the
primary level. Since 1950 substantial increases have occurred at this level, with
enrollment increasing to 1,616,626 in 1950 and reaching 4,790,183 in 1968,
thereby achieving an enrollment ratio of 90.86 percent for the age bracket 5-14.
This enrollment ratio is misleading, for what is of crucial importance is the
content of the education. The enrollment at the high school level was only
849,533 (18.11 percent), and the figure for higher education was a meagre
160,334 (130,531 males, 29,803 females), or 4.93 percent.[153]   In higher
education, scientific and technological studies have increased more slowly than
the social sciences, which are reported to have high prestige value. The slowest
growing field has been agriculture, which does not provide enough motivation.[154]
Most observers have felt that Turkey faces "a shortage of skills and that existing
imbalances and practices within higher education represent a major obstacle to
the country's future development."[155]

Religious thought in Turkey was rarely studied in the preceding centuries. Not
until 1928 was a project begun to translate the Qur'an into Turkish, and even
then it was abandoned in the face of heavy opposition.[156] The mass of the
Turkish population did not understand Arabic and, therefore, in Turkey's prior
history we can conclude that very few people would have studied the Qur'an,
without which the whole philosophy of Islam and the Islamic values cannot be
understood.   Mustafa Kemal Atatürk had believed that the translation of the
Qur'an "would be the greatest event of the Revolution."[157]

In the beginning, therefore, Atatürk was fully aware of the importance of
religious thought and its impact on the polity. He also realized that the
contemporary Western civilization was compatible with the authentic Islamic
worldview. The adoption of Western civilization required fundamental changes
in the society's value systems, which meant a reinterpretation of Islamic
religious thought wherein lay embedded the existing value systems. Atatürk had
also recognized that for the revival of Islam it was essential to disengage it from
the condition of being a political instrument. Mere separation was not enough,
however. What was required was the creation of an intellectual environment in
which the reformation of Islamic religious thought could eventually have taken
place, which meant an active and systematic study of the Qur'an by the masses.
This could not have occurred in a secular setting. Given the serious nature of
the issue, the prior Turkish history of several centuries, and Atatürk's general
approach to religion, it appears that this was not clear to him and he had not
fully thought the issue through. Even so, it was the obstinate and unenlightened
opposition of religious circles which made him and his associates finally declare

the republic secular in 1928. In the circumstances that he found himself in, the alternative he faced was, basically, to continue the society in the same manner as was the case during the Ottoman empire. We arrive at this conclusion from the opposition he faced even in the matter of translating the Qur'an into Turkish.

The first translation of the Qur'an had appeared in 1923, but the Department of Piety disapproved it for its inaccuracies. A few more translations appeared until 1927, when private and hasty translations were discouraged. The question was then taken up by Atatürk and the National Assembly. The Islamist poet Mehmed Akif, who was known to Atatürk and was believed to be able to produce a reliable as well as a literary translation, was invited by the National Assembly to assume the task; Akif, however, sabotaged the idea because of his "Islamism," even though at first he accepted the commission. Since 1923, he had sensed the future direction of Atatürk's policies and had been under the influence of the al-Azhar ulema and other Egyptian personalities. The dean of the Egyptian Modernists, Shaikh Muhammad Rashid Rida, declared the attempt to translate the Qur'an a kufr (sin). Thereafter Akif refused the commission and settled in Egypt.

Atatürk renewed his invitation to Akif as late as 1936 but was rejected. A number of other issues had come up in the reform of religion, but none was resolved and controversies ensued. A development of most serious consequences occurred when, due to the attitude of the religious circles and strong differences among the intellectuals on several religious issues, Atatürk "ceased to evince interest in reforming religion after 1928 and came to the conclusion that the course of development of the religious consciousness of the people could not and should not be led by the state or by secular personalities."[158] Thereafter the possibility of reforming religious thought in Turkey was skipped and left in suspension. Later, the awareness grew that official neglect of religion had gone too far, and Atatürk was made the scapegoat.[159] As we have seen above, the blame falls squarely on the religious circles. With this background in view, we will now examine Turkey's developmental efforts.

ASSESSMENT OF THE DEVELOPMENT PLANS AND MODERNIZATION GOALS OF THE STATE

After the ravages of war for nearly a decade in which 2.5 million Turks were killed, the republic started with a low level of income and dependent upon mineral and agricultural exports for the supply of manufactured goods. Rapid industrialization was undertaken in the 1930s to solve many problems.[160] Beginning in 1948, an ambitious economic development was undertaken by the state and the results were impressive for the period 1948-1958. Gross national product in terms of 1948 prices increased by 57.7 percent. On a per capita basis, the increase in real product was about 3 percent, with an average population increase of nearly 3 percent.   Although gains in agricultural production were uneven and erratic, still production increased by 32.5 percent. The industrial sector reported increases of 65.9 percent in manufacturing, 163.8 percent in mining, and 235.0 percent in public utility production. The emphasis was "on industrialization with the objective of meeting western European standards of production and on stimulation of agricultural productivity."[161]

Although substantial real gains were made in production and income, they were "accompanied and affected by economic instability generated by lack of a coordinated development plan and by the pressures of excess demand."[162] In its developmental efforts, the state did not follow any basic thesis such as self-sufficiency or balanced growth, nor was there any overall plan. Growth occurred in all areas in an uncoordinated manner; compulsory savings did play a part in this effort, but it was undertaken primarily by exhausting gold stocks and foreign exchange reserves, by extending national credit beyond reasonable limits, and through economic aid.[163]   The government created a number of coordinating agencies, but a central economic coordinating agency was missing and decisions tended "to be made on a day-to-day basis by diverse agencies. Under such a system resources tend to be allocated, at least in part, on the basis of subjective evaluation of national need or political criteria, with the accompanying dangers of misallocation."[164]   Poor planning is also reflected in depending on wheat as a major cash crop in the future, even though its production remains unreliable for a number of reasons.   The potential in other areas like fishing and forest products industries "which could result in exports or reduction of imports, is still basically untouched."[165]

To offset the balance-of-trade deficit, U.S. economic aid and foreign credits were utilized. U.S.-paid shipments "increased from $30.8 million in 1953 to $91.2 million in 1957, while programmed economic aid of all types, to include Public Law 480 surplus commodities, rose from $57.5 million to $175.5 million during the same period."[166]   The country's debt rose from 716.8 million to 1,574.3 million Turkish lira (the rate of exchange of the lira fluctuated rapidly in this period), or by 120 percent from 1950 to 1956.[167] Economic management and planning in Turkey (as well as in Pakistan and Egypt) show that "if sound concepts of growth are to be followed and the economic experiences of others are to be exploited in promoting expansion . . . , the question is not whether planning and control systems should be created, but rather what kind of plans should be made and how they should be applied."[168]   The planning needs to cover such aspects of life as how to make life in villages rewarding, productive, and interesting, how to control the growth of population, and how to reduce glaring income inequalities, just to name a few.

In Turkey, nearly 78 percent of the people living in villages want to migrate to cities, and 57.2 percent of the families wish to migrate because of poverty and landlessness. In the villages, old attitudes and traditions are still pervasive. Nearly 72 percent of young women are married by the time they are 19 years old, with 31.1 percent marrying as early as 14 or 15. The value and attitude characteristics of villagers are still basically as they were in the past; only 28.7 percent of villagers, for example, favor higher education for girls. Over 86 percent of men in the villages still do not allow their wives to go out without a scarf, and in the cities, the figure is still 36 percent. Over 45 percent of the men in villages still do not allow men and women to sit together while visiting. The rapid population increase in the rural areas has offset whatever increases in rural income had taken place in recent years.[169]

Development in Turkey has been so skewed that over 40 percent of villagers have reported difficulty in understanding the language spoken on the radio. Aside from the glaring income inequalities and poverty, a serious elite-mass gap remains in communication, language, and concepts.[170] Poor planning and developmental programs have kept the literacy level in rural areas at a very low level. After half a century of reforms, literacy was only 38.1 percent with rural literacy markedly lower. A survey found that more than one-third of those interviewed had left school before they graduated. In 1968 only 26.9 percent of males and 8.8 percent of females were primary school graduates, and among these many had graduated from only a three-grade primary school.[171]

In 1972 the province of Istanbul still had 45 percent of Turkey's private manufacturing plants and employed 54 percent of all workers in the private sector.[172] In 1977, 20 percent of the nonagricultural labor force was unemployed. Excluding extensive underemployment in the agriculture sector, 8 percent of the agricultural labor force was unemployed. The percentages translate into 1.5 million workers unemployed. Because of massive unemployment and poor incentives, nearly 1 million Turks are working in European countries, a situation that is staggering, for it means that 33 to 35 percent of all Turkey's nonagricultural workers have gone abroad. If we add to this figure the waiting list of those who want to work abroad, 85 percent of Turkish workers would be working outside the country![173] Workers' remittances in 1972, 1973, and 1974 were "only slightly less than total Turkish export earnings, and in excess of the deficit in visible trade."[174] With regard to living conditions in Turkey, in 1975 about 4.5 million Turks, or more than a quarter of the urban population, lived in squatter housing, making Turkish cities rank among the highest in the world in terms of percentage of squatter housing. In 1975, 47.9 percent of urban housing lacked electricity, and 56.7 percent were without city water.[175]

In a country's development process, the kind of value systems in operation in the society matters a great deal, for it shapes the entire structure of the society. In the case of Turkey, the ancient value system that was based primarily on traditions rather than on an intelligently worked out ethical system and a developed system of thought, remained embedded in the fabric of the society. Secularism did not erode it, nor could it have; it further confused an already confused society. "The end result was 'the real impoverishment of Turkish culture'; among the intelligentsia this state of affairs [has] led to a type of human relations which have been vacuous, sentimental and yet devoid of compassion."[176] The existing state of the society provides sufficient testimonials to substantiate the above conclusion. It is even doubtful that the Turkish elites have understood or accepted the underlying value systems of democracy. At best, it seems that the acceptance has been of the form rather than the substance. Earlier we referred to the conditions in rural areas where the bulk of Turkish population lives. It does not appear that the state has been particularly concerned about changing those conditions. Thus, a Turkish observer noted: "The 1966 annual program of the Five Year Development Plan vaguely repeats the need for a land reform in a general way. The pendulum appears to have swung against enactment of any effective reform bill in the foreseeable future."[177]

The agrarian situation in Turkey is similar to that in Pakistan and Egypt. All three countries have a strong agricultural base that remains unexploited for the general good of the societies, but is exploited by the rich landed classes. The exploitation by the landlords is so massive as to put Marx's criticism of capitalism to shame. For its part, capitalism, as we noted earlier, has successfully canceled out the Marxist critique to a considerable degree through the development of the corporate political system. The blatant exploitation of the landed classes in these three Muslim countries shows that the elites do not subscribe to any ethical system. Indeed, it demonstrates that they neither have any idea of what the ethical system of Islam is supposed to be or what it demands—nor do they care to know. It also fully justifies the criticism that the elites of Muslim societies, with the exception of some individuals, are not Muslims. In the practical sphere, the elites show that they are not willing to let an Islamic society emerge by continuously attacking the roots of Islamic ideology as contained in the Qur'an.

Table 7.2 shows the distribution of landholdings in Turkey. Although the distribution is based on a 1952 survey, the pattern has held over the years, the only change being that the condition of the small shareholders has worsened because of rapid increases in population. In his annual messages of 1936 and 1937 to the National Assembly, Atatürk drew attention to the issue by pointing out that it would have been appropriate to liquidate the remnants of the Ottoman statutes. It was absolutely urgent, he informed the house, that every Turkish farming family own as much land as it could live and work on. On this principle rested the foundations and development of the country. He wanted every farmer to have his own land and under no circumstances did he want to break up a farmer's holding which was just enough for his living. As for the large farmers, their landholding "should be limited according to the population density and soil fertility of each region."[178]

The present agrarian structure is a real obstacle to the development of the Turkish economy. There is very little saving from this sector, and as a result a minuscule amount is available for investment in the industrial sector, which

Table 7.2

Size of Farm Units in Turkey, 1952 Fall Survey

Size in Decares	No. of Farmers	Percent	Cultivated (hectares)	Percent	Average size per Farm in Decares[a]
1-20	773,000	30.6	836,000	4.3	10.8
21-50	797,000	31.5	2,790,000	14.3	35.0
1-50	1,570,000	62.1	3,626,000	18.6	23.0
51-75	336,000	13.3	2,097,000	10.8	62.4
1-75	1,906,000	75.4	5,723,000	29.4	30.0
76-150	384,000	15.3	4,023,000	20.7	104.8
151-500	199,000	7.8	4,880,000	25.1	245.2
Over 500	38,000	1.5	4,826,000	24.8	1,270.0
TOTAL	2,527,000	100.0	19,452,000	100.0	

[a]Ten decares equals 1 hectare; 1 hectare equals 2.471 acres.

Source: Resat Aktan, "Problems of Land Reform in Turkey," *The Middle East Journal* 20, No. 3 (Summer 1966): 322.

results in heavy borrowing from other countries and international agencies. As Table 7.2 shows, one-third of Turkish farmers owned less than 5 percent and nearly two-thirds owned less than 20 percent of the total cultivated land. Three-fourths of the farmers operated less than 30 percent of the land. One-fourth of the farmers owned more than 70 percent of the land, and 38,000 farmers owned almost 5 million hectares, or one-fourth of the arable land. In 1952 nearly a million farmers were either landless or owned insufficient land. In addition, at least 100,000 new families per year entered the farming class in the next twelve years.[179] Over the years, large numbers of additional families have continued to grow in this class.

The agricultural sector suffers from excessive fragmentation of landholdings. On average, one farm consisted of seven field parcels located in different areas. Such fragmentation makes it impossible to cultivate the land rationaly and efficiently. As for the large landholdings, most of them are divided into small pieces and are rented to sharecroppers or, rarely, to cash tenants. The sharecroppers are usually in heavy debt to their landlords, use primitive methods, and make the least amount of capital investment. The disinterest of the parties concerned results in low productivity, and depletion of natural resources as well as of human beings. This system of land operation benefits only the owners of large lands. The income of absentee landlords is spent elsewhere. The lands continuously deteriorate for lack of interest and maintenance.[180]

Turkey's low level of productivity, as well as its increasing population, has caused a continuous drop in farm income. The gap between the city and village has widened, and unemployment in the rural areas has mushroomed. As a result, the frustrated masses run to the cities, creating further economic, social, administrative, judicial, and political problems.[181] The agrarian sector is beset with disputes; of the 4 million annual court cases, more than half are related to land. This creates an atmosphere of insecurity that adversely affects production. Crops are not cared for, and fields are even left idle; this also leads to much hostility and social unrest. These disputes stem from the lack of cadastral surveys and inadequate title registration. Very few of the lands have been surveyed. "The experts estimate that, to finish the job with the present organization and speed, the work may take 50 to 100 or even 200 years."[182] The landlord system itself breeds feuding. Nur Yalman describes the agricultural picture in eastern Turkey in these terms:

When nobody knows to whom the land will eventually belong . . . long-term improvements of any capital expenditure is naturally out of the question. This is one of the reasons one hardly ever sees any trees planted in the villages, let alone elsewhere.

It should certainly not be thought that the villager is incapable of capital expenditure for land improvement. . . . the excellent orchard of Abdullah Bey was watered by a motor pump. . . . This simple pump had created an oasis out of the desert. Its cost was about 2,500 TL [Turkish lira]. Was a village of 100 households incapable of buying some pumps to ease the water situation? Let me merely mention that the bride-price . . . of a village girl among the Shafi population of Diyarbakir starts at 5,000 TL. This is the cost of the girl to the shepherd. A man of means would have to pay 10,000 TL or much more. The lack of incentive for capital improvements cannot be sought in the general poverty of the villager but must be seen in connection with the insecurity of tenure.[183]

This picture also describes the prevalence of social ills that are a legacy of the Ottoman empire and that continue unabated in the republic.[184] The villagers still greatly respect the role of religious or pious personages as against the judges who are identified with the national administration. In this region of the country, linguistic barriers separate villagers and administration, and the distinction between national codes and local custom persists. "The European type legal codes of the country have not been brought into line with the customary and Islamic legal arrangements in the countryside."[185] Notwithstanding the official proclamation of secularism, in the countryside religious orders thrive, "which provide an acceptable local legal system for their followers and effectively insulate the villagers from the European induced singularities of the administration."[186]

To be sure, the state did prepare a Land Reform Bill in 1960, for it considered land reform to be a prerequisite of agricultural development. Yet, nothing came of it because large landlords and farmers set the agenda in all political parties. All political parties are opposed to land reform although they do not openly say so. The largest, the Justice party, chants "agricultural development" but without land reform. The Federation of Farmers' Organization, controlled by large landowners, uses every trick to oppose reform. It sees agricultural development through government investment. The Union of Chambers of Commerce and Industry also released a highly critical report in 1966 that virtually killed the whole attempt at reform.[187]

All this suggests that the Turkish society's opportunity structure for the mass of its population is virtually closed, with powerful ramifications in all spheres of life. Changes in a nation's opportunity structure have a direct and strong impact on political and economic modernization. For national development, changes in opportunity structure are just as much required as are better education, increased availability of capital for investment, increased productivity and profitability in the agricultural sector, increased exports, and a host of other factors. An expanded opportunity structure makes it possible for individuals to enter more promising, challenging, and satisfying jobs in the newly emerging sectors of the economy.[188]

Turkey's first and second five-year-plans, formulated in 1963 and 1968, had visualized "that Turkey would increase exports and domestic savings sufficiently to maintain a high rate of growth without requiring foreign aid on concessional terms. "[189]   However, between 1960 and 1973, Turkey received $3.7 billion in loans, and private inflows for investment totaled only $1.3 billion. From 1979 to 1983 it received foreign aid worth over $2 billion annually.[190]   In 1978 Turkey had reached a stage where its debt could not be serviced and had to renegotiate the terms of its outstanding debt. Of the $8.2 billion borrowed between 1973 and 1978, over $6.9 billion was short term, with a maturity of under three years.[191]

Regular deficits in the current account of the balance of payments leads to greater external debt, which in turn produces increasing debt service payments. Higher interest payments contribute to the further deterioration of the current balance. "Between 1980 and 1986, the level of external debt as a share in GNP rose from 27.8 to 53.5 per cent."[192] In such a situation, impressive yearly GNP increases of 4.1 percent (1981), 4.5 percent (1982), 3.3 percent (1983), 5.9 percent (1984), 5.1 percent (1985), and 8.0 percent (1986) are robbed of their potential good effects on the society. As far as domestic savings for investment are concerned, an interesting feature of "the fiscal system has been that incomes in agriculture have, until recently, remained largely untaxed."[193]   Of the total workforce, 57.3 percent are employed in the agricultural sector. Turkey has an unemployment ratio of over 19 percent. Because of high population growth (2 1/4 percent), it is estimated that "an annual growth of real GNP of roughly 6 1/4 percent is required just to keep unemployment unchanged."[194]   In the industrial sector, Turkey has made major gains. In 1986 the share of industrial production in the gross national product was TL 11365.1 billion, whereas the agricultural sector had a share of TL 6484.8 billion.[195]   Turkish goods lack competitiveness because in the international market the product structure needs improvement. In addition, greater diversification and a shift from unprocessed goods to processed goods are required.[196] It is reform at the structural level of the society, however, which is crucial in the country's quest for development and modernization.   Table 7.3, which shows the income distribution in the society, illustrates the point and illumines the serious nature of the issue.

Among the 10 percent of households that constitute the richest group,[197] 13.6 percent are "capitalists, 12.3 percent are government employees, but as much as 46.7 percent are farmer households."[198]   As Table 7.3 shows, 55.6 percent of the very poor are farmers. They and other socioeconomic groups in the income bracket of 12,000 TL and less "are extremely poor, unlikely to be able to feed themselves adequately and unable to enjoy even the minimum standards of a dignified human life."[199]   Households earning more than 72,000 TL a year (excluding taxes) constitute nearly 5 percent of the population: "Farmers dominate this category, while urban capitalists constitute twenty percent of the wealthy group."[200]

Table 7.3

Composition of Income Ranges by Socioeconomic Groups (percent)

Socioeconomic Group	12,000TL and less	12,000–24,000TL	24,000–72,000TL	72,000TL and more
Capitalists 1	0.0	0.0	0.1	6.5
Capitalists 2	0.0	0.0	1.5	14.9
Professionals	0.0	0.0	0.5	5.0
Government employees	5.5	14.5	18.1	8.2
White collar workers	0.1	0.7	2.2	1.7
Rentiers	0.7	0.7	0.9	1.2
Skilled labor	4.4	15.2	14.5	2.2
Unskilled labor	16.6	14.3	6.5	0.8
Artisans	13.2	18.4	18.4	10.1
Farmers	55.6	34.8	37.0	49.2
Rural labor	3.2	1.4	0.3	0.0

Note: An income of 72,000 TL was taken to define the wealthy group; in 1973 dollar terms, it amounts to nearly $8,000; households below 24,000 TL are definitely poor; households of 12,000 TL and below are extremely poor.

Source: Kemal Derviş and Sherman Robinson, "The Structure of Income Inequality in Turkey (1950-1973)," in Ergun Özbudun and Aydin Ulusan, eds., *The Political Economy of Income Distribution in Turkey* (New York: Holmes and Meier, 1980), p. 110.

CONCLUSION

When Turkey became a republic in 1923, it was beset with serious problems, the origins of which were religious. Atatürk recognized it well and sought to change the situation. Given Turkey's social conditions at that time, which were heavily dominated by the religious circles, Atatürk concluded that if religion was allowed to play the same kind of role as was the case until then, the country could not develop and modernize. To prevent that situation, Atatürk and his associates opted for secularism, and in doing so, they understood and interpreted it too literally.

The society's socioeconomic structure reveals that it is steeped in irrationality. Much of the elite or the rich class, which comprises 5 percent of the population, engages in blatant exploitation of the masses. The major problem in the Turkish case is that the value systems of the society have not changed. These value systems are based on a system of thought that has falsely been identified with Islam. Although the state's policy of secularism has prohibited religion from entering the public domain, in reality it affects every aspect of life. It could not be otherwise, for the people's basic conceptions of life are molded by such practices, ideas, and traditions that have wrongly been attributed to Islam. It was important, therefore, to address this issue and to create a situation in which reformation of Islamic religious thought could take place. That would be a necessary condition for bringing about changes in the society's value systems.

The need in Turkey, as in Pakistan and Egypt, is to end a dual system of education, the one secular and the other religious, and to achieve an intelligent balance of the two. More importantly, a major change must be made in the basic conception of religious education. Thus far, it has been confined to the ritualistic aspect of it; the need is to intelligently study and understand the serious thought that is contained in the Qur'an. The behavior of the elites in Turkey, as well as in Pakistan and Egypt, shows (again with isolated honorable exceptions) that they are not familiar with the most basic elements of the ideology of Islam as contained in the Qur'an. For meaningful changes to occur in Turkey's developmental efforts, a new look at secularism is called for. Real secularism would emerge only when religion is first of all intelligently understood. The overall picture that emerges from the economic activity of the society is that developmental programs are basically purposeless and lack clearly stated goals beyond a vague desire to make the country modern. It also appears that the elites have no clear conception of what modernization means and entails.

8

CONCLUSION

The main finding that emerges from this study is that the existing ideas and conceptions of life which are presented, propagated, and inculcated as Islamic religious thought, practices, way of life, orientations, and traditions are a major obstacle to the development of Pakistan, Egypt, and Turkey. The same is true for all other Muslim countries, for the situation is the same throughout the Muslim world. In some cases, it is worse because of other operating factors. Another part of this finding is that Muslim societies can develop and progress only through Islam. Islamic religious thought, as contained in the Qur'an, is an exceedingly powerful productive force which Muslim societies have not yet realized and utilized.

Islam fully sanctions, and indeed requires, that people acquire material prosperity. To be successful in this world is vitally important for the Qur'an, a point Muslim societies have not really grasped; and one measure of this success is certainly prosperity. For Islamic societies to become progressive, it is of crucial importance that changes in Muslims' ideas about Islam occur. These changes cannot be brought about through fiat, as Turkey's example illustrates. They can occur only through changes in the realm of thought, which alone can redeem Islam from the highly distorted ideas that, through the centuries, have wrongly been attributed to it. It is the distorted Islam which Muslims have adhered to in the last several centuries which has resulted in the present conditions of Muslim societies. Given the way Islam is understood by the mass of Muslim populations, including the elites (barring some outstanding exceptions, of course), it is a serious mistake to think that Muslim societies are developing; a recognition of this fact needs to be made by the societies concerned before they can begin to develop. A few changes here and there—in literacy or in the gross national product, or in the installation of some industrial units—do not amount to much, for the underlying structures and worldviews of the societies basically remain unchanged.

The literature on development and modernization is, to some degree, misleading with regard to Muslim societies. The literature has tended to focus on the more recent history of the West. Muslim societies, as some of the leading political and intellectual figures of the societies have observed, have not yet broken away from their medieval period. And the reason for this, beyond doubt, is religious, as our studies of Pakistan, Egypt, and Turkey have demonstrated. On the whole, the literature on development and modernization is relevant, provided we keep the historical background of Muslim societies in full view; it can provide useful lessons and directions.

Scholars have made a serious mistake in linking secularization of culture, as commonly understood, with modernization, or in making it a necessary condition for development and progress. This is particularly so in the case of Muslim societies. The modernizers of Turkey, as our study has shown, faulted on this score. Even though Turkey has been secular for nearly seventy years, it has not progressed in any real sense; in fact, secularism became a powerful weapon in the hands of the wealthy Turkish class to exploit the masses. Material prosperity has occurred in Turkey only in the case of the richest 10 percent of households. The majority of the rest of the population lives in abject poverty. Secularism has prevented reform of the value systems, which are still grounded in medievalism. The same is true of Pakistan and Egypt. And the reason in all three cases is the same: religious thought has remained unreformed, undeveloped.

In Turkey, secularism prevented the possibility of reform of religious thought, although Atatürk did carry out major and needed reforms in the society. Their impact was slight, however, for the mass of the population still adhered to old religious conceptions and traditions. Through secularism, religion became a private affair, which in any case was the situation before, as far as religious education was concerned. Atatürk's reforms were thus frozen at whatever stage they were. Further reform of Islamic religious thought could not take place because Islam was taken out of the intellectual environment.

To be sure, Atatürk had believed that the reform of Islam was essential for progress to take place in Turkey. To some extent he was prevented from moving in that direction by the intransigence of the traditional Islamic religious leaders and circles. The classic example is the opposition of these circles to Atatürk's attempt to have the Qur'an translated into the Turkish language, so that the mass of the population could read and understand the Qur'an first hand. This could dispel those practices, ideas, and traditions which are wrongly attributed to Islam. Finding the religious circles unwilling to change and fearing that they would regain their lost power if the status quo continued, thereby holding the society in bondage, as was the case before, Atatürk opted for secularism. It is difficult, therefore, to apportion blame on him for opting for secularism in those unusual circumstances. The objective conditions were such that he considered it to be the best course of action. Nevertheless, it seems to be the case that the Kemalists did not fully think the issue through.

Subsequent political leaders have not reexamined the issue of secularism beyond allowing some religious courses at the elementary level of education. At the mass level, religious education is, in any case, in the hands of the traditional Islamic educators. Thus, the content of religious education in the country is the same as it was in the Ottoman period. The basic orientations of the people, including the elites, toward the most fundamental aspects of life, therefore, remain unchanged. Secularism further ensures that it remains so.

The dichotomous system of education, secular and religious, prevails in all three countries. Religious education in all three countries is in the hands of religious functionaries whose education is based on medieval Islamic religious thought. Their understanding of Islam is based heavily on the voluminous corpus of the hadith literature, most of which several modern Muslim scholars have themselves pointed out to be fabricated or highly suspect. Western scholars who have examined the issue have also reached the same conclusion. As far as systematic and intelligent study of the Qur'an is concerned, which is the real source of Islam, traditional religious teachers and leaders do not carry it out; the syllabi followed in religious educational institutions testify to that fact. At best, their understanding of the Qur'an is based on a literal interpretation of the Qur'anic verses which, as Fazlur Rahman has pointed out, is "far removed from any genuine insight into the depths of the Qur'an."

The magnitude of the negative impact on the masses of Muslim societies, who receive their religious education at the hands of such individuals, can be well imagined. The dichotomous system of education does not affect negatively the masses of the Muslim populations alone; it also affects the elites and the middle classes who receive modern education. The vast majority of them have the same conceptions of Islam as the general population, for they too, at an early age, receive religious education from the same group of religious functionaries. Moreover, in their adult lives, through the ritualist aspects and religious celebrations where the orthodox are at the helm of affairs, they are conditioned in the same way as the general population. Therefore, secularism, in the Islamic context, only further strengthens the influence of the orthodox and makes the problem worse.

The crying need in Muslim societies is to end the dual system of education and to make religious education, that is *independent* study of the Qur'an, a compulsory part of the curriculum at the high school level and beyond. Through this approach, it does not mean at all that religion will enter politics. Quite the contrary, in the Islamic context in addition to authentic and required religious education, it will provide an effective way to keep religion out of politics. The main purpose of secularism is thus not only successfully achieved, but the benefits are even greater for the society and the individuals. Moreover, it is in this intellectual environment that "reconstruction of religious thought in Islam," as Iqbal put it, can take place. It is in this environment, too, that religious thought can be intelligently understood. The reconstruction of religious thought in Islam is actually the most fundamental condition for Muslim societies to develop and to advance further. As our study has shown, in all three cases the state has been content to enhance merely the literacy ratio in the society. The issue is far more serious. The requirement is to make at least high school education available to the masses. Beyond that, the state must provide higher education to a larger proportion of the population.

The development of a society rests fundamentally on moral questions, and the biggest moral question involved in a society is how resources are distributed among its people. Underlying the concept of development is the idea of self-perfection, which necessitates material prosperity for all. In fact, the two go hand in hand and provide the opportunity to further enhance each other. Healthy materialism is necessary to guard against escapism, which denigrates material wants and views misery in such terms as to make God responsible for it. Materialism, however, needs to be mediated by ethical norms that, in the case of Muslim societies, Islam provides. To this end, an ethical system needs to be first worked out from the Qur'an, clearly stated, taught, and enforced. As Fazlur Rahman has pointed out, this has not yet been done, the evidence for which is provided by the three societies we have examined in this study. In all three cases, a very rich class virtually exploits the mass of the population which lives in abject poverty.

All three countries have a strong agricultural base that remains unexploited for the general good of the societies, but is exploited by the rich landed classes who have prevented the state from carrying out any meaningful land reforms. The blatant exploitation by the rich classes in the three Muslim countries we have studied shows, in fact, that the elites do not subscribe to any ethical system. Indeed, it provides evidence that they neither have any idea of what the ethical system of Islam is supposed to be or what it demands. Nor do they care to know. It also provides full justification to the criticism of those who argue that the elites of Muslim societies, barring some individuals, are not really Muslim.

In the practical sphere, the elites show that they are not willing to let an Islamic society emerge (which, incidentally, is entirely different from the society preached by the ulema or the religious leaders). They continuously attack the roots of Islamic ideology as contained in the Qur'an.

The benefits of whatever economic development has taken place in the societies have gone disproportionately to the richer part of the population. This fact provides evidence that the elites have paid no attention to the idea of socioeconomic justice which the Qur'an so heavily emphasizes. It further provides evidence that, by and large, the elites have no clear conception of the Qur'anic doctrine, which again links up with the serious nature of the problem inherent in the dichotomous system of education prevalent in Muslim societies. The elites' neglect of the masses, in fact, bears out the Qur'anic message that "one major cause of the decay of societies is the neglect into which they are cast by the prosperous members." The manner in which wealth is distributed in the three countries we have studied is also in clear violation of the Qur'anic principle that wealth should not circulate only among the rich. Such serious matters which are raised in the Qur'an are completely ignored by the ruling elites in Muslim societies, and Islam is advocated and practiced in terms of some rituals, which indicates the magnitude of intellectual bankruptcy within the ruling circles.

Exploitation of the masses by the rich classes in all three countries also shows that dependency theories are severely flawed at their core. Dependency theories tend to provide mere rationalizations for the existing state of affairs in Muslim societies, as the study of the three Muslim societies shows. Economic development and avoidance of dependency are contingent on the state's ability to generate domestic savings for investment in development projects. External borrowing, which leads to dependency, occurs because the ruling circles avoid the hard questions of domestic resource mobilization and extraction. By resorting to heavy deficit financing, the state also avoids facing and resolving deep-seated societal problems that cause external borrowing to take place in the first place. It translates into a lack of political will among the elites and an unawareness of the society's ills, which lie in the thought processes of the individuals forming the society.

Dependency theories do not address the core issues that exist in the structures and fabrics of societies and which thwart attempts to develop or modernize. Their message amounts to encouraging passivity and apathy at all levels, particularly for the elites, who find in such studies a ready explanation for the conditions existing in their societies, and the acceptance of the status quo. The biggest problem with the dependency theory is that with one stroke it rules out the possibility of substantial progress in all the developing countries. Dependency theory argues, in effect, that as long as the current world economy is structured as it is, the developing countries will find it well-nigh impossible to change their economic conditions. Such a conclusion completely ignores the inner dynamics of developing countries—the way they are structured, organized, and run, and the kind of ideas which are prevalent and propagated—which are far more directly related to the state of a society than any other outside factor. On the basis of our study of the three countries, dependency theories lose their validity.

Modernization is not achieved by merely extending the past with some cosmetic changes into the present. Rather, it involves systemic transformation, which means, first of all, the desire, commitment, and the will to change the existing paradigm on which the society is based. Transformation of societies is akin to the processes involved in scientific revolutions. In the construction of a new paradigm on which the society is to be based in a modern setting, changes at the core of the old paradigm are required, which obviously is no longer viable, or else the need to change would not have been felt. Fortunately, in the modern world, the new paradigm that has existed in the more developed part of the world for quite some time now can be observed at close distance. Therefore, as far as the need to change is concerned, it is already manifestly established.

The question is no longer whether the old paradigm needs to be changed; the question is how to make the transition from the old paradigm to a new one. In the process of transition, there is undoubtedly an overlap between the outer parameters of the two paradigms, but at the core there are some basic changes. Only then can the transition be accomplished successfully. Otherwise, there will be a continuous clash both between the old and new paradigms operating in the external environment, or the world, and within the societies where the new paradigm seeks to oust the old one. In the transformation of a society's old paradigm, what is involved is a transformation at all levels of the society—political, economic, social, religious, educational, intellectual, and psychological.

Because of the nature of the changes involved in acquiring modernity, modernization is an outgrowth of social revolution. And just as scientific revolutions require the commitment, persistence, and honesty of the scientists, modernization, to be successful, requires primarily the commitment, persistence, and honesty of the ruling elites who exercise direct control on political resources that have a profound impact on the social and economic systems. The crisis of legitimacy, "both of political elites and social systems," which is so widespread in Muslim societies,

has been reinforced by the failure of [Islamic] governments to make good on their promises of achieving development and social justice. With the exception of the [recently] wealthy Gulf states, economic problems have increasingly plagued the Islamic countries. Among the factors responsible for this economic crisis are elite incompetence and corruption, inflation, high rates of population growth, as well as the pervasive lack of developmental ideologies for economic planning and mass mobilization. Nor are the oil producing countries free from economic problems, because of the lack of effective mechanisms of balanced economic development and income distribution. . . . It is significant that in no less than 13 countries of the Islamic orbit the *per capita* income is below $800.00.[1]

Because of the ruling elite's lack of commitment to development, the mass of the population does not view itself as having any stake in the developmental projects undertaken by the state. Consequently, there is a lack of commitment and effort on the part of the general population also. The state must create the cognitive image of change in different spheres of life so as to be believable by its promises. And the images have to be real; only then will necessary support and effort be forthcoming from the masses.

In evaluating development in what are generally termed the developing countries, the important question to ask is what has been happening to poverty, unemployment, and inequality. Growth in gross national product or per capita income is no proof that development in any real sense has taken place. Even if per capita income doubles, but high rates of poverty, unemployment, and inequality persist, it would be strange to call such a society "developing."

As Inkles and Smith have described, underdevelopment is a state of mind. For development to occur, a change in attitudes and values, at both the individual and the societal level is needed. For societies to become modern, it is of crucial importance that individuals having the characteristics of a modern person (as explained in Chapter 2) are widely diffused in the population. Diffusion of modern persons throughout the population is the essence of development.

Modern persons are not typical to any particular culture; it is their number, however, which ultimately determines the state of a particular society. It is the creation of such persons in the society, both urban and rural, which is state's responsibility and which creates a modern society. As John Stuart Mill observed a long time ago, the worth of the individuals determines the worth of a state. In the development of societies, this element is far more important than all the other elements contained in a developmental plan. For the creation of modern persons, the answers lie in the educational field; and in the case of Muslim societies, this aspect of societal activity gains even more importance given the influence of centuries of distorted Islamic religious education, the impact of which has been both strong and exceedingly harmful.

The task is, therefore, even more difficult and yet urgent. The task is first to erase the traditional conceptions of Islam and to replace it with the teachings of Islam as contained in the Qur'an. It calls for the elimination of the dichotomous system of education and its replacement with a comprehensive modern system of education in which the study of the Qur'an is an integral part.[2] As our study has shown, a comprehensive modern system of education in which the study of the Qur'an is an integral part does not exist in Pakistan, Egypt, and Turkey. Nor does such a system exist in any other Muslim country.

The process of development or modernization should be viewed as a triad relationship between the individual, the economic system or conditions, and the political system. In this triad relationship the individual plays the preeminent role. Because of the impact of material conditions on life, economic development for all members of a society, which is the purpose of the entire developmental process, is vitally important. Individuals, affected by economic conditions, in turn affect the functioning and development or nondevelopment of the economic, social, cultural, and political aspects of life, and thereby society itself.

Religion is a very powerful force. It can work both positively and negatively, depending on the content of the religious doctrine, how it is interpreted and understood, and how it is applied in real life. Examination of the developments in the Western and Islamic societies shows two similar and contrasting results.

In the Western experience, it hindered progress as long as it remained dogmatic and the exclusive domain of some people. When philosophers wrestled with profound issues and critically examined their relevance in the operation of societies, their analysis provided useful insights that made it possible for societies to move forward. It is important that an environment should exist in which it is possible to discuss and evaluate religious issues intelligently, dispassionately, and in a scholarly way. In the case of Muslim societies, this has so far not happened, and the result has been that the grossly distorted ideas that have been attributed to Islam in the preceding several centuries have played a negative role in the functioning of the societies. Our studies of Pakistan, Egypt, and Turkey substantiate this conclusion. Moreover, because Islam has been kept out of the intellectual environment, serious, thoughtful, and critical study of religious ideas has not taken place. As a consequence, the implications of religious ideas have generally not been understood, which has led to a situation in which thought itself has remained undeveloped.

In the Christian West, it was the Reformation that stemmed the rot that had settled in Christian societies and that made it possible for the societies to develop and progress. The Reformation, above all, diminished the power and influence of the clergy and thus paved the way for the development of the European intellect. In Muslim societies a similar reformation is long overdue, which would be the basis for the societies to move forward. This reformation can occur only in an intellectual environment in which intelligent study of the Qur'an becomes a vigorous societal activity. This reformation is needed, above all, to check the illegitimate power and influence of a class that masquerades as ulema or religious leaders but that actually is a clergy. This clergy is illegitimate and un-Islamic, for the Qur'an does not sanction it.

As is apparent from Chapter 4, Islamic doctrine is a powerful force for development and progress. The chapter also shows where the main problem lies. The biggest problem so far has been that Islam has been in the exclusive hands of the ulema and religious functionaries who have dogmatically adhered to an interpretation which was made in medieval times. The Qur'an itself provides testimony that this interpretation is wrong, which shows that the Qur'an has not been intelligently studied by the ulema. The curricula of Islamic religious education in the religious institutions of Pakistan and Egypt provide further corroborative evidence on this score, if one were needed.

The situation in Turkey is similar, for al-Azhar of Egypt was the mentor of the ulema of Turkey in the period of the Ottoman empire that did not end until 1923. In secular Turkey, the successors of the ulema and religious functionaries of the Ottoman period have provided religious education to the masses. In short, then, the content of religious education in all three countries has remained the same as it was in the medieval period. Sadat was to the point when he said that the task facing him was to move Egypt forward from the medieval period in which it still lived; the same would apply to the other two countries—indeed, all Muslim countries—barring elements of the educated classes.

For Muslim societies to develop in any meaningful way, it is of crucial importance that the Qur'an is taken out of the hands of the so-called religious leaders, so to say, and placed squarely in the hands of the people; and not to revere but to study and understand, which was the purpose of the Qur'an; reverence should follow from there. The ulema and religious functionaries, by giving a literal interpretation of isolated Qur'anic verses and using them out of context, have grossly distorted the message of the Qur'an. It is due to practices such as these that no systematic exposition of the Qur'an has ever taken place, with the consequence that gross misunderstanding exists, at both the elite and mass level, about the teachings of the Qur'an.

This misunderstanding is compounded and reinforced by the religious teachers' heavy reliance on the so-called traditions of Islam, a vast majority of which are believed to be forgeries and distortions. The prevalent ideas and practices in vogue in Islamic societies are largely derived from such traditions. One of the main requirements for progressive changes to take place in Muslim countries is to discard the bulk of these traditions, which not only control everyday activity but also prevent the growth of fresh ideas. The ideas generated by the vast hadith literature, which is the source of these traditions, occupy Muslim consciousness. The strength of the impact of these ideas is illustrated by the example of Turkey which, though secular, retains the influence of the ideas generated by the traditions. The Turkish example also illustrates the necessity of studying the Qur'an at the high school level and beyond in the modern system of education.

The educational system which a people evolve is one of the most important and the most characteristic institutions of its corporate life. . . . Once established, it becomes a powerful formative factor in its further development, and thus helps to perpetuate its ideals and its pattern of intellectual life. Considered from this (philosophical) point of view, the system of Muslim education becomes a matter of deep import.[3]

For Islamic societies to become progressive, changes in the Muslims' ideas about Islam are crucial. These changes can occur only if the source of Islam, the Qur'an, is studied, and the bulk of the hadith literature, which is of questionable validity, is weeded out. As far as the Qur'an is concerned, there is nothing in it which prevents a person, male or female, from living life in a vigorous manner. In the eyes of the Qur'an, a society's failure in this world reflects punishment by God. A measure of a society's success is material prosperity, albeit not singularly but mediated by the overall message of the Qur'an. To put it another way, a Muslim society's failure in the material sphere is proof of its failure in understanding and applying the Qur'anic doctrine. In the words of Iqbal:

It is one of the most essential teachings of the Qur'an that nations are collectively judged, and suffer for their misdeeds here and now. In order to establish this proposition the Qur'an constantly cites historical instances, and urges upon the reader to reflect on the past and present experience of mankind [and learn from it].[4]

Modern Muslim scholars have analyzed the situation in Muslim societies quite comprehensively. Considerable literature is available, some of which has been brought out in the course of our studies of Pakistan, Egypt, and Turkey. It is a measure of the negligence of the elites in these and other Muslim countries that this literature does not form part of the curriculum in their educational systems. One cannot help reaching the conclusion, therefore, that this "negligence" is at least in part a deliberate attempt to keep the masses uninformed so as to maintain the status quo in which the chief beneficiaries are the elites. A major part of the reason for this state of affairs is that the elites themselves, with few exceptions, are not familiar with most of this literature, for they too are the products of the existing educational system.

Developmental planning in Pakistan, Egypt, and Turkey has been marked by the lack of a comprehensive statement and strategy. It shows the lack of any overall purpose and direction. It also shows the lack of will or willingness on the part of the state to bring about the necessary changes which, though difficult, are possible and essential. Such changes are, in fact, a precondition for modernization efforts to have any meaning and success. In the modernization and development of societies, fundamental changes are required in all the systems through which societies are organized. It requires "the psychological and intellectual no less than the political or economic, to undergo transformation."[5] Our study of Pakistan, Egypt, and Turkey has found that this change is not noticeable except in isolated individuals of a small educated class.

Traditional Islamic conceptions of life are rampant at both the elite and mass levels which, when evaluated on the terms of the Qur'an and considered as a whole, are not Islamic. The emphasis has been primarily on symbolic practices and ceremonies, the underlying ideas and purposes behind which have been grossly misunderstood, while the major teachings of the Qur'an have largely been neglected and not understood. Islam has been understood and propagated in such a way as to mean that as long as one carried out some rituals one was a Muslim, while almost the entire doctrine of the Qur'an has been brushed aside by not paying attention to the most serious issues which are raised in the Qur'an. The symbolic practices and ceremonies, in fact, have been taught and practiced in such a way as to give them magical powers.

The state, in all three cases, continues to reinforce these conceptions through the continuation of the traditional curriculum and system of religious education. The economic conditions of the masses in all three countries cannot be significantly altered without extensive social change. And in the absence of Islamic reform, socioeconomic reforms cannot be brought about, for reforms of any kind are directly related to the conceptions of life that are heavily conditioned by the existing state of Islamic religious thought.

NOTES

CHAPTER 1

1. In this category would also fall most of the writings of dependency theorists like Samir Amin of Egypt. Other dependency theorists like Immanuel Wallerstein did not examine Islamic societies in any systematic manner and based their conclusions regarding dependency on what they observed at the surface level. Their theories of dependency are, therefore, seriously flawed insofar as Islamic societies are concerned and, in fact, lose their validity. This is illustrated in the studies of the three Muslim societies as carried out in this book.

2. Donald Eugene Smith, *Religion and Political Development* (Boston: Little Brown, 1970), p. xi.

3. Ibid., p. 5.

4. Theda Skocpol, *States and Social Revolutions: A Comparative Analysis of France, Russia, and China* (Cambridge: Cambridge University Press, 1979), p. 36.

5. Ibid.

6. Ibid.

7. Joachim Wach, *The Comparative Study of Religions* (New York: Columbia University Press, 1958), p. 12.

8. Ibid., p. 16.

CHAPTER 2

1. Harry Eckstein, "The Idea of Political Development: From Dignity to Efficiency," *World Politics* 34 (July 1983): 455. Explaining the shortcomings of the older version of a universal social science of development, Wiarda points out that earlier development studies were "elevated almost to the status of near-universal social science laws of development and modernization, when in fact the world was much more diverse . . . " Howard J. Wiarda, ed., "Future Directions in Comparative Politics," in *New Directions in Comparative Politics* (Boulder, Colo.: Westview Press, 1985), p. 205; see

also pp. 34-36. Because of the diversity of the world, development and modernization theories are likely to be mediated by specific societal factors, and hence an all-encompassing grand theory is unlikely to emerge in the field. A similar conclusion is reached by Warren F. Ilchman and Norman Thomas Uphoff in *The Political Economy of Change* (Berkeley: University of California Press, 1969), p. 17.

2. Ibid., p. 463.

3. Even Immanuel Wallerstein's *The Capitalist World Economy* (Cambridge: Cambridge University Press, 1980) has a very limited explanatory value for the conditions existing in the "Third World." A more comprehensive explanation would appear to rest within the societies concerned. According to him, "the basic problem is one concerning the structure of inequality of the present world-system (p. 131)." While this may be so to a degree, I think the basic problem is more acutely related to the social structures of the societies concerned. James Weaver and Kenneth Jameson also point out that "the call for a new international economic order is essentially a sham. . . . a new international economic order . . . is not enough; for much of the problem is within the poor countries themselves." James Weaver and Kenneth Jameson, *Economic Development: Competing Paradigms* (Lanham, Md.: University Press of America, 1981), p. 73.

4. Daniel Lerner, *The Passing of Traditional Society* (Glencoe, Ill.: Free Press of Glencoe, 1958), pp. 46-47.

5. Gabriel A. Almond and G. Bingham Powell, Jr., *Comparative Politics*, 2nd ed. (Boston: Little, Brown, 1978), p. 50.

6. Peter Sederberg, "The Betrayed Ascent: The Crisis and Transubstantiation of the Modern World," *The Journal of Developing Areas* 13, No. 2 (January 1979): 135-136. The qualities that Almond and Powell attribute to secularization (*Comparative Politics,* 2nd ed., p. 19) have no a priori reason to be so.

7. Jason L. Finkle and Richard E. Gable, *Political Development and Social Change*, 2nd ed. (New York: John Wiley, 1971), pp. vii-viii.

8. The frustrations often expressed in the literature regarding the field of developmental studies seem to relate to it.

9. David Apter, *The Politics of Modernization* (Chicago: University of Chicago Press, 1965), p. 461. In this context, Geertz highlights the relationship between economic progress and social development: "What looks like a quantum jump from a specifically economic point of view is, from a generally social one, merely the final expression in economic terms of a process which has been building up gradually over an extended period of time." See Clifford Geertz, *Peddlers and Princes* (Chicago: University of Chicago Press, 1963), p. 2.

10. Robert A. Nisbet, *Social Change and History: Aspects of the Western Theory of Development* (New York: Oxford University Press, 1969). In an earlier study, Morris Ginsberg made similar observations; see Morris Ginsberg, *The Idea of Progress: A Revaluation* (London: Methuen and Co., 1953), p. 5.

11. Apter, *The Politics of Modernization*, p. 43.

12. Ginsberg, *The Idea of Progress*, p. 7.

13. Ibid., pp. 8-10.

14. Quoted in ibid., p. 17.

15. Ibid., p. 22.

16. Ibid., p. 20.

17. Denis Goulet, *The Cruel Choice: A New Concept in the Theory of Development* (New York: Atheneum, 1978), p. vii.

18. Ibid., p. viii; Goulet explains that "in the final analysis, economic, political, and cultural development are means for obtaining the good life"; ibid., p. 215.

19. Eric Fromm, *Escape from Freedom* (New York: Holt, Rinehart and Winston, 1941), p. 271.

20. Christian Bay, *The Structure of Freedom* (Stanford: Stanford University Press, 1958), p. 54.

21. Ibid. Eric Fromm's view is virtually the same; See Fromm, *Escape from Freedom*, p. 271.

22. Goulet, *The Cruel Choice,* p. 243.

23. Ibid.

24. Ibid., p. 257.

25. Ibid., p. 218.

26. Ibid., p. x.

27. Ibid., p. 271.

28. Apter, *The Politics of Modernization,* p. 64. Modernity "functions as the dialectical rather than the *historical* opposite of tradition." Modernity itself is transitional "in the sense that it is not a fixed arrangement, but an arrangement in which history continues to have meaning." See Leonard Binder, "The Crisis of Political Development" in Binder et al., *Crises and Sequences in Political Development* (Princeton, N.J.: Princeton University Press, 1971), p. 21. Customs are an inherent part of traditions, and in the long run, if remained unexamined and unchecked, can be passed on as a part of religion. Mill observed this when he said, "custom, in the East, is a religion." See John Stuart Mill, *On Liberty* (Indianapolis: Hackett Publishing Co., 1978), p. 83.

29. Joseph R. Gusfield, "Tradition and Modernity: Misplaced Polarities in the Study of Social Change," in Finkle and Gable, eds., *Political Development and Social Change*, p. 22. Pye points out, however, that traditional systems may provide the "basis for subsequent development if they provide a people with a firm sense of identity, but the strength of the traditional order will impede development to the degree that it makes impossible the infusion of any new or modern elements of political culture." Lucian W. Pye, "Introduction: Political Culture and Political Development," in Lucian W. Pye and Sidney Verba, *Political Culture and Political Development* (Princeton, N.J.: Princeton University Press, 1965), p. 21.

30. Neil J. Smelser, "Mechanisms of Change and Adjustment to Change," in Finkle and Gable, eds., *Political Development and Social Change,* p. 29.

31. Ibid., pp. 31-33.

32. Ibid., p. 33.

33. Ibid., p. 37.

34. Ibid., p. 38.

35. Ibid., p. 34.

36. S. M. Lipset, *Political Man* (New York: Doubleday, 1959), pp. 45-58.

37. Everett E. Hagen, "How Economic Growth Begins: A Theory of Social Change," in Finkle and Gable, eds., *Political Development and Social Change,* p. 74.

38. Ibid., p. 75.

39. Ibid., p. 76.

40. David C. McLelland, *The Achieving Society* (Princeton, N.J.: Van Nostrand Co., 1961).

41. David C. McLelland, "The Achievement Motive in Economic Growth," in Finkle and Gable, eds., *Political Development and Social Change*, pp. 98-99.

42. Alex Inkles and David H. Smith, *Becoming Modern* (Cambridge, Mass.: Cambridge University Press, 1974), p. 312.

43. Ibid., p. 313.

44. Ibid.

45. Ibid., p. 302.

46. Ibid., pp. 290-291, 310-311.

47. Ibid., pp. 291, 312-313.

48. Ibid., pp. 289, 296-297.

49. Ibid., p. 296.

50. Ibid., pp. 315-316.

51. Mill, *On Liberty*, pp. 111-113.

52. Inkles and Smith, *Becoming Modern*, pp. 16-17.

53. Karl Marx, "The German Ideology," in David McLellan, ed., *Karl Marx: Selected Writings* (Oxford: Oxford University Press, 1977), p. 164.

54. Ralph Braibanti, "Values in Institutional Process," in Harold Lasswell, Daniel Lerner, and John Montgomery, eds., *Values and Development: Appraising Asian Experience* (Cambridge, Mass.: MIT Press, 1976), pp. 135-136.

55. See, for example, Pye, "Introduction" in Pye and Verba, *Political Culture and Political Development*, pp. 11-12.

56. Samuel P. Huntington, *Political Order in Changing Societies* (New Haven, Conn.: Yale University Press, 1968), p. 140.

57. Sayeeda Ahmad Chaudhry, "Female Labor Force Participation and its Relationship to Fertility Rate: Some Policy Implications for Developing Countries," Ph.D. dissertation, George Washington University, 1983, p. 17.

58. Ibid., pp. 33-34.

59. Ibid., p. 125.

60. Edward Shills, "Political Development in the New States," *Comparative Studies in Society and History* Vol. II, 1959-1960, p. 282.

61. Thomas S. Kuhn, *The Structure of Scientific Revolutions* (Chicago: University of Chicago Press, 1962), p. 76.

62. Ibid.

63. Ibid., pp. 77, 84.

64. Ibid., p. 85.

65. Ibid., pp. 84-85.

66. Manfred Halpern, "The Rate and Costs of Political Development," *The Annals of the American Academy of Political and Social Science* 358 (March 1965): 21-22.

67. Kuhn, *The Structure of Scientific Revolutions*, p. 91.

68. Ilchman and Uphoff, *The Political Economy of Change*, p. 32.

69. Ibid., pp. 30-31. In this context, it is important to bear in mind the impact of political structure or system on political culture, for the political system itself is "a source of individuals' attitudes toward that system." Gabriel A. Almond and Sidney Verba, *The*

Civic Culture (Princeton, N.J.: Princeton University Press, 1963), p. 368. For a definition and discussion of the civic culture, see ibid., pp. 6-40 and Ch. 15. Carole Pateman also emphasizes the importance of the impact of political structure on political culture. See Carole Pateman, "The Civil Culture: A Philosophic Critique," in Gabriel A. Almond and Sidney Verba, eds., *The Civic Culture Revisited* (Boston: Little, Brown, 1980), Ch. III. Dudley Seers explains how the political and economic systems are closely interrelated. See Dudley Seers, "The Meaning of Development," in Norman T. Uphoff and Warren F. Ilchman eds., *The Political Economy of Development* (Berkeley: University of California Press, 1972), p. 126.

70. Ilchman and Uphoff, *The Political Economy of Change*, pp. 50-51.

71. Ibid., p. 33.

72. Ibid., p. 34.

73. Ibid., p. 35.

74. Lars G. Björk, "The Function of Cognitive Images in Facilitating Organizational Change," *Journal of Human Behavior and Learning* 2, No. 1 (1985): 44.

75. Ibid., p. 46.

76. Ibid., p. 48.

77. United Nations Development Assistance Committee, in its review of 1982, has reported that the fundamental development policies are those that "activate the material aspirations and energies of [people]", and that the basic "resource requirement for development is an adequate supply of literate, trained and motivated manpower." See Bradford Morse and Uner Kirdar, "Human Resource Development: Challenge for the '80s," *Journal of the Society for International Development* 1 (1984): 52.

78. Ibid., p. 57.

79. Seers, "The Meaning of Development," in Uphoff and Ilchman eds., *The Political Economy of Development*, p. 123.

80. Timothy and Leslie Nulty, "Pakistan: An Appraisal of Development Strategy," in ibid., p. 142.

81. Seers, "The Meaning of Development," in ibid., p. 123.

82. Timothy and Leslie Nulty, "Pakistan," in ibid., p. 134.

83. Seers, "The Meaning of Development," in ibid., p. 124.

84. Timothy and Leslie Nulty, "Pakistan," in ibid., p. 135.

85. Seers, "The Meaning of Development," in ibid., p. 124.

86. Ibid., p. 125.

87. Simon Kuznets, *Modern Economic Growth: Rate, Structure, and Spread* (New Haven, Conn.: Yale University Press, 1966), p. 452.

88. Ibid., pp. 6-7, 452-453.

CHAPTER 3

1. Donald Eugene Smith, *Religion and Political Development,* (Boston: Little, Brown, 1970), p. 2.

2. Ibid., p. xi.

3. Delos B. McKown, *The Classical Marxist Critiques of Religion: Marx, Engels, Lenin, Kautsky* (The Hague: Martinus Nijhoff, 1975), p. 17.

4. Smith, *Religion and Political Development*, pp. 11-12.

5. Ibid., p. 19. The thrust of Max Weber's argument in his analysis of religion and society was in the same direction; that is, "each of the major religions of the world develops its own distinctive orientation toward all the major phases of human activity, and thus comes to exercise an influence on the development of other major institutional systems in society, an influence which cannot be accounted for merely in economic terms." See Gerhard Lenski, *The Religious Factor* (Garden City, N.Y.: Doubleday, 1961), p. 322.

6. Samuel S. Cohen, *What We Jews Believe* (Cincinnati: Union of American Hebrew Congregations, 1931), p. 3.

7. Thomas Luckmann, "On Religion in Modern Society: Individual Consciousness, World View, Institution," *Journal for the Scientific Study of Religion* 2, No. 2 (April 1963): 151.

8. Ibid., pp. 152-153.

9. Ibid., p. 153.

10. Ibid., pp. 158-160. In this context it is of interest to note that Durkheim believed that "there is a definite limit to the individualizing trend in social evolution". His central concern was "the spiritual and moral dignity of human life" in which spiritual values played a decisive role. See Theodore M. Steeman, "Durkheim's Professional Ethics," in ibid., pp. 171, 181.

11. Kalman H. Silvert, ed., *Churches and States: The Religious Institution and Modernization* (New York: American Universities Field Staff, 1967), p. vi.

12. Quoted in Jeremy Bernstein, *Einstein* (New York: Viking Press, 1973), p. 15.

13. J. A. Franquiz, "Albert Einstein's Philosophy of Religion," *Journal for the Scientific Study of Religion* 4, No. 1 (October 1964): 65. It appears that Einstein did not fully understand the meaning of the omnipotence of God. See ibid., p. 66, for his observations on this and other points.

14. Franklin L. Baumer, *Religion and the Rise of Skepticism* (New York: Harcourt, Brace and Co., 1960), p. 4; and W.E.H. Lecky, *History of the Rise and Influence of the Spirit of Rationalism in Europe* (London: Longmans, Green, and Co., 1866), pp. 52-53. Whereas in Europe "for two or three centuries, most of the great works in Christendom bore some marks of Averroes," the reaction against Averroes in the Muslim world was so great and the panic so widespread "that the theologians pronounced logic and philosophy to be the two great enemies of their profession, and ordered all books on those dangerous subjects to be burnt." Lecky, footnote on p. 53.

15. Lecky, *History of the Rise and Influence*, p. 56.

16. Ibid., p. 52.

17. Ibid., pp. 53-54.

18. Ibid., pp. 54-55.

19. Ibid., p. 62.

20. Ibid., p. 63.

21. Ibid., p. 61.

22. Ibid., pp. 447, 440-441.

23. Baumer, *Religion and the Rise of Skepticism*, p. 45.

24. Felix Gilbert, *Machiavelli and Guicciardini: Politics and History in Sixteenth Century Florence* (Princeton, N.J.: Princeton University Press, 1965), p. 7.

25. J. H. Hexter, *The Vision of Politics on the Eve of the Reformation: More, Machiavelli, and Seysell* (New York: Basic Books, 1973), p. 3.

26. Ibid., p. 4.

27. Ibid.

28. Mulford Q. Sibley, *Political Ideas and Ideologies* (New York: Harper and Row, 1970), p. 298.

29. W. K. Marriot, trans., *The Prince* (London: J. M. Dent and Sons, 1938), p. 144; Sibley, *Political Ideas*, pp. 302-303.

30. Leslie J. Walker, trans., *The Discourses of Niccolo Machiavelli* Vol. 1 (London and Boston: Routledge and Kegan Paul, 1975), p. 26.

31. Leo Strauss, "Machiavelli the Immoralist," in Robert M. Adams, trans., ed., *The Prince: A New Translation, Backgrounds, Interpretations* (New York: Norton and Co., 1977), p. 66.

32. Ibid., pp. 182-183.

33. Baumer, *Religion and the Rise of Skepticism*, pp. 12-13.

34. Ibid., pp. 46-47.

35. Ibid., pp. 47-48.

36. Ibid.

37. Ibid., pp. 51-56.

38. Ibid., p. 67.

39. This passage is based on pp. 110-121 in ibid.

40. Dieter Henrich, "Some Historical Presuppositions of Hegel's System," in Darrel E. Christensen, ed., *Hegel and the Philosophy of Religion: The Wofford Symposium* (The Hague: Martinus Nijhoff, 1970), p. 32.

41. Raymond Keitt Williamson, *Introduction to Hagel's Philosophy of Religion* (Albany: State University of New York Press, 1984), p. 301.

42. Andrew Prior, *Revolution and Philosophy: The Significance of the French Revolution for Hegel and Marx* (Cape Town: David Philip, Publisher, 1972), p. 14.

43. Ibid., pp. 14-15.

44. Ibid., p. 16.

45. Robert L. Perkins, "Hegel and the Secularization of Religion," *International Journal for Philosophy of Religion* 1, No. 3 (Fall 1970): 133-135.

46. Ibid., p. 134.

47. Ibid.

48. Ibid., p. 146.

49. Frederick Gregory, *Scientific Materialism in Nineteenth Century Germany* (Dordrecht, Holland: D. Reidel Publishing Co., 1977), p. 28.

50. Ibid., p. 3.

51. Ibid.

52. Ibid.

53. Ibid.

54. Ibid., pp. 3-4.

55. Ibid., p. 189.

56. Ibid., p. 5.

57. Ibid.

58. Ibid., pp. 6-9.

59. Ibid., pp. 147, 149.

60. Ibid., p. 151.

61. Willard Huntington Wright, *What Nietzsche Taught* (New York: B. W. Huebsch, 1915), pp. 52-53.

62. Ibid., p. 95.

63. Ibid., pp. 127, 174.

64. Ibid., pp. 186, 192.

65. Karl Jaspers, *Nietzsche and Christianity* (U.S.: Henry Regency Co., 1963), pp. 31-33, 38.

66. Wright, *What Nietzsche Taught*, pp. 241, 299.

67. Baumer, *Religion and the Rise of Skepticism*, pp. 13-14.

68. Ibid., p. 14.

69. Ibid., p. 15.

70. Ibid.

71. McKown, *The Classical Marxist Critiques*, p. 4.

72. Karl Marx and Friedrich Engels, *On Religion* (New York: Schocken Books, 1964), pp. 15, 73-75.

73. Ibid., p. 40.

74. Ibid., p. 34.

75. Ibid., p. 42.

76. Ibid., p. 50.

77. Ibid., pp. 147-148.

78. Frederick Engels, *Feuerbach: The Roots of the Socialist Philosophy*, trans. Austin Lewis (Chicago: Charles H. Kerr and Co., 1903), pp. 25, 119.

79. Trevor Ling, *Karl Marx and Religion: In Europe and India* (New York: Harper and Row, 1980), pp. 30-31.

80. Ibid., p. 30; McKown, *The Classical Marxist Critiques*, p. 15.

81. McKown, *The Classical Marxist Critiques*, p. 16.

82. Ibid.

83. Ibid., pp. 16-17.

84. Ibid., p. 19-20.

85. Ibid., p. 17.

86. For a discussion of McKown's arguments, see pp. 23-31 in ibid.

87. Ibid., pp. 97-98.

88. Ibid., p. 161.

CHAPTER 4

1. Translated from Ghulam Ahmed Parwez, *Asbab-e Zawal-e Ummat (Causes of the Downfall of the Community of Muslim Peoples)*, 4th ed. (Lahore: Adara Taloo-e Islam, 1966), pp. iv-vi.

2. Ibid., pp. 1-6.

3. Bryan S. Turner, *Weber and Islam: A Critical Study* (London/Boston: Routledge and Kegan Paul, 1974), p. 20. Alasdaire MacIntyre has pointed out that, in explaining the relationship between beliefs and actions, sociologists often start with a strong thesis

and end with a compromise. Marx and Pareto considered beliefs to be of secondary importance, while Weber held beliefs to be independent and influential. Weber, however, "slips into a 'facile interactionism' in which beliefs cause actions and actions cause belief." Ibid., p. 9.

4. Ibid., p. 16.

5. Ibid., p. 11.

6. Salem Azzam, "Introduction," in Islamic Council of Europe, *Islam and Contemporary Society* (London/New York: Longman Group Ltd., 1982), p. viii.

7. Albert Hourani, *Arabic Thought in the Liberal Age* (London: Oxford University Press, 1962), p. 129.

8. Fazlur Rahman, *Major Themes of the Qur'an* (Minneapolis: Bibliotheca Islamica, 1980), p. xii.

9. Ibid., pp. xi, xv.

10. Ibid., p. xii.

11. Syed Ameer Ali, *The Spirit of Islam* (1890; reprinted, London: Chatto and Windus, 1974), 10th ed., pp. 183-185.

12. Donald Eugene Smith, *Religion and Political Development* (Boston: Little, Brown, 1970), p. 85.

13. In a discussion of four religious systems—Hinduism, Buddhism, Islam, and Catholicism—Smith makes a similar point. The four religious systems provide very different raw materials for the development of religious ideologies of change; for this purpose the ahistorical-historical distinction is critical. Whereas Catholicism and Islam are conducive to social change, the ahistorical Indic religious systems, Hinduism and Buddhism, lack the raw materials for developing a convincing ideology of social change. Donald Eugene Smith, ed., "Religion and Political Modernization: Comparative Perspectives," in *Religion and Political Modernization* (New Haven, Conn.: Yale University Press, 1974), p. 24.

14. Jacob M. Landau, *Radical Politics in Modern Turkey* (Leiden, Netherlands: E. J. Brill, 1974), p. 171.

15. Ibid., p. 172.

16. Ervin I.J. Rosenthal, *Islam in Modern National State* (Cambridge: Cambridge University Press, 1965), p. 51.

17. Ibid., p. 52.

18. Ibid., p. 55.

19. Ibid.

20. Thomas Luckmann observes that "the institutional specialization of religion [in the West] resulted in the relativization of the Church as an institution among other institutions." Thomas Luckmann, "On Religion in Modern Society: Individual Consciousness, World View, Institution," *Journal for the Scientific Study of Religion* 2, No. 2 (April 1963): 158.

21. *The Pakistan Times*, Overseas Weekly, June 28, 1987.

22. In such an arrangement the government will have to resist attempts by the ulema to be the arbiters of all matters pertaining to religion. Historically, the ulema, in general, have displayed an intransigent orthodoxy. For example, in 1955 the government of Pakistan appointed a Commission on Marriage and Family Laws to review existing practices and to make recommendations. Of the seven members of the commission, only

one was from the ulema, who strongly dissented with the recommendations of the commission even though they were based on a very reasonable interpretation of the Qur'anic injunctions on the matter. For details, see Donald Eugene Smith, *Religion, Politics, and Social Change in the Third World* (New York: Free Press, 1971), pp. 71-79.

23. Ibid., p. 73.

24. Fazlur Rahman, "Some Key Ethical Concepts of the Qur'an," *The Journal of Religious Ethics*, 2, No. 2, (Fall 1983): 183-184.

25. Quoted from Pakistan Government, "Resolution on the Report of the Commission," 1959, in Rosenthal, *Islam in Modern National State*, p. 350.

26. Ibid.

27. Charles S. Liebman and Eliezer Don-Yehiya, *Religion and Politics in Israel* (Bloomington: Indiana University Press, 1984), p. 15. Daniel Crecelius equates modernization with secularism: "Secularization has been identified as an integral part of the modernization process."; "Most studies on the process of modernization or secularism . . . . " Daniel Crecelius, "The Course of Secularization in Modern Egypt," in Smith, ed., *Religion and Political Modernization*, pp. 67, 91; see also pp. 93-94.

28. Liebman and Don-Yehiya, *Religion and Politics in Israel*, p. 15.

29. Ibid., p. 16.

30. Ibid.

31. To cite just two examples, "in the expansion of Islam, the Sufi orders tended frequently to tolerate and even absorb the non-Islamic religious beliefs and practices of the new converts"; Donald Eugene Smith, *Religion and Political Development* (Boston: Little, Brown, 1970), p. 49; "Through its people scattered over the world, Judaism has been able to receive the impact of the spiritual experiences of human civilization." Leo Baeck, *The Essence of Judaism* (New York: Schocken Books, 1967), p. 9. "Judaism . . . was subjected to the influence of an alien culture and religion, Arabic Islam, in an interplay which shaped its forms of expression and patterns of thought significantly and creatively." Charles J. Adams, *A Reader's Guide to the Great Religions* 2nd ed. (New York: Free Press, 1977), p. 323.

32. R. J. Zwi Werblowsky, *Beyond Tradition and Modernity: Changing Religions in a Changing World* (London: Athlone Press, 1976), pp. 72-73.

33. Turner, *Weber and Islam*, p. 153.

34. Ibid., p. 154.

35. Ibid., p. 152.

36. Ibid., p. 153.

37. Ibid.

38. Ibid., p. 155.

39. Ibid., pp. 155-156.

40. Ibid., p. 159.

41. Ibid., p. 158.

42. Sir Muhammad Iqbal, *The Reconstruction of Religious Thought in Islam* (Lahore: Sh. Mohammad Ashraf, 1962), pp. 154-155.

43. Ibid., p. 184.

44. Ibid., p. 189.

45. Fazlur Rahman, *Islam and Modernity* (Chicago: University of Chicago Press,

1982), p. 2.

46. Ibid., p. 14.

47. Ibid., pp. 14-15.

48. Ibid., p. 15.

49. Ibid., p. 2.

50. Ibid., pp. 2-4.

51. Professor Muhammad Qutb, "Islam as a Supreme Doctrine" in *Islam and Contemporary Society* (London/New York: Published by Longman in association with the Islamic Council of Europe, 1982), p. 1.

52. Rahman, *Major Themes of the Qur'an,* p. 20.

53. Quoted from the Qur'an in ibid., p. 8.

54. Ibid., p. 23.

55. Immanuel Wallerstein, *The Capitalist World Economy* (London: Cambridge University Press, 1979), p. 132.

56. Rahman, *Major Themes of the Qur'an,* pp. 23-24, 14.

57. Rahman, *Islam and Modernity,* pp. 16-17.

58. Ibid., pp. 18-19.

59. Ibid., p. 31.

60. Ibid., pp. 136-137.

61. Ibid., p. 20.

62. Sheila McDonough, *The Authority of the Past: A Study of Three Muslim Modernists* (Pennsylvania: American Academy of Religion, 1970), p. 10.

63. Ibid.

64. Rahman, *Major Themes of the Qur'an,* p. 30.

65. Ibid., p. 27; see also pp. 23-26.

66. Rahman, *Islam and Modernity,* p. 139.

67. Ibid., pp. 139-140.

68. Ibid., p. 141.

69. Ibid.

70. Ibid., pp. 142-143.

71. An outstanding and pioneering work in that direction is by Fazlur Rahman, *Major Themes of the Qur'an.* Similar works are required dealing with specific issues. In addition, the entire hadith literature (compilations of sayings attributed to the Prophet Muhammad or a description of his deeds. The compilation also includes attributions to the Prophet's Companions and their Successors) needs to be reexamined critically to weed out such attributions that are highly questionable, or have no validity at all. In any case, the Qur'an alone is of primary importance.

72. Rahman, *Islam and Modernity,* p. 156. An astonishing fact to be noted here is that "Muslim scholars have never attempted an ethics of the Qur'an, systematically or otherwise." Ibid., p. 154. The Qur'an's ethics, however, "is its essence, and it is also the necessary link between theology and law. . . . The Muslims' failure to make a clear distinction between Qur'anic ethics and law has resulted in a confusion between the two. Neither ethics nor law ever became a discipline in itself. Islamic law, in fact, is not law in a modern sense." Ibid., pp. 154-155.

73. Oliver Leaman, *An Introduction to Medieval Islamic Philosophy* (Cambridge: Cambridge University Press, 1985), p. 17.

74. Ibid., pp. 20-21.
75. Ibid., p. 58.
76. Ibid.
77. Ibid., p. 47.
78. Ibid., p. 190.
79. Ibid.
80. Ibid., p. 191.
81. Rahman, *Islam and Modernity*, pp. 157-159.
82. Ibid., p. 138.
83. Rahman, *Major Themes of the Qur'an*, pp. 40-41.
84. Ibid., pp. 38-39.
85. Ibid., p. 39.
86. G.H.A. Juynboll, *Muslim Tradition: Studies in Chronology, Provenance and Authorship of Early Hadith* (Cambridge: Cambridge University Press, 1983), pp. 1-2.
87. See, for instance, the study quoted under the previous footnote. See also G.H.A. Juynboll, *The Authenticity of the Tradition Literature: Discussions in Modern Egypt* (Leiden: E. J. Brill, 1969); and Alfred Guillaume, *The Traditions of Islam* (Oxford: Oxford University Press, 1924). For a sample of the hadiths, see Muhammad Azizullah, *Glimpses of the Hadith* (Karachi: Crescent Publications, 1980), 4th printing. In describing the traditions, the author says that "it has been established that Hadith was nothing short of revelation"; ibid., p. 17.
88. Juynboll, *Muslim Tradition*, p. 8.
89. Ibid., pp. 20, 134.
90. Ibid., p. 5. See also Chapter 4 which analyzes some commonly accepted names of hadith transmitters. Thus, Juynboll points out that "there is undeniable evidence in support of the theory that certain key figures in *hadith* transmission, such as Ibn Shihab az-Zuhri, constitute in reality a collection of persons who have all played a part in *hadith* and whose common name is used or misused in *isnads* [chain of transmitters] either by themselves or by otherwise anonymous *hadith* forgers." Ibid., p. 160.
91. Ibid., pp. 163, 269.
92. Ibid., p. 29; see also pp. 24-30.
93. Ibid., p. 21.
94. Guillaume, *The Traditions of Islam*, pp. 28-32.
95. Ibid., pp. 33-35.
96. Juynboll, *Muslim Tradition*, p. 12; see also p. 131.
97. Rahman, *Islam and Modernity*, p. 147.
98. In this context see also John Thomas Cummings et al., "Islam and Modern Economic Change" in John L. Esposito, ed., *Islam and Development* (Syracuse, N.Y.: Syracuse University Press, 1980), pp. 25-47.
99. Rahman, *Islam and Modernity*, p. 146.
100. Ibid., p. 16.

CHAPTER 5

1. For background to the independence movement, see K. K. Aziz, *The Making of*

Pakistan: A Study in Nationalism (London: Chatto and Windus, 1967); Syed Sharifuddin Pirzada, ed., *Foundations of Pakistan: All-India Muslim League Documents—1906-1947* Vol. II (Karachi: National Publishing House Ltd., 1970). A very important study is by Chaudhri Muhammad Ali, *The Emergence of Pakistan* (New York: Columbia University Press, 1967).

2. *Quaid-i-Azam Muhammad Ali Jinnah: Speeches as Governor General* (Karachi: Pakistan Publications, 1963), p. 65.

3. Pirzada, ed., *Foundations of Pakistan,* p. 290.

4. Aziz Ahmad and G. E. Von Grunebaum, *Muslim Self-Statement in India and Pakistan: 1857-1968* (Wiesbaden: Otto Harrassowitz, 1970), p. 113.

5. G. W. Choudhry, *Documents and Speeches on the Constitution of Pakistan* (Dacca: Green Book House, 1967), pp. 21-22.

6. Pirzada, ed., *Foundations of Pakistan,* p. 485.

7. See, for instance, Saleem M.M. Qureshi, "Iqbal and Jinnah: Personalities, Perceptions and Politics," in C. M. Naim, ed., *Iqbal, Jinnah, and Pakistan: The Vision and the Reality* (Syracuse:, N.Y.: Syracuse University Press, 1979), pp. 11-39. Binder substantiates the argument presented here; see Leonard Binder, *Religion and Politics in Pakistan* (Berkeley: University of California Press, 1961), p. 144.

8. Pirzada, ed., *Foundations of Pakistan,* p. 35.

9. Sir Mohammad Iqbal, *The Reconstruction of Religious Thought in Islam* (Lahore: Sh. Mohammad Ashraf, 1962), p. 7.

10. Pirzada, ed., *Foundations of Pakistan,* p. 453.

11. Ibid., p. 485.

12. Choudhry, *Documents and Speeches,* pp. 21-22.

13. Ibid., p. 24.

14. Wilfred Cantwell Smith, *Pakistan as an Islamic State* (Lahore: Shaikh Muhammad Ashraf, 1951), pp. 6-7. Gibb had thought that "the great majority of the conservative theologians know what it is they are defending but do not know . . . what they are defending it against." H.A.R. Gibb, *Modern Trends in Islam* (Chicago: University of Chicago Press, 1947), p. 71. On the basis of what we have seen in the preceding chapter, however, we reach the inescapable conclusion that the conservative theologians do not know what they are defending.

15. Binder, *Religion and Politics,* p. 114.

16. Choudhry, *Documents and Speeches,* p. 25.

17. Munir D. Ahmed, "Pakistan: The Dream of an Islamic State," in Carlo Caldarola ed., *Religion and Societies: Asia and the Middle East* (Berlin: Mouton, 1982), p. 264.

18. It may be useful here to mention what the term *ulama* or *ulema* means. The term *ulama* is the plural of the Arabic word *alim,* its root being ILM. Ilm means knowledge, and therefore ulama means those who possess knowledge. This word is twice used in the Qur'an. The term is also used in the hadith collections. However, the term has also developed a technical meaning. In this sense, it is applied to those who are well conversant with all or any branch of "Islamic" learning, like jurisprudence (fiqh), theology (kalam), tradition (hadith), Qur'anic exegesis (tafsir), and others. These subjects are taught in religious seminaries, and those who receive degrees from the seminaries are generally known as ulema/ulama. Manzooruddin Ahmad, "The Political

Role of the Ulama in the Indo-Pakistan Sub-continent," *Islamic Studies* 6 (1967): 327. In the collection of the traditions, there is an astonishing tradition which states that "the ulama are the successors of the prophet"; ibid., p. 347, n. 3.

19. Keith Callard, *Pakistan: A Political Study* (Britain: Allen and Unwin, 1957), p. 210, n. 1.

20. Choudhry, *Documents and Speeches,* p. 25.

21. Ibid.

22. Detlev H. Khalid, "Theocracy and the Location of Sovereignty," *Islamic Studies* 11, No. 3 (September 1967): 198.

23. Ibid., pp. 198-199.

24. Rahman, "Iqbal, the Visionary; Jinnah, the Technician; and Pakistan the Reality," in Naim, ed., *Iqbal, Jinnah, and Pakistan,* p. 8.

25. Ibid., pp. 7-8.

26. Ibid., p. 7.

27. Fazlur Rahman reaches the same conclusion: "The principles enunciated in the Qur'an are justice and fair play. This is precisely the meaning of accepting the 'Sovereignty of God,' since the standards of justice are objective and do not depend on or even necessarily conform to, the subjective wishes of a people." "Implementation of the Islamic Concept of State in the Pakistani Milieu," *Islamic Studies* 6, No. 3 (September 1967): 209.

28. Manzooruddin Ahmed, "Sovereignty of God in the Constitution of Pakistan: A Study in the Conflict of Traditionalism and Modernism," *Islamic Studies* 4, No. 2 (June 1985): 205. See also Manzooruddin Ahmed, "Islamic Aspects of the New Constitution of Pakistan," *Islamic Studies* 2, No. 2, (June 1963): 251.

29. Ahmed, "Sovereignty," *Islamic Studies* 4, No. 2 (June 1965): 210.

30. Rahman, "Implementation of the Islamic Concept," *Islamic Studies* 6, No. 3 (September 1967): 208-209.

31. Binder, *Religion and Politics,* pp. ix, 7.

32. Rahman, "Implementation of the Islamic Concept," *Islamic Studies* 6, No. 3 (September 1967): 206.

33. Ibid., pp. 216-217.

34. Ibid., p. 217. The ulema have influenced some people so greatly, however, that one writer states: "The *mujtahidun* comprise jurist-theologians who are competent to resolve difficult questions of law through independent interpretation of the Qur'an and the *Sunnah,"* as if it is their prerogative to have "independent interpretation." Ahmed, "Islamic Aspects," *Islamic Studies* 2, No. 2 (June 1963): 277, n. 38.

35. Rahman, "Implementation of the Islamic Concept," *Islamic Studies,* 6, No. 3 (September 1967): 218.

36. Binder, *Religion and Politics,* p. 156.

37. Ibid., pp. 179, 181-182.

38. Ibid., p. 175.

39. Ibid., p. 220. For details and discussion of some of the other principles, see pp. 216-232.

40. Choudhry, *Documents and Speeches,* p. 198.

41. Rahman, "Implementation of the Islamic Concept," *Islamic Studies* 6, No. 3 (September 1967): 212.

42. Binder, *Religion and Politics*, pp. 283-284.

43. Ibid.

44. Ibid., p. 184.

45. Ibid.

46. Ibid., pp. 188, 211.

47. Ibid.; see also p. 189.

48. Mahfuzul Haq, "Some Reflections on Islam and Constitution-Making in Pakistan: 1947-56," *Islamic Studies* 5, No. 2 (June 1966): 219.

49. Smith, *Pakistan as an Islamic State*, pp. 98-99, 75, 70.

50. Ibid., p. 86.

51. Ahmed, "Islamic Aspects," *Islamic Studies* 2, No. 2 (June 1963): 252-253.

52. Ibid., p. 256.

53. Choudhry, *Documents and Speeches*, p. 576.

54. Ibid., pp. 576-577.

55. Ibid., p. 841.

56. Ibid., p. 842.

57. Ibid., p. 862.

58. Sardar Muhammad Ishaq Khan, *The Constitution of the Islamic Republic of Pakistan* (Lahore: Khyber Law Publishers, 1973), p. 1.

59. Munir D. Ahmed, "Pakistan" in Caldarola, ed., *Religion and Societies*, p. 265.

60. Erwin I.J. Rosenthal, *Islam in the Modern National State* (Cambridge: Cambridge University Press, 1965), p. xvii.

61. Ibid.

62. Quoted by Kemal A. Faruki, "Pakistan: Islamic Government and Society," in John L. Esposito ed., *Islam in Asia* (New York: Oxford University Press, 1987), p. 60. *Chaddar* and *Chardivari* literally mean shawl and the four walls. It is "an alliterative allusion to the concept of women's seclusion originally given currency soon after the promulgation of martial law by General Zia-ul-Haq himself." Ibid., p. 76, n. 8.

63. Freeland Abbot, *Islam and Pakistan* (Ithaca, N. Y.: Cornell University Press, 1968), p. 84.

64. Ibid.

65. Ibid., p. 85.

66. Ibid., p. 79.

67. Ibid.

68. Ibid., p. 80.

69. Ibid., p. 30.

70. Ibid., p. 80.

71. Thus, an Arab writer, in an article in *Arab News* (November 25, 1988), a publication of Saudi Arabia, makes the astonishing statement in his discussion of polygamy: "It is well known that Islam allows a man to marry up to four wives at a time." The Qur'an, in fact, does not allow that and specifically mentions that man cannot do justice to more than one wife at a time. The provision regarding more than one wife was only in the context of orphaned girls who were in someone's custody, that is, to prevent the custodians to usurp orphaned girls' inherited wealth by marrying them only to possess their wealth. Such custodians were told that if they feared that they could not do justice to the rights of orphaned girls regarding their inheritance and were tempted

to marry them only to keep their inheritance, they should marry other women whom they liked, whether two, three, or four. They were also told that, in such an eventuality, if they feared they could not do justice to more than one wife, they should marry only one. The important point in all of this was to prevent the exploitation of the orphaned girls, and this provision of more than one wife, was *only* in the context of orphaned girls and was specifically meant in only those situations as they existed in the then Arabia. This provision was in no way meant to be a license for everyone to have more than one wife at a time. The Qur'anic stipulation is absolutely clear on the matter. To this day, however, religious teachers use the Qur'anic verse out of context. See 4:2-3; also see Fazlur Rahman, "The Controversy Over the Muslim Family Laws," in Donald Eugene Smith, ed., *South Asian Politics and Religion* (Princeton, N.J.: Princeton University Press, 1966), pp. 416-420.

72. A.A.A. Fyzee, "Recent Developments in Islam," *Islamic Culture* Vol. 1, 1927, p. 436.

73. Ibid.

74. J.M.S. Baljon, *Modern Muslim Koran Interpretation (1880-1960)* (Leiden: E. J. Brill, 1961), p. 3.

75. Ahmad and Grunebaum, *Muslim Self-Statement,* p. 3.

76. Ibid., p. 4.

77. Bashir Ahmad Dar, *Religious Thought of Sayyid Ahmad Khan* (Lahore: Institute of Islamic Culture, 1957), p. 270.

78. Ibid., p. 271.

79. Ibid., pp. 273-274.

80. Ibid., p. 274.

81. Ibid., p. 276.

82. Sheila McDonough, *The Authority of the Past: A Study of Three Muslim Modernists* (Pennsylvania: American Academy of Religion, 1970), p. 14.

83. Ibid.

84. Ibid.

85. Ibid., p. 12.

86. Ahmad and Grunebaum, *Muslim Self-Statement,* p. 25.

87. McDonough, *The Authority of the Past,* p. 15.

88. Ahmad and Grunebaum, *Muslim Self-Statement,* p. 5.

89. Ibid.

90. Ibid., p. 49. As outstanding as some of Chiragh Ali's critique and ideas were regarding the contemporary religious thought in Islam, he became associated with the founder of the Ahmadiyya movement, which eventually disclosed itself as an heretical sect. Pakistan declared this sect to be non-Muslim in 1974. Apparently, Chiragh Ali was not aware how the movement would evolve. In the beginning of this movement Iqbal himself "had hopes of good results following from this movement." Soon, however, he found it to be totally un-Islamic and declared it to be so. Syed Abdul Vahid, ed., *Thoughts and Reflections of Iqbal* (Lahore: Sh. Muhammad Ashraf, 1964), p. 297. See also pp. 269-276.

91. Ahmad and Grunebaum, *Muslim Self-Statement,* p. 49.

92. Ibid., pp. 49-50.

93. Ibid., pp. 50, 52. See p. 51 for the schema.

94. Ibid., p. 50, n. 3.
95. Ibid., p. 50.
96. Ibid., p. 52.
97. Ibid., p. 53.
98. Ibid.
99. Ibid., p. 52.
100. Iqbal, *The Reconstruction of Religious Thought,* p. 97.
101. Ibid.
102. Ibid., p. 14.
103. Javid Iqbal, *Ideology of Pakistan* (Karachi: Ferozsons Ltd., 1971), p. 83.
104. Ibid.
105. Ibid., p. 82.
106. Ibid., p. 281-282.
107. Iqbal, *The Reconstruction of Religious Thought,* p. 176.
108. Ibid., pp. 178-179.
109. Ibid., p. 178.
110. Ibid., pp. 171-172.
111. Ibid., 156.
112. Ibid.
113. McDonough, *The Authority of the Past,* p. 23.
114. Iqbal, *The Reconstruction of Religious Thought,* p. 126.
115. McDonough, *The Authority of the Past,* pp. 24-25; See also Vahid, ed., *Thoughts and Reflections of Iqbal,* pp. 36-42.
116. Ibid., p. 33.
117. Ibid., p. 28.
118. One of the outstanding exceptions in the political leadership of Pakistan has been its founder, the Quaid-i-Azam, who observed that "certain evil customs had crept into Muslim society and were eating into the vitals of the body politic. . . . those customs had neither the sanction of Islam nor did common sense justify their perpetuation." *Dawn,* November 5, 1946.
119. Iqbal, *The Reconstruction of Religious Thought,* p. 85.
120. Ibid., p. 138.
121. McDonough, *The Authority of the Past,* p. 36.
122. Ibid., pp. 37-46.
123. Ghulam Ahmed Parwez, *Asbab-e Zawal-e Ummat (Causes of the Downfall of the Community of Muslim Peoples),* 4th ed. (Lahore: Adara Taloo-e Islam, 1966), p. 162.
124. Ibid., pp. 162-163.
125. Sayyid Abul A'la Maududi, *The Islamic Law and Constitution,* 8th ed., translated and edited by Khurshid Ahmad (Lahore: Islamic Publications Ltd., 1983), p. 52.
126. Aziz Ahmad, *Islamic Modernism in India and Pakistan* (London: Oxford University Press, 1967), p. 247.
127. Ibid., p. 248.
128. Ibid.
129. Ibid., p. 247.
130. M. Munir and M. R. Kayani, *Report of the Court of Inquiry to Enquire into the Punjab Disturbances of 1953* (Lahore: Superintendent, Government Printing, 1954), p.

232. The report is commonly known as the Munir Report. The report, though valuable on several counts, is surprisingly biased and sympathetic toward Ahmadis or Qadianis, a sect that was created toward the end of the nineteenth century and began to call itself Islamic. The agitators in the 1953 disturbances were correctly demanding that the sect be declared non-Muslim. The National Assembly under Bhutto's administration in 1974 eventually declared the sect to be non-Muslim.

131. In 1959 President Ayub Khan wrote in the foreword to Javid Iqbal's *The Ideology of Pakistan and Its Implementation* (Lahore: Sh. Ghulam Ali and Sons, 1959): "In our ignorance we began to regard Islamic ideology as synonymous with bigotry and theocracy, and subconsciously began to fight shy of it."

132. Munir and Kayani, *Report of the Court of Inquiry,* p. 231.

133. The 1983-1984 economic survey by the government states that fertility "has displayed imperviousness to policy measures." Government of Pakistan, *Pakistan: Economic Survey 1983-1984* (Islamabad: 1984), p. 107. The survey acknowledges that the persistently high growth rate in population indicates an undue emphasis on clinical measures "to the neglect of the determinants underlying the reproductive behavior of the people [which] appears to be a major responsible factor." Ibid., p. 113.

134. Ibid.

135. *The Constitution of the Republic of Pakistan* (Karachi: Government of Pakistan Press, 1962), p. 95.

136. Ahmad, "Islamic Aspects," *Islamic Studies* 2, No. 2 (June 1963): Appendix B, p. 279.

137. Ibid., Appendix A, p. 278.

138. Ibid., Appendix B, p. 279.

139. Ibid., Appendix B, p. 282.

140. Ibid., Appendix C, p. 283.

141. Ibid. p. 266.

142. Ibid., p. 271.

143. Khalid Bin Sayeed, "Islam and National Integration in Pakistan," in Smith, ed., *South Asian Politics and Religion,* p. 413.

144. Ibid.

145. Freeland Abbot, "Pakistan and the Secular State," in ibid., p. 364. For detailed discussion of this ordinance, see Fazlur Rahman, "The Controversy Over the Muslim Family Laws," in ibid., pp. 414-427.

146. Abbot, "Pakistan and the Secular State," in Smith ed., *South Asian Politics and Religion,* p. 362.

147. Ibid.

148. In 1979 Fazlur Rahman had observed: "There can be no doubt that fundamentalism will be short-lived because being essentially a reaction, it can offer little positive, but its brief career probably will not end without doing great damage to Pakistan in several ways. . . . " See Rahman, "Iqbal the Visionary," in Naim, ed., Iqbal, *Jinnah, and Pakistan,* p. 8.

149. Wayne A. Wilcox, "Ideological Dilemmas in Pakistan's Political Culture," in Smith, ed., *South Asian Politics and Religion,* p. 351.

150. Sayyid Abul A'la Maududi, *First Principles of the Islamic State,* translated and edited by Khurshid Ahmad (Lahore: Islamic Publications Ltd., 1974), p. 4.

151. Ibid., pp. 3-5.

152. Ibid., pp. 10, 12. See also pp. 5-10. See also by the same author, *Political Theory of Islam* (Lahore: Islamic Publications Ltd., 1976), lines four through seven from the bottom of the footnote on p. 46. The author, in this and in the book quoted at n. 150, places heavy emphasis on the sunnah. Thus, he says:

"(i) It would be *ultra vires* of the parliament or the legislature to enact any law which is repugnant to the Qur'an and the *Sunnah*.

(ii) The Qur'an and the *Sunnah* would be the chief sources of the public law of the land." *Political Theory of Islam*, p. 36, n. 30.

153. Munir D. Ahmed, "Pakistan: The Dream of an Islamic State," in Caldarola, ed., *Religion and Societies*, pp. 278-279.

154. Ibid., pp. 279-280.

155. Ibid., pp. 280-281.

156. Ibid., p. 281.

157. Ibid.

158. Ibid., pp. 282-285.

159. Ahmad, "The Political Role of the Ulama," *Islamic Studies* 6 (1967): 335.

160. Choudhry, *Documents and Speeches*, p. 450.

161. Manzooruddin Ahmad, "The Political Role of the Ulama," Islamic Studies 6 (1967): 338-339.

162. William L. Richter, "The Political Meaning of Islamization in Pakistan: Prognosis, Implications, and Questions," in Anita M. Weiss, ed., *Islamic Reassertion in Pakistan* (Syracuse, N.Y.: Syracuse University Press, 1986), p. 131. In this context Zia's statement immediately after the coup is revealing. Explaining that he had no political ambitions, he said: "I was obliged to step in to fill the vacuum created by the political leaders. I have accepted this challenge as a true soldier of Islam." Dawn, July 6, 1977. That Zia may have been contemplating the overthrow of the government in power for some time is indicated by a remark he made in a conference of army officers, attended by this writer, several months before the coup. An officer in discussing a problem complained that the government was not allocating sufficient funds, and hence the problem was likely to remain unresolved. Zia, without discussing the problem, thundered: "Who's the government? I am the government."

163. The first politician who released a press statement welcoming Zia's usurpation of power was the Jamaat-i-Islami chief, Mian Tufail Mohammed, "who assured Gen. Zia of all cooperation and help to him in keeping the promises he [had] made in the broadcast." *Dawn*, July 6, 1977.

164. In August 1978 Zia associated himself with four of the nine parties of the Pakistan National Alliance to help him enforce Nizam-i-Mustafa (system of the Prophet). Two of these parties were fundamentalist religious parties—the Jamaat-i-Islami, and the Jamia-ul-Ulama-i-Islam. The principle on which these parties were selected was not explained, nor did the parties themselves explain "why they had joined the Martial Law Government except that . . . they shared General Muhammad Ziaul Haq's objective to enforce Islam and to restore democracy in the country." Muhammed Munir, *From Jinnah to Zia* (Lahore: Vanguard Books Ltd., 1980), p. 135. Through the First Shariat Benches order, P.O. 22 of 1978, the government "promised that a *shariat* bench will be set up at each High Court and a *shariat* Appellate Bench in the Supreme Court. Their

functions would be to declare a law invalid if it was repugnant to the Qur'an and sunnah. The measure was hailed by Maulana Maududi and others [ulema] as a landmark in the history of the country." Later, at the suggestion of Mian Tufail Mohammad, head of the Jamaat-i-Islami, Zia "amended the Constitution by adding the Shariat Benches Order as Chapter 3A to Part VII of the Constitution." Ibid., p. 141.

165. Ibid., p. xx.

166. *Dawn,* September 2, 1977.

167. Ibid.

168. Munir, *From Jinnah to Zia,* p. xii.

169. Weiss, ed., *Islamic Reassertion,* p. 11.

170. Keesing's Publications, *Keesing's Contemporary Archives,* Vol. XXVII (London: 1981), p. 31070.

171. Ibid. "A manifestation of Zia-al-Haq's 'Islamization' was the press interviews of a regular speaker on Islamic subjects on the TV who had chosen to accept nomination to the Majlis-i-Shoora [Majlis-i-Shoora means consultative assembly—it was one of those labels that Zia had introduced to "Islamize" Pakistan]. He [came] out with the retrogressive idea that the doors of various professions should be closed on Pakistani women on the ground that they should not mingle with male members of society and should confine themselves strictly to the four walls of their homes." Mohammad Asghar Khan, *Generals in Politics: Pakistan 1958-1982* (London: Croom Helm, 1983), p. 219.

172. As Faruki has observed, "Zia-ul-Haq [had] prescribed 'national' dress for officials that merely [accentuated] provincial and ethnic differences. This hostility to contemporary clothing of international design [was] also symptomatic of an unhealthy xenophobia that [had] infected the country to the detriment of culture and knowledge." Kemal A. Faruki, "Pakistan: Islamic Government and Society," in Esposito ed., *Islam in Asia,* p. 74.

173. Weiss, ed., *Islamic Reassertion,* p. 13. See also pp. 14-15.

174. *The Pakistan Times,* overseas weekly, July 10, 1988.

175. Ibid.

176. Keesing's, Vol. XXVII (1981), p. 31070. In 1982 the government instituted "a pre-admission test in Islamic ideology for college and university [Muslim] students." Ibid., Vol. XXXIII (1987), p. 34992.

177. Grace Clark, "Pakistan's Zakat and 'Ushr as a Welfare System," in Weiss, ed., *Islamic Reassertion,* p. 93. In 1984 the amount raised by the zakat levy was "about Rs 1 billion ($75 million) compared to the state's secular revenues of Rs 60 billion ($4.5 billion). . . . it has not eliminated poverty in the past and the amount being collected by government is unlikely to do so, let alone serve as a substitute for secular taxes for administration and development." Faruki, "Pakistan: Islamic Government," in Esposito, ed., *Islam in Asia,* p. 63.

178. Shahid Javed Burki, "Economic Management Within an Islamic Context," in Weiss, ed., *Islamic Reassertion,* p. 50.

179. Ibid.

180. Ibid., pp. 51-52. The passage is reintegrated from these pages.

181. Ibid., p. 53.

182. Ibid., p. 51.

183. Keesing's, Vol. XXXIII (1987), p. 34992.

184. Burki, "Economic Management," in Weiss, ed., *Islamic Reassertion*, p. 50.

185. Ibid., p. 51.

186. Weiss, ed., *Islamic Reassertion*, p. xv.

187. Weiss, "The Historical Debate on Islam and the State in South Asia," in Weiss, ed., *Islamic Reassertion*, p. 15.

188. Burki, "Economic Management," in Weiss, ed., *Islamic Reassertion*, p. 55.

189. Ibid. At present, it is the ninth most populous country in the world.

190. Keesing's, Vol. XXXIII (1987), p. 34992.

191. Ibid.

192. Smith, *Pakistan as an Islamic State*, pp. 96-97.

193. Ibid., p. 97.

194. Ibid., p. 98.

195. Ibid., pp. 97-98.

196. *Speeches and Statements by Field Marshal Mohammad Ayub Khan*, Vol. III, July 1960-June 1961, p. 139.

197. Ibid.

198. Hafiz Nazar Ahmed, *Ja'iza-ei Madaris-e 'Arabiyyah Islamyyah Maghrabi Pakistan (Survey of Arabic Islamic Schools of West Pakistan)* (Lahore: Muslim Academy, 1972), p. 13.

199. Ibid., p. 628.

200. Ibid., p. 611.

201. Ibid., p. 610.

202. Ibid., p. 614.

203. Ibid.

204. Ibid., p. 650.

205. Ibid., p. 690.

206. *The Economist*, September 3, 1988, p. 16.

207. Ibid., p. 17.

208. Rafique Akhtar, *Pakistan Year Book*, 13th ed., (Karachi: East and West Publishing Co., 1985), pp. 6-8.

209. Ibid., p. 277.

210. Ibid., p. 289.

211. Saghir Ahmad, "Islam and Pakistani Peasants," in Aziz Ahmad ed., *Contributions to Asian Studies*, Vol. 2, (Leiden: E. J. Brill, 1971), p. 96.

212. Hafeez Malik, "The Spirit of Capitalism and Pakistani Islam," in ibid., p. 68.

213. Ibid., p. 69; Khalid B. Sayeed, *The Political System of Pakistan* (Boston: Houghton Mifflin Co., 1967), p. 152.

214. Sayeed, *The Political System*, p. 149.

215. Burki, "Economic Management," in Weiss, ed., *Islamic Reassertion*, p. 54.

216. Sayeed, *The Political System*, pp. 148-149.

217. Asghar Khan, *Generals in Politics*, pp. 194-195.

218. Ibid.

219. Burki, "Economic Management," in Weiss, ed., *Islamic Reassertion*, p. 54.

220. Ibid.

221. Government of Pakistan, *Pakistan: Economic Survey 1983-84* (Islamabad: Ministry of Finance, 1984), p. xiv.

222. Akhtar, *Pakistan Year Book,* 13th ed., p. 331.

223. Asghar Khan, *Generals in Politics,* p. 195.

224. Ibid.

225. Ibid., p. 196.

226. Ibid.

227. Ibid., p. 197.

228. For details, see Victoria Schofield, *Bhutto—Trial and Execution* (London: Cassell, 1981).

229. Asghar Khan, *Generals in Politics,* p. 147; see also pp. 205-207, 219-224. The sixth five year plan made no provision for the redistribution of landownership, although landless peasants form the bulk of the rural population. No agricultural income tax was proposed, and no serious measures were suggested to reduce income inequality. See S. M. Huda, "Did it Work in Pakistan?," *Development* 4 (1985): 75.

230. Shahid Javed Burki and Robert Laporte, Jr., eds., "The Political and Social Environment for Development," in *Pakistan's Development Priorities: Choices for the Future* (Karachi: Oxford University Press, 1984), p. 13.

231. Rafique Akhtar, *Pakistan Year Book,* 10th ed. (Karachi: East and West Publishing Co., 1982-1983), p. 285.

232. Ibid., 13th ed., 1985-1986, pp. 253-254.

233. Ibid., pp. 254-255.

234. *Pakistan: An Official Handbook, 1984* (Islamabad: Ministry of Information and Broadcasting, 1985), p. 58.

235. Shahid Javed Burki, "A Historical Perspective on Development," in Burki and Laporte, Jr., eds., *Pakistan's Development Priorities,* p. 32.

236. Ibid.

237. Ibid., pp. 32-33.

238. Ibid., p. 33.

239. Ibid., p. 34.

240. Faruki, "Pakistan: Islamic Government," in Esposito, ed., *Islam in Asia,* p. 61.

241. Burki, "A Historical Perspective," in Burki and Laporte, eds., *Pakistan's Development Priorities,* p. 39.

242. Ibid., p. 29.

243. Gibb, *Modern Trends in Islam,* p. 3.

244. Theda Skocpol, *States and Social Revolutions: A Comparative Analysis of France, Russia, and China* (Cambridge: Cambridge University Press, 1981), p. 29.

245. Ibid., p. 3.

246. Ibid.

247. Ibid., pp. 292-293.

248. Mazheruddin Siddiqi, "Trends of Muslim Thought in Pakistan," in *Colloquium on Islamic Culture in its Relation to the Contemporary World* (Princeton, N.J.: Princeton University Press, 1953), p. 87.

249. Burki, "A Historical Perspective," in Burki and Laporte, eds., *Pakistan's Development Priorities,* p. 31.

250. Karl Marx, "The Eighteenth Brumaire of Louis Bonaparte," in McLellan, ed., *Karl Marx: Selected Writings* (Oxford: Oxford University Press, 1977), reintegrated from pp. 302, 300.

CHAPTER 6

1. Richard F. Nyrop, ed., *Egypt: A Country Study* (Washington, D.C.: American University, 1983), 4th ed., pp. 161-162.

2. President Nasser's foreword in Anwar el Sadat, *Revolt on the Nile* (New York: John Day Co., 1957), p. 6.

3. Ibid., p. 60.

4. Louis J. Cantori, "Religion and Politics in Egypt," in Michael Curtis, ed., *Religion and Politics in the Middle East* (Boulder, Colo.: Westview Press, 1981), p. 80.

5. Ibid., see also Sadat, *Revolt on the Nile,* pp. 91-92.

6. H. B. Sharabi, *Government and Politics of the Middle East in the Twentieth Century* (Princeton, N.J.: D. Van Nostrand, 1963), p. 202.

7. Ibid., pp. 202-203.

8. Ibid., p. 203.

9. John S. Badeau, "Introduction" in Gamal Abdel Nasser, *The Philosophy of the Revolution* (Buffalo, N.Y.: Smith, Keynes and Marshall, 1959), p. 17.

10. Nasser, *The Philosophy of the Revolution,* p. 32.

11. Ibid., p. 34.

12. Ibid., p. 35. But Nasser himself had no clear idea how the society was to be reformed and reconstructed. As Badeau has observed, Nasser's coup was aimed at the overthrow of a corrupt and unstable government, but little thought was given to what would replace the old order. Nasser "speaks as though a new plan for national life would miraculously spring from the minds of the intelligentsia, like the fabled Egyptian phoenix arising from the ashes of its own death." John S. Badeau, "A Role in Search of a Hero: A Brief Study of the Egyptian Revolution," *The Middle East Journal* 9, No. 4 (Autumn 1955): 375.

13. Nasser, *The Philosophy of the Revolution,* p. 36.

14. Sharabi observes that "lacking a definite doctrine, the Free Officers acted by rule of thumb." Sharabi, *Government and Politics,* p. 209. Nasser seems to have been more concerned with external affairs and image-making than with serious domestic problems. Thus, Wheelock's analysis shows that Nasser was more interested in foreign affairs than in pressing issues of internal development. Keith Wheelock, *Nasser's New Egypt* (New York: Praeger, 1960).

15. Nyrop, ed., *Egypt,* p. 26.

16. Ibrahim Ibrahim, "Islamic Revival in Egypt and Greater Syria," in Cyriac K. Pullapilly, ed., *Islam in the Contemporary World* (Notre Dame, Ind.: Cross Roads Books, 1980), p. 163.

17. Ibid.

18. Ibid.

19. Dan Hofstadter, ed., *Egypt and Nasser: Volume I, 1952-56* (New York: Facts on File, 1973), p. 56.

20. Ibid.

21. Ibid., pp. 57-60. A day after the agreement was concluded, the Brotherhood had charged, on solid grounds, that "the new agreement bound Egypt to unfavorable conditions at a time when the 1936 Anglo-Egyptian Agreement had almost expired."

Wheelock, *Nasser's New Egypt*, p. 43.

22. Ibid., pp. 60-61.

23. Harold B. Barclay, "Egypt: Struggling with Secularization," in Carlo Caldarola, ed., *Religion and Societies: Asia and the Middle East* (Berlin: Mouton, 1982), p. 127.

24. Ibid., p. 134.

25. Bruce M. Borthwick, "Religion and Politics in Israel and Egypt," *The Middle East Journal* 33, No. 2 (Spring 1979): 153.

26. Ibid., p. 156.

27. Ibid.

28. Ibid., p. 158.

29. Ibid.

30. "Constitution of the Arab Republic of Egypt," *The Middle East Journal* 26, No. 1 (Winter 1972): 55.

31. Joseph P. O'Kane, "Islam in the New Egyptian Constitution: Some Discussions in al-Ahram," *The Middle East Journal* 26, No. 2 (Spring 1972): 138.

32. Ibid., p. 141.

33. Ibid., p. 139.

34. Ibid., pp. 139-140.

35. Ibid., p. 145.

36. Ibid., p. 148.

37. "Constitution," *The Middle East Journal* 26, No. 1 (Winter 1972): 55.

38. Borthwick, "Religion and Politics," *The Middle East Journal* 33, No. 2 (Spring 1979): 159.

39. Ibid.

40. Ibid., p. 160.

41. Ibid., pp. 156-157.

42. Ibid., p. 162.

43. P. J. Vatikiotis, *The Egyptian Army in Politics* (Bloomington: Indiana University Press, 1961), pp. 190-191.

44. Borthwick, "Religion and Politics," *The Middle East Journal* 33, No. 2 (Spring 1979): 157.

45. Barclay, "Egypt," in Caldarola, ed., *Religion and Societies,* p. 137.

46. Ibid.

47. Fred De Jong, "Aspects of the Political Involvement of *Sufi* Orders in Twentieth Century Egypt (1907-1970)—An Exploratory Stock-Taking," in Gabriel R. Warburg and Uri M. Kupferschmidt, eds., *Islam, Nationalism and Radicalism in Egypt and the Sudan* (New York: Praeger, 1983), p. 196.

48. Ibid.

49. Ibid. For a good study of the Sufi orders in Egypt, see Michael Gilsenan, *Saint and Sufi in Modern Egypt* (Oxford: Oxford University Press, 1973).

50. Charles C. Adams, *Islam and Modernism in Egypt* (1933; reprinted., New York: Russell and Russell, 1968), p. 188.

51. Ibid., p. 189.

52. Ibid.

53. Warburg and Kupferschmidt, eds., *Islam, Nationalism and Radicalism,* p. 197.

54. Ibid.

55. For details see ibid., pp. 198-205.

56. Ibid., pp. 201-202.

57. Ibid., pp. 203-204.

58. Barclay, "Egypt," in Caldarola, ed., *Religion and Societies*, p. 139.

59. Cantori, "Religion and Politics," in Curtis, ed., *Religion and Politics*, p. 83.

60. Ibid., p. 85.

61. Ibid., p. 83.

62. Barclay, "Egypt," in Caldarola, ed., *Religion and Societies*, p. 139.

63. Cantori, "Religion and Politics," in Curtis, ed., *Religion and Politics*, p. 84.

64. Ibid., p. 86.

65. Ibid., p. 83.

66. Vatikiotis, for instance, suggests that leadership should "remove religion from the public realm altogether and relegate it to the realm of private belief." P. J. Vatikiotis, "Religion and State," in Warburg and Kupferschmidt, eds., *Islam, Nationalism and Radicalism*, p. 69. He himself also acknowledges that from 1820 to 1923 religion in Egypt was in the retreat (pp. 57-58), which is to say that for all practical purposes Egypt was a secular state in which "state primary, secondary, and higher education grew with curricula modeled along European lines" (p. 57).

67. Daniel Crecelius, "Al-Azhar in the Revolution," *The Middle East Journal* 20, No. 1 (Winter 1966): 32.

68. Ibid., p. 33.

69. Ibid., p. 36.

70. Ibid., p. 33.

71. Ibid., p. 39.

72. Ibid., p. 36.

73. Ibid., p. 40.

74. Vatikiotis, "Religion and State," in Warburg and Kupferschmidt, eds., *Islam, Nationalism and Radicalism*, p. 68.

75. Ibid.

76. Ibid., p. 69.

77. Ibid.

78. Nabil A. Khoury, "Islam and Modernization in the Middle East: Muhammad Abduh, an Ideology of Development," Ph.D. dissertation, State University of New York at Albany, 1976, p. 18.

79. Nadav Safran, *Egypt in Search of Political Community* (Cambridge, Mass.: Harvard University Press, 1961), p. 63.

80. Ibid., pp. 64-65.

81. Ibid., p. 63.

82. Ibid.

83. Ibid., p. 72.

84. Ibid., pp. 71-72.

85. Ibid., p. 76; see also p. 74.

86. Richard N. Frye, *Islam and the West: Proceedings of the Harvard Summer School Conference on the Middle East* (The Hague: Mouton, 1957), pp. 166-167.

87. Ibid., p. 167.

88. Ibid., pp. 167-168.

89. Ibid., p. 170.

90. Albert Hourani, *Arabic Thought in the Liberal Age: 1798-1939* (London: Oxford University Press, 1962), pp. 161-162.

91. Ibid., p. 168.

92. Ibid., pp. 168, 175-176.

93. Ibid., pp. 168-169.

94. For details, see ibid., p. 225.

95. Ibid., p. 228.

96. Ibid.

97. Ibid., p. 236.

98. Ibid., p. 233.

99. Ibid., p. 239.

100. Adams, *Islam and Modernism*, pp. 185-186.

101. Ibid., p. 190.

102. Ibid., pp. 195-196.

103. Menahem Milson, "Taha Husayn's 'The Tree of Misery': A Literary Expression of Cultural Change," *Asian and African Studies* 3 (1967): 88.

104. Ibid., p. 82.

105. Israel Gershoni, "Egyptian Intellectual History and Egyptian Intellectuals in the Interwar Period," *Asian and African Studies* 19, No. 3 (November 1985): 342-343.

106. Ibid.

107. Ibid., pp. 343, 345.

108. Ibid., p. 347.

109. Fazlur Rahman, "Islamic Studies and the Future of Islam," in Malcolm H. Kerr ed., *Islamic Studies: A Tradition and its Problems* (Malibu, Calif.: Undena Publications, 1980), p. 130.

110. Ibid.

111. Ibid.

112. Ibid., pp. 132-133.

113. Gershoni, "Egyptian Intellectual," *Asian and African Studies* 19, No. 3 (November 1985): 347-348.

114. Ibid., p. 348. For a good example of the ideology of religious groups in Egypt, see Michael Youssef, *Revolt Against Modernity: Muslim Zealots and the West* (Leiden: E. J. Brill, 1985), pp. 69-75, Chapter 11, and Appendix I.

115. Khalid M. Khalid, *From Here We Start*, trans. Ismail R. el-Faruqi (Washington, D.C.: American Council of Learned Societies, 1953), pp. 3-9.

116. Ibid., p. 4.

117. Ibid., pp. 103-104; see also pp. 97-102, 105-109.

118. Ibid., p. 18.

119. Ibid., pp. 109-110.

120. Ibid., p. 113. In this context, however, Khalid himself quotes two rather strange traditions and believes them. Ibid.

121. Ibid., p. 65.

122. P. J. Vatikiotis, *The Modern History of Egypt* (New York: Praeger, 1969), p. 323.

123. Daniel Crecilius, "The Course of Secularization in Modern Egypt," in John L.

Esposito, ed., *Islam and Development: Religion and Sociopolitical Change* (Syracuse, N.Y.: Syracuse University Press, 1980), p. 66.

124. Ibid.

125. Ibid., pp. 66-67.

126. Ibid., p. 67.

127. Rahman, "Islamic Studies" in Kerr, ed., *Islamic Studies,* p. 132.

128. Ibid.

129. Ibid.

130. Crecilius, "The Course of Secularization," in Esposito, ed., *Islam and Development,* p. 67.

131. Ibid.

132. Crecilius seems to make this argument. He also strongly advocates the separation of religion and politics, and he sees secularism as the key to modernization (ibid., pp. 68-70). But secularism cannot bring modernization to Muslim societies. The need there is of a different nature: the resolution, first of all, of the ideological confusion, and widespread understanding of the ideology in the population, which means an active and intelligent study of the source of Islam — the Qur'an. It is disastrous, therefore, for Muslim societies to separate religion from the polity in that sense. It does not, however, mean that religion should become an object of politics. In that sense, therefore, there is a strong case for the separation of religion from politics. Such a separation cannot be brought about by mere declarations. An awareness of such a separation, and the separation itself, can emerge only when the contents of the Qur'an are widely understood in the population. In such a situation, however, the separation, in an ultimate sense, breaks down. This is so because "Islam . . . is marked by fundamental unity. The distinction between . . . the spiritual and the temporal, is meaningless in Muslim doctrine, since one and the same text, the Qur'an, revealed by God to the Prophet Muhammad, contains both the rules regulating relations between man and God and the principles governing social life." Gilles Kepel, *Muslim Extremism in Egypt: The Prophet and Pharaoh* (Berkeley: University of California Press, 1985), p. 228.

133. It is totally wrong to think that modernity can be achieved in Muslim countries without Islam, as Gabriel Warburg suggests: "The resurgence of Islam may be a purely defensive phenomenon or perhaps a religious backlash that is no more than a holding operation against modernity. Indeed, many Muslim scholars both in Egypt and elsewhere argue that Islam is fighting a losing battle." Warburg, "Introduction," in Warburg and Kupferschmidt, eds., *Islam, Nationalism and Radicalism,* p. 8.

134. Vatikiotis, "Religion and State," in ibid., p. 61.

135. Eventually, the religious groups were to acquire such power and legitimacy that they were able "to challenge and frighten state authority to such a degree as to require massive and brutal suppression by the state." See ibid.

136. Ahmed M. Gomaa, "Islamic Fundamentalism in Egypt during the 1930s and 1970s: Comparative Notes," in ibid., p. 147.

137. Ibid.

138. Ibid.

139. Warburg, "Introduction," in ibid., p. 10.

140. Ibid., p. 11.

141. Guenter Levy, "Nasserism and Islam: A Revolution in Search of Ideology," in Donald Eugene Smith, ed., *Religion and Political Modernization* (New Haven, Conn.:

Yale University Press, 1974), p. 277.

142. Osman Amin, *Muhammad Abduh,* trans. Charles Wendell (Washington, D.C.: American Council of Learned Societies, 1953), p. 77.

143. Ibid., p. 78.

144. Ibid., p. 85.

145. Hava Lazarus-Yafeh, "Contemporary Religious Thought Among the Ulama of Al-Azhar," *Asian and African Studies* 7, Special Number (1971): 214-215.

146. Ibid., p. 215.

147. A. L. Tibawi, *Islamic Education* (New York: Crane, Russak and Co., 1972), pp. 119-120.

148. Ibid., p. 117.

149. Lazarus-Yafeh, "Contemporary Religious Thought," *Asian and African Studies* 7, Special Number (1971): 159.

150. Ibid., p. 185.

151. Ibid., pp. 184-185.

152. Ibid., pp. 164-165.

153. Ibid., p. 166.

154. Ibid., p. 170.

155. Ibid., pp. 170-174.

156. Ibid., pp. 177-183.

157. Crecelius, "Al-Azhar," *The Middle East Journal* 20, No. 1 (Winter 1966): 39.

158. Jörg Kraemer, "Tradition and Reform at Al-Azhar University," *Middle Eastern Affairs* 7, No. 1 (1956): 89.

159. Crecelius, "Al-Azhar," *The Middle East Journal* 20, No. 1 (1966): 48.

160. J. Heyworth-Dunne, *An Introduction to the History of Education in Modern Egypt* (1939; reprint ed., London: Frank Cass and Co., 1968), p. 41.

161. Ibid., pp. 75, 71. For details of subjects covered and the material used in these institutions, see ibid., pp. 72-75, 43-44.

162. In 1966 there were 4,000 Muslim missions from other countries studying at al-Azhar. Crecelius, "Al-Azhar," *The Middle East Journal* 20, No. 1 (Winter 1966): 46-47.

163. Morroe Berger, *Islam in Egypt Today* (Cambridge: Cambridge University Press, 1970), pp. 38, 42.

164. Ibid., p. 61.

165. Ibid.

166. Ibid., p. 129.

167. Richard P. Mitchell, *The Society of the Muslim Brothers* (London: Oxford University Press, 1969), p. 284.

168. Ibid., p. 285.

169. Ibid., p. 286.

170. Joseph S. Szyliowicz, *Education and Modernization in the Middle East* (Ithaca, N.Y.: Cornell University Press, 1973), pp. 261-262.

171. Ibid., p. 262.

172. Ibid., pp. 263-264.

173. Ibid., p. 265.

174. Ibid., p. 266.

175. Ibid., p. 268.

176. Ibid., p. 272.

177. The above two paragraphs are based on pp. 269-305 in ibid. Egypt has not made any significant progress in female education since 1960; enrollment in primary schools has increased only by 4 percent over the 1960 figure when it stood at 52 percent for this age group. See Byron G. Massialas and Samir Ahmed Jarrar, *Education in the Arab World* (New York: Praeger, 1983), p. 258.

178. Szyliowicz, *Education and Modernization,* p. 307.

179. Jack H. Thompson and Robert D. Reischauer, eds., *Modernization of the Arab World* (Princeton, N.J.: D. Van Nostrand, 1966), p. 64.

180. Ibid., p. 68.

181. Mitchell, *The Society of the Muslim Brothers,* pp. 282-283.

182. Thompson and Reischauer, eds., *Modernization of the Arab World,* pp. 68-69.

183. Ibid., p. 71.

184. Ibid., pp. 73-74.

185. Hans E. Tütsch, *From Ankara to Marakesh: Turks and Arabs in a Changing World* (London: Allen and Unwin, 1964), pp. 122-123.

186. Ibid., pp. 119-120.

187. Bent Hansen, "Planning and Economic Growth in the UAR (Egypt), 1960-5," in P. J. Vatikiotis, ed., *Egypt Since the Revolution* (New York: Praeger, 1968), pp. 32-33.

188. John Waterbury, *The Egypt of Nasser and Sadat: The Political Economy of Two Regimes* (Princeton, N.J.: Princeton University Press, 1983), p. 33.

189. Ibid.

190. Thompson and Reischauer, eds., *Modernization of the Arab World,* p. 68.

191. Ibid., p. 84.

192. William J. Burns, *Economic Aid and American Policy Toward Egypt: 1955-1981* (Albany: State University of New York Press, 1985), p. 21.

193. Waterbury, *The Egypt of Nasser and Sadat,* p. 32.

194. Ibid.

195. Ibid., pp. 32-33.

196. Ibid., p. 33.

197. Ibid., p. 34.

198. Ibid., pp. 31-32.

199. Ibid., p. 36.

200. Mark N. Cooper, *The Transformation of Egypt* (London: Croom Helm, 1982), p. 91.

201. Ibid., pp. 94-101.

202. Ibid., pp. 106-107.

203. Ibid., p. 120.

204. For a good illustration of the present value systems and the state of the society, see Unni Wikan, *Life Among the Poor in Cairo* (London: Tavistock Publications, 1980).

205. Waterbury, *The Egypt of Nasser and Sadat,* pp. 41-43.

206. Ibid., p. 45.

207. Alan C. Kelley et al., *Population and Development in Rural Egypt* (Durham, N.C.: Duke University Press, 1982), pp. 3-4. The book analyzes the population

problem in Egypt in great depth and highlights the prevalent attitudes in the masses on this serious issue.

208. Ibid., pp. 48-49.
209. Ibid., p. 52.
210. Ibid., pp. 254-257.
211. Ibid., p. 256.
212. Ibid., p. 260.
213. Ibid., p. 434.
214. Ibid. See also Khalid Ikram, *Egypt: Economic Management in a Period of Transition* (Baltimore: Johns Hopkins University Press, 1980), pp. 68-69. This book is a detailed and excellent analysis of Egypt's economy with policy recommendations.
215. Ikram, *Egypt: Economic Management,* p. 52.
216. Ibid.
217. Derek Hopwood, *Egypt: Politics and Society, 1945-1984* (Boston: Allen and Unwin, 1985), p. 189.
218. Waterbury, *The Egypt of Nasser and Sadat,* p. 121.
219. Ibid., pp. 242, 245.
220. Halim Barkat, "Ideological Determinants of Arab Development," in I. Ibrahim, ed., *Arab Resources: The Transformation of a Society* (London: Croom Helm, 1983), p. 182.
221. Ibid., p. 173.
222. For illustration of this point, see Gabriel R. Warburg, "Islam and Politics in Egypt: 1952-80," *Middle East Studies* 18, No. 2 (April 1982): 131-157.
223. Khoury, "Islam and Modernization," Ph.D. dissertation, p. 120.
224. Ibid., p. 123.
225. Ibid., p. 32.

CHAPTER 7

1. H. B. Sharabi, *A Handbook of the Contemporary Middle East* (Washington, D.C.: Georgetown University, 1956), pp. 86-87.
2. Meral Güclü, *Turkey* (Oxford: Clio Press, 1981), pp. xxv-xxvii.
3. Albert Hourani, *Arabic Thought in the Liberal Age: 1798-1939* (London: Oxford University Press, 1962), p. 185.
4. Ibid.
5. Ibid.
6. Wilfred Cantwell Smith, *Pakistan as an Islamic State* (Lahore: Shaikh Muhammad Ashraf, 1951), pp. 87-88.
7. Ibid., p. 69.
8. Ibid., pp. 74-75.
9. Ibid., pp. 48, 47.
10. Ibid., pp. 48-49.
11. Hourani, *Arabic Thought in the Liberal Age,* p. 184.
12. Ibid.; see also pp. 184-192.
13. Sharabi, *A Handbook of the Contemporary Middle East,* pp. 87-88.

14. Elanor Bisbee, *The New Turks: Pioneers of the Republic, 1920-1950* (Philadelphia: University of Pennsylvania Press, 1956), 3rd printing, p. 23.

15. Ibid., p. 24.

16. Ibid., p. 21.

17. Donald Everett Webster, *The Turkey of Atatürk: Social Process in the Turkish Reformation* (Philadelphia: American Academy of Political and Social Science, 1939), p. 20.

18. Fazlur Rahman, "Implementation of the Islamic Concept of State in the Pakistani Milieu," *Islamic Studies* 6, No. 3 (September 1967): 212-213.

19. E.W.F. Tomlin, *Turkey: The Modern Miracle* (London: Watts and Co., 1940), p. 35.

20. Webster, *The Turkey of Atatürk*, pp. 169-170.

21. *A Speech Delivered by Ghazi Mustapha Kemal, President of the Turkish Republic, October 1927* (Leipzig: K. F. Koehler, 1929), p. 684.

22. Ibid., p. 721.

23. Ibid.

24. Tomlin, *Turkey*, p. 36.

25. *A Speech Delivered by Ghazi Mustapha Kemal*, p. 722.

26. Ibid.

27. Ibid., p. 718.

28. Ibid., pp. 717-718.

29. Ibid., p. 717.

30. Ibid.; see also pp. 62, 259-261.

31. Ibid., p. 720.

32. Webster, *The Turkey of Atatürk*, p. 171.

33. Ibid.

34. Ibid. Atatürk emphasized the crucial role of leadership in such undertakings. In all great enterprises, he observed, the condition of success is that there must be a leader available who possesses special qualifications and untiring energy. See *A Speech Delivered by Ghazi Mustafa Kemal*, p. 62.

35. *A Speech Delivered by Ghazi Mustafa Kemal*, p. 16.

36. Ibid., p. 158.

37. Ibid., pp., 158-159.

38. Ibid., p. 160.

39. Ibid., p. 78.

40. Ibid., p. 80.

41. E.W.F. Tomlin, *Life in Modern Turkey* (London: Thomas Nelson and Sons, 1946), pp. 71-72.

42. Ibid., pp. 72-73.

43. Binnaz Sayari, "Religion and Political Development in Turkey," Ph.D. dissertation, City University of New York, 1976, p. 171.

44. Ibid; see also p. 145, n. 39, in ibid.

45. John Grant, *Through the Garden of Allah* (London: John Gifford Limited, 1938), pp. 56-57.

46. Niyazi Berkes, "Ziya Gökalp: His Contribution to Turkish Nationalism," *The Middle East Journal* 8 No. 4 (Autumn 1954): 375.

47. Ibid., pp. 375-376.
48. Ibid., pp. 376-377.
49. Ibid., p. 379.
50. Ibid.
51. Ibid., p. 384.
52. Ibid.
53. Ibid.
54. Ibid., pp. 385-388.
55. Ibid., p. 388.
56. Ibid.
57. Ibid., p. 389.
58. Ibid., p. 387.
59. Ibid., p. 390.
60. Gökalp considered secularism to be a condition for Turkey to become a modern country. Niyazi Berkes, trans. and ed., *Turkish Nationalism and Western Civilization: Selected Essays of Ziya Gökalp* (London: Allen and Unwin, 1959), p. 144.
61. Ibid., p. 185.
62. Lilo Linke, *Allah Dethroned: A Journey Through Modern Turkey* (London: Constable and Co., 1937), p. 30.
63. Ibid., pp. 36, 50.
64. Berkes, ed., *Turkish Nationalism and Western Civilization*, p. 199.
65. Ibid., pp. 199-200.
66. Ibid., p. 201.
67. Taha Parla, *The Social and Political Thought of Ziya Gökalp: 1876-1924* (Leiden: E. J. Brill, 1985), p. 121.
68. Ibid.
69. In this context, several philosophers' conclusion "that beliefs and opinions are not mere passive ideas, but effective forces, creative or destructive," is apt. See ibid., p. 41.
70. Uriel Heyd, *Foundations of Turkish Nationalism: The Life and Teachings of Ziya Gökalp* (London: Luzac and Co., 1950), p. 82.
71. The responsibility for this also falls on Gökalp. On this point, therefore, I disagree with Heyd and Parla (Heyd, p. 82; Parla, p. 38).
72. Heyd, *Foundations of Turkish Nationalism*, p. 85.
73. This view is further reinforced because of Gökalp's reliance on "traditions", which he occasionally quotes in his writings. See, for instance, pp. 87 and 98 in ibid. However, he did say that law should be modified according to the requirements of the age or the collective consciousness of society. Ibid., pp. 85, 86.
74. Ibid., p. 89.
75. Ibid., p. 91.
76. For Gökalp's views on the positive and negative symbolic practices and ceremonies, see ibid., p. 84.
77. Parla, *The Social and Political Thought of Ziya Gökalp*, pp. 73, 70.
78. Ibid., p. 70.
79. Ibid., p. 72.
80. Niyazi Berkes, *The Development of Secularism in Turkey* (Montreal: McGill

University, 1964), p. 264.

81. Parla, *The Social and Political Thought of Ziya Gökalp*, p. 42.

82. Ibid., p. 46.

83. Ibid., pp. 50, 51, 49.

84. Berkes, *The Development of Secularism in Turkey*, p. 290.

85. Ibid., p. 259. Compare this with the "Islamization program" of the Zia regime in Pakistan as noted in Chapter 5. Zia personally instituted the practice of worshipping in offices.

86. Parla, *The Social and Political Thought of Ziya Gökalp*, p. 7.

87. Ibid., p. 120.

88. Ibid., pp. 93, 121, 125.

89. Ibid., p. 121.

90. Ibid., p. 93.

91. Berkes, *The Development of Secularism in Turkey*, pp. 210-211.

92. Ibid., p. 213.

93. Ibid.

94. Ibid., pp. 216, 218.

95. Ibid., pp. 217-218.

96. For details see ibid., pp. 223-250.

97. John Robert Barnes, *An Introduction to Religious Foundations in the Ottoman Empire* (Leiden: E. J. Brill, 1987), p. 110 and elsewhere. The book provides a good account of the development of religious foundations under the Ottoman empire. The author's main conclusion from the study however, is astounding: "The decline of this institution in the nineteenth century led to the general material impoverishment of Islam that is witnessed today" (p. ix). Actually, the reverse is true.

98. Ibid., pp. 42-43.

99. Ibid., p. 110.

100. Ibid.

101. Ibid., p. 153.

102. Ibid., p. 152.

103. Ibid., p. 152.

104. Berkes, *The Development of Secularism in Turkey*, pp. 501-502.

105. Ibid., p. 501.

106. Ibid., p. 502.

107. Ibid., pp. 502-503.

108. Sayari, "Religion and Political Development," Ph.D. dissertation, p. 214, n. 31.

109. Ibid.

110. Ibid., pp. 160-161. Sayari takes unnecessary issue with the fact that Atatürk had also utilized the then powerful Islamic symbols, the sultanate and the caliphate, in the liberation effort and later abandoned them (pp. 161-162). Atatürk, in his Six-Day Speech has explained that it was politically essential at that time to do so. See also Dankwart A. Rustow, "Politics and Islam in Turkey 1920-1955" in Richard N. Frye, ed., *Islam and the West* (The Hague: Mouton, 1957), p. 70.

111. Sayari, "Religion and Political Development," Ph.D. dissertation, pp. 161-162, 175.

112. Ibid., pp. 163-164.

113. Ibid., p. 166.

114. Atatürk, in a speech at the opening of the new law school in Ankara on November 5, 1925, explained how prevalent religious laws and their exponents had brought ruination to the country. It took three centuries before the printing press was allowed into Turkey. The "greatest and . . . the most insidious enemies of the revolutionaries" were the "rotten laws and their decrepit upholders." See Bernard Lewis, *The Emergence of Modern Turkey* (London: Oxford University Press, 1961), pp. 268-269. Metin Heper thinks that the ambivalence toward Islam shown by the present-day educated elite in Turkey is "due primarily to the fact that they, rather than the masses, had been under the cast-iron theory of Islam." See Metin Heper, "Islam, Polity and Society in Turkey: A Middle Eastern Perspective," *The Middle East Journal* 35, No. 2 (Summer 1981): 358. Actually, the reason for this is that the "educated elite" are ignorant of Islam.

115. During the Kemalist era, for example, the influential Dr. Riza Nur (1879-1942) "called for a return to Ottomanism. While he accepted the Republican form of government, he wanted Islam to be the official state religion." Jacob M. Landau, *Radical Politics in Modern Turkey* (Leiden: E. J. Brill, 1974), p. 193.

116. Serif Mardin, "Turkey: Islam and Westernization," in Carlo Caldarola, ed., *Religion and Societies: Asia and the Middle East* (Berlin: Mouton, 1982), p. 180. Islam, however, has a direct concern with material life and worldly concerns.

117. Ibid., pp. 180-181.

118. Ibid., p. 181.

119. Sayari, "Religion and Political Development," Ph.D. dissertation, pp. 176, 182.

120. Ibid., pp. 182-183.

121. Ibid., pp. 184-185.

122. Ibid., pp. 185-186.

123. Ibid., pp. 186-187.

124. In 1945 a widespread religious order, called Nurcular or "disciples of Nur" following the name of its leader Saidi Kurdi, sometimes called Saidi Nursi, came to the fore. The religious order continued its activities mostly underground and demanded in the 1950s, 1960s and 1970s that the outlawed sharia be made the law of Turkey. Citing Saudi Arabia as an example, it claimed that there was no need for any constitution save the Qur'an. It "recommended polygamy, traditional dress and other measures consonant with the *seria* [sharia]." See Landau, *Radical Politics in Modern Turkey*, pp. 183-185.

125. Sayari, "Religion and Political Development," Ph.D. dissertation, pp. 187-188.

126. The above two paragraphs are based on pp. 189-195 in ibid.

127. Ibid., p. 202. Sayari's conclusion that religion as a source of mass mobilization has been an important factor in the political development of Turkey (p. 211) is seriously flawed and misleading.

128. Hans E. Tütsch, *From Ankara to Marakesh: Turks and Arabs in a Changing World* (London: Allen and Unwin, 1964), pp. 20, 27.

129. Walker F. Weiker, *The Modernization of Turkey: From Ataturk to the Present Day* (New York: Holmes and Meier, 1981), p. 105.

130. Mardin, "Turkey: Islam and Westernization," in Caldarola, ed., *Religion and*

Societies, p. 182.

131. Ibid.

132. Ibid., pp. 182, 184.

133. Ibid., p. 188.

134. Ibid., p. 189. Abadan-Unat and Yücekök, in their study have found that in the underdeveloped areas of Turkey, that is, the rural areas, the Islamic religion is in the hands of classes that benefit from underdevelopment. For details, see Nermin Abadan-Unat and Ahmet N. Yücekök, "Religious Pluralism in Turkey," *Turkish Yearbook of International Relations*, 10 (1969-1970): 24-49. See also Dogu Ergil, "Secularization as Class Conflict: The Turkish Example," *Asian and African Affairs* 62, Part I (February 1975): 69-79.

135. Mardin, "Turkey: Islam and Westernization," in Caldarola, ed., *Religion and Societies*, p. 188.

136. Ibid., p. 189.

137. Ibid., p. 191.

138. Ibid., p. 190.

139. Ibid. By 1971 these schools were given the status of professional schools of the lycee level. See ibid.

140. Mardin, "Turkey: Islam and Westernization," in Caldarola, ed., *Religion and Societies*, p. 189.

141. Ibid., pp. 189-190.

142. Andreas M. Kazamias, *Education and the Quest for Modernity in Turkey* (London: Allen and Unwin, 1966), pp. 134-135; 136-137, 152.

143. Ibid., pp. 127-128. One major reason why vocational and technical education does not appeal to students is that the rewards after graduation from such schools are not enticing. For such professions to be attractive, social and cultural changes are required. See ibid., pp. 153-154.

144. Ibid., p. 148.

145. Joseph S. Szyliowicz, *Education and Modernization in the Middle East* (Ithaca, N.Y.: Cornell University Press, 1973), p. 331. Tütsch described the educational situation in Turkey as one of "criminal neglect." Hans E. Tütsch, *From Ankara to Marakesh: Turks and Arabs in a Changing World* (London: Allen and Unwin, 1964), p. 27.

146. Ibid., pp. 330-331. For figures of educational development in the period 1923-1972, see pp. 464-465.

147. Kazamias, *Education and the Quest for Modernity*, p. 158; see also, pp. 154-157.

148. W. M. Watt, "Islam and the West," in Denis MacEoin and Ahmed Al-Shahi, eds., *Islam in the Modern World* (London: Croom Helm, 1983), p. 4.

149. Ibid., pp. 4, 6.

150. Ghulam Nabi Saqib, *Modernization of Muslim Education in Egypt, Pakistan, and Turkey: A Comparative Study* (Lahore: Islamic Book Service, 1983), p. 160.

151. Ibid., p. 280.

152. Ibid, p. 141.

153. Ibid., pp. 150-151, 153, 277.

154. Ibid., p. 153.

155. Szyliowicz, *Education and Modernization in the Middle East,* p. 372.

156. Weiker, *The Modernization of Turkey,* p. 106.

157. Berkes, *The Development of Secularism in Turkey,* p. 488.

158. The above two paragraphs are based on ibid., pp.487-496.

159. A. Haluk Ulman and Frank Tachau, "Turkish Politics: The Attempt to Reconcile Rapid Modernization with Democracy," *The Middle East Journal* 19, No. 1 (Winter 1965): 164. The writers tend to blame Atatürk for "official neglect of religion."

160. James A. Morris, "Recent Problems of Economic Development in Turkey," *The Middle East Journal* 14, No. 1 (Winter 1960): 1.

161. Ibid., pp. 3, 2.

162. Ibid., p. 8.

163. Ibid., p. 3.

164. Ibid., p. 4.

165. Ibid., p. 5.

166. Ibid. p. 9.

167. Ibid., pp. 10-11.

168. Ibid., pp. 12-13.

169. Weiker, *The Modernization of Turkey,* pp. 55-57.

170. Ibid., p. 57.

171. Ibid, pp. 57-58.

172. Ibid., p. 65.

173. Ibid., pp. 81-82.

174. Ibid., pp. 84-85.

175. Ibid., pp. 65-66.

176. Heper, "Islam, Polity and Society in Turkey," *The Middle East Journal* 35, No. 2 (Summer 1981): 360-361.

177. Resat Aktan, "Problems of Land Reform in Turkey," *The Middle East Journal* 20, No. 3 (Summer 1966): 334.

178. Ibid., p. 320.

179. Ibid., p. 322.

180. Ibid., p. 323.

181. Ibid., p. 325.

182. Ibid., p. 324.

183. Nur Yalman, "On Land Disputes in Eastern Turkey," in Girdhari L. Tikku, ed., *Islam and its Cultural Divergence* (Urbana: University of Illinois Press, 1971), p. 207.

184. Ibid., p. 217. There has been virtually no change in this matter since the days of Ziya Gökalp, who described it thus: "The principal reason for the lack of economic development and the moral regression in Diyarbakir for some time is this miserable state of agriculture. There is almost no real agriculture in our province. There is only one active and continuous concern in this unfortunate country: land disputes." Quoted in ibid., p. 180.

185. Ibid., pp. 216, 215.

186. Ibid., p. 215.

187. Aktan, "Problems of Land Reform," *The Middle East Journal* 20, No. 3 (Summer 1966): 329-331.

188. Leslie L. Roos and Noralou P. Roos, *Managers of Modernization: Organizations*

and Elites in Turkey (1950-1969) (Cambridge, Mass.: Harvard University Press, 1971), p. 219. Roos and Roos conclude, based on a per capita increase of 4 percent annually in the period 1962-1967, that the opportunity structure in Turkey was expanding (p. 218). My conclusion is just the reverse of it.

189. Ron Ayres and T. C. Thompson, *Turkey: A New Era* (London: Euromony Publications, 1984), p. 92.

190. Ibid.

191. Ibid., p. 93.

192. OECD Economic Surveys, 1986/87, *Turkey* (Paris: OECD, 1987), p. 25.

193. Ibid., p. 57.

194. Ibid., p. 11.

195. Ibid., p. 74.

196. Ibid., p. 61.

197. See Kemal Dervis and Sherman Robinson, "The Structure of Income Inequality in Turkey (1950-1973)" in Ergun Özbudun and Aydin Ulusan, eds., *The Political Economy of Income Distribution in Turkey* (New York: Holmes and Meier, 1980), pp. 108-109 for composition of Turkish society in group percentages.

198. Ibid., p. 107.

199. Ibid., p. 110.

200. Ibid., pp. 110-111.

CHAPTER 8

1. R. Hrair Dekmejian, "Anatomy of Islamic Revival: Legitimacy Crisis, Ethnic Conflict and the Search for Islamic Alternatives," *The Middle East Journal* 34, No. 1 (Winter 1980): 6-7.

2. For the curriculum of religious education, besides the Qur'an, the works of Fazlur Rahman are indispensable.

3. Khalifa Shujauddin, "Religion in Muslim Countries with Special Reference to Religious Education," in *Colloquium on Islamic Culture in its Relation to the Contemporary World* (Princeton, N.J.: Princeton University Press, 1953), p. 39.

4. Sir Mohammad Iqbal, *Reconstruction of Religious Thought in Islam* (Lahore: Sh. Mohammad Ashraf, 1962), p. 138.

5. Daniel Crecelius, "Secularization in Modern Egypt," in Donald Eugene Smith ed., *Religion and Political Modernization* (New Haven, Conn.: Yale University Press, 1974), p. 91.

BIBLIOGRAPHY

THEORETICAL AND CONTEXTUAL

Adams, Charles J. *A Reader's Guide to the Great Religions.* 2nd ed. New York: Free Press, 1977.

Adams, Robert M. (trans., ed.) *The Prince: A New Translation, Backgrounds, Interpretations.* New York: Norton and Co., 1977.

Ali, Syed Ameer, *The Spirit of Islam.* 10th ed. London: Chatto and Windus, 1974.

Almond, Gabriel A., and Powell, G. Bingham, Jr. *Comparative Politics.* 2nd ed. Boston: Little, Brown, 1978.

Almond, Gabriel A., and Verba, Sidney, eds. *The Civic Culture.* Princeton, N.J.: Princeton University Press, 1963.

————. *The Civic Culture Revisited.* Boston: Little, Brown, 1980.

Apter, David. *The Politics of Modernization.* Chicago: University of Chicago Press, 1965.

Azizullah, Muhammad, *Glimpses of the Hadith.* 4th printing. Karachi: Crescent Publications, 1980.

Baumer, Franklin L. *Religion and the Rise of Scepticism.* New York: Harcourt, 1960.

Bay, Christian. *The Structure of Freedom.* Stanford, Calif.: Stanford University Press, 1958.

Bernstein, Jeremy. *Einstein.* New York: Viking Press, 1973.

Binder, Leonard, et al. *Crises and Sequences in Political Development.* Princeton, N.J.: Princeton University Press, 1971.

Björk, Lars G. "The Function of Cognitive Images in Facilitating Organizational Change." *Journal of Human Behavior and Learning* 2, No. 1 (1985).

Chaudhry, Sayeeda Ahmad. "Female Labor Force Participation and its Relationship to Fertility Rate: Some Policy Implications for Developing Countries." Ph.D. dissertation, George Washington University, July 1983.

Christensen, Darrel E., ed. *Hegel and the Philosophy of Religion: The Wafford Symposium.* The Hague: Martinus Nijhoff, 1970.

Dekmejian, R. Hrair. "Anatomy of Islamic Revival: Legitimacy Crisis, Ethnic Conflict and the Search for Islamic Alternatives." *The Middle East Journal* 34, No. 1 (Winter 1980).

Eckstein, Harry. "The Idea of Political Development: From Dignity to Efficiency." *World Politics* 34 (July 1983).

Engels, Frederick. *Feuerbach: The Roots of the Socialist Philosophy.* Chicago: Charles H. Kerr and Co., 1903. Translated by Austin Lewis.

Esposito, John L., ed. *Islam and Development.* Syracuse, N.Y.: Syracuse University Press, 1980.

Finkle, Jason L., and Gable, Richard E., eds. *Political Development and Social Change.* 2nd ed. New York: John Wiley, 1971.

Franquiz, J. A. "Albert Einstein's Philosophy of Religion." *Journal for the Scientific Study of Religion.* 4, No. 1 (October 1964).

Fromm, Eric. *Escape from Freedom.* Stanford, Calif.: Stanford University Press, 1958.

Geertz, Clifford. *Peddlers and Princes.* Chicago: University of Chicago Press, 1963.

Gilbert, Felix. *Machiavelli and Guicciardini: Politics and History in Sixteenth Century Florence.* Princeton, N.J.: Princeton University Press, 1965.

Ginsberg, Morris. *The Idea of Progress: A Revaluation.* London: Methuen and Co., 1953.

Goulet, Denis. *The Cruel Choice: A New Concept in the Theory of Development.* New York: Atheneum, 1978.

Gregory, Frederick. *Scientific Materialism in Nineteenth Century Germany.* Dordrecht, Holland: D. Reidel Publishing Co., 1977.

Guillaume, Alfred. *The Traditions of Islam.* Oxford: Oxford University Press, 1924.

Halpern, Manfred. *The Politics of Social Change in the Middle East and North Africa.* Princeton, N.J.: Princeton University Press, 1963.

————."The Rate and Costs of Political Development." *The Annals of the American Academy of Political and Social Science* 358 (March 1965).

Hexter, J. H. *The Vision of Politics on the Eve of the Reformation: More, Machiavelli, and Seysell.* New York: Basic Books, 1973.

Hourani, Albert. *Arabic Thought in the Liberal Age.* London: Oxford University Press, 1962.

Huntington, Samuel P. *Political Order in Changing Societies.* New Haven, Conn.: Yale University Press, 1968.

Ilchman, Warren F., and Uphoff, Norman Thomas. *The Political Economy of Change.* Berkeley: University of California Press, 1969.

Inkles, Alex, and Smith, David H. *Becoming Modern.* Cambridge, Mass.: Cambridge University Press, 1974.

Iqbal, Sir Muhammad. *The Reconstruction of Religious Thought in Islam.* Lahore: Sh. Mohammad Ashraf, 1962.

Islamic Council of Europe. *Islam and Contemporary Society.* London/New York: Longman Group Limited, 1982.

Jaspers, Karl. *Nietzsche and Christianity.* U.S.: Henry Regency Co., 1963.

Juynboll, G.H.A. *Muslim Tradition: Studies in Chronology, Provenance and Authorship of Early Hadith.* Cambridge: Cambridge University Press, 1983.

————. *The Authenticity of the Tradition Literature: Discussions in Modern Egypt.* Leiden: E. J. Brill, 1969.

Kuhn, Thomas S. *The Structure of Scientific Revolutions.* Chicago: University of Chicago Press, 1962.

Kuznets, Simon. *Modern Economic Growth: Rate, Structure, and Spread.* New Haven, Conn.: Yale University Press, 1966.

Landau, Jacob M. *Radical Politics in Modern Turkey.* Leiden: E. J. Brill, 1974.

Lasswell, Harold; Lerner, Daniel; and Montgomery, John, eds. *Values and Development: Appraising Asian Experience.* Cambridge, Mass.: MIT Press, 1976.

Leaman, Oliver. *An Introduction to Medieval Islamic Philosophy.* Cambridge: Cambridge University Press, 1985.

Lecky, W.E.H. *History of the Rise and Influence of the Spirit of Rationalism in Europe.* London: Longmans, Green, and Co., 1866.

Lenski, Gerhard. *The Religious Factor.* Garden City, N.Y.: Doubleday, 1961.

Lerner, Daniel. *The Passing of Traditional Society.* Glencoe, Ill.: Free Press of Glencoe, 1958.

Liebman, Charles S., and Don-Yehiya, Elazer. *Religion and Politics in Israel.* Bloomington: Indiana University Press, 1984.

Ling, Trevor. *Karl Marx and Religion: In Europe and India.* New York: Harper and Row, 1980.

Lipset, S. M. *Political Man.* New York: Doubleday, 1959.

Luckman, Thomas. "On Religion in Modern Society: Individual Consciousness, World View. Institution." *Journal for the Scientific Study of Religion* 2, No. 2 (April 1963).

Marriot, W. K., trans. *The Prince.* London: J. M. Dent and Sons, 1938.

Marx, Karl, and Engels, Frederich. *On Religion.* New York: Schocken Books, 1964.

McDonough, Sheila. *The Authority of the Past: A Study of Three Muslim Modernists.* Pennsylvania: American Academy of Religion, 1970.

McKown, Delos B. *The Classical Marxist Critiques of Religion: Marx, Engels, Lenin, Kautsky.* The Hague: Martinus Nijhoff, 1975.

McLellan, David, ed. *Karl Marx: Selected Writings.* Oxford: Oxford University Press, 1977.

McLelland, David C. *The Achieving Society.* Princeton, N.J.: Van Nostrand Co., 1961.

Mill, John Stuart. *On Liberty.* Indianapolis: Hackett Publishing Co., 1978.

Morse, Bradford, and Kirdar, Uner. "Human Resource Development: Challenge for the '80s." *Journal of the Society for International Development* 1 (1984).

Nisbet, Robert A. *Social Change and History: Aspects of the Western Theory of Development.* New York: Oxford University Press, 1969.

Parwez, Ghulam Ahmad. *Asbab-e-Zawal-e Ummat (Causes of the Downfall of the Community of Muslim Peoples).* 4th ed. Lahore: Adara Taloo-e Islam, 1966.

Perkins, Robert L. "Hegel and the Secularization of Religion." *International Journal for Philosophy of Religion* 1, No. 3 (Fall 1970).

Prior, Andrew. *Revolution and Philosophy: The Significance of the French Revolution for Hegel and Marx.* Cape Town: David Philip, Publisher, 1972.

Pye, Lucian W., and Verba, Sidney. *Political Culture and Political Development.* Princeton, N.J.: Princeton University Press, 1965.

Rahman, Fazlur. *Major Themes of the Qur'an.* Minneapolis: Bibliotheca Islamica, 1980.

——————. *Islam and Modernity.* Chicago: University of Chicago Press, 1982.

——————. "Some Key Ethical Concepts of the Qur'an." *The Journal of Religious Ethics*

2, No. 2 (Fall 1983).

Rosenthal, Ervin I.J. *Islam in Modern Nation State.* Cambridge: Cambridge University Press, 1965.

Sederberg, Peter C. "The Betrayed Ascent: The Crisis and Transubstantiation of the Modern World." *The Journal of Developing Areas* 13, No. 2 (January 1979).

Sibley, Mulford Q. *Political Ideas and Ideologies.* New York: Harper and Row, 1970.

Silvert, Kalman H., ed. *Churches and States: The Religious Institution and Modernization.* New York: American Universities Field Staff, 1967.

Skocpol, Theda. *States and Social Revolutions: A Comparative Analysis of France, Russia, and China.* Cambridge: Cambridge University Press, 1979.

Smith, Donald Eugene. *Religion and Political Development.* Boston: Little, Brown, 1970.

————, ed. *Religion and Political Modernization.* New Haven, Conn.: Yale University Press, 1974.

————. *Religion, Politics, and Social Change in the Third World.* New York: Free Press, 1971.

Steinberg, Milton. *Basic Judaism.* New York: Harcourt, Brace, 1947.

Stowasser, Barbara Freyer. *Religion and Political Development: Some Comparative Ideas on Ibn Khaldun and Machiavelli.* Washington, D.C.: Center for Contemporary Studies, Georgetown University, 1983.

Turner, Bryan S. *Weber and Islam: A Critical Study.* London/Boston: Routledge and Kegan Paul, 1974.

Uphoff, Norman T., and Ilchman, Warren F., eds. *The Political Economy of Development.* Berkeley: University of California Press, 1972.

Wach, Joachim. *The Comparative Study of Religions.* New York: Columbia University Press, 1958.

Walker, Leslie J., trans. *The Discourses of Niccolo Machiavelli.* Vol. 1. London and Boston: Routledge and Kegan Paul, 1975.

Wallerstein, Imanuel. *The Capitalist World Economy.* London: Cambridge University Press, 1979.

Weaver, James, and Jameson, Kenneth. *Economic Development: Competing Paradigms.* Lanham, Md.: University Press of America, 1981.

Werblowsky, R.J. Zwi. *Beyond Tradition and Modernity: Changing Religions in a Changing World.* London: Athlone Press, 1976.

Wiarda, Howard J., ed. *New Directions in Comparative Politics.* Boulder, Colo.: Westview Press, 1985.

Williamson, Raymond Keitt. *Introduction to Hegel's Philosophy of Religion.* Albany: State University of New York Press, 1984.

Wright, Willard Huntington. *What Nietzsche Taught.* New York: B. W. Huebsch, 1915.

PAKISTAN

Abbot, Freeland. *Islam and Pakistan.* Ithaca, N. Y.: Cornell University Press, 1968.

Ahmad, Aziz. *Islamic Modernism in India and Pakistan.* London: Oxford University Press, 1967.

Ahmad, Manzooruddin. "The Political Role of the Ulama in Indo-Pakistan Sub-continent." *Islamic Studies* 6 (1967).

Ahmed, Aziz., ed. *Contributions to Asian Studies.* Vol. 2. Leiden: E. J. Brill, 1971.

Ahmed, Aziz, and Grunebaum, G. E. Von. *Muslim Self-Statement in India and Pakistan: 1857-1968.* Wiesbaden: Otto Harrassowitz, 1970.

Ahmed, Hafiz Nazar. *Ja'iza-e Madaris -e 'Arabiyyah Islamyyah Maghrabi Pakistan (Survey of Arabic Islamic Schools of West Pakistan).* Lahore: Muslim academy, 1972.

Ahmed, Manzooruddin. "Sovereignty of God in the Constitution of Pakistan: A Study in the conflict of Traditionalism and Modernism." *Islamic Studies* 2, No. 2 (June 1963).

————. "Islamic Aspects of the New Constitution of Pakistan." *Islamic Studies* 2, No. 2 (June 1963).

Akhtar, Rafique. *Pakistan Year Book.* 13th ed. Karachi: East and West Publishing Co., 1985.

————. *Pakistan Year Book.* 10th ed. Karachi: East and West Publishing Co., 1982-83.

Ali, Chaudhri Muhammad. *The Emergence of Pakistan.* New York: Columbia University Press, 1967.

Aziz, K. K. *The Making of Pakistan: A Study in Nationalism.* London: Chatto and Windus, 1967.

Baljon, J.M.S. *Modern Muslim Koran Interpretation (1880-1960).* Leiden: E. J. Brill, 1961.

Binder, Leonard. *Religion and Politics in Pakistan.* Berkeley: University of California Press, 1961.

Burki, Shahid Javed, and Laporte, Robert., eds. *Pakistan's Development Priorities: Choices for the Future.* Karachi: Oxford University Press, 1984.

Caldarola, Carlo, ed. *Religion and Societies: Asia and the Middle East.* Berlin: Mouton, 1982.

Callard, Keith. *Pakistan: A Political Study.* Britain: Allen and Unwin, 1957.

Choudhry, G. W. *Documents and Speeches on the Constitution of Pakistan* Dacca: Green Book House, 1967.

Colloquium on Islamic Culture in its Relation to Contemporary World. Princeton, N.J.: Princeton University Press, 1953.

The Constitution of the Republic of Pakistan. Karachi: Government of Pakistan Press, 1962.

Dar, Bashir Ahmad. *Religious Thought of Sayyid Ahmad Khan.* Lahore: Institute of Islamic Culture, 1957.

Esposito, John L., ed. *Islam in Asia.* New York: Oxford University Press, 1987.

Fyzee, A.A.A. "Recent Developments in Islam." *Islamic Culture* 1, 1927.

Government of Pakistan. *Pakistan: Economic Survey 1983-84.* Islamabad: 1984.

————. *Pakistan: Economic Survey 1983-84.* Islamabad: Ministry of Finance, 1984.

Haq, Mahfuzul. "Some Reflections on Islam and Constitution-Making in Pakistan: 1947-56." *Islamic Studies* 5, No. 2 (June 1966).

Huda, S. M. "Did It Work In Pakistan?" *Development* 4 (1975).

Iqbal, Javid. *Ideology of Pakistan.* Karachi: Ferozsons Ltd., 1971.

————. *The Ideology of Pakistan and its Implementation.* Lahore: Sh. Ghulam Ali and sons, 1959.

Keesing's Contemporary Archives. Bristol/London: Keesing's Publications Ltd., 1931-89.

Khalid, Detlev H. "Theocracy and the Location of Sovereignty." *Islamic Studies* 11, No. 3 (September 1967).

Khan, Mohammad Asghar. *Generals in Politics: Pakistan 1958-1982.* London: Croom Helm, 1983.

Khan, Sardar Muhammad Ishaq. *The Constitution of the Islamic Republic.* Lahore: Khyber Law Publishers, 1973.

Maududi, Sayyid Abul A'la. *First Principles of the Islamic State.* Translated and edited by Khurshid Ahmad. Lahore: Islamic Publications Ltd., 1974.

————. *Political Theory of Islam.* Lahore: Islamic Publications Ltd., 1976.

————. *The Islamic Law and Constitution.* 8th ed. Translated and edited by Khurshid Ahmad. Lahore: Islamic Publications Ltd., 1983.

Munir, Muhammed. *From Jinnah to Zia.* Lahore: Vanguard Books Ltd., 1980.

Munir, M., and Kayani, M. K. *Report of the Court of Inquiry to Enquire into the Punjab Disturbances of 1953.* Lahore: Superintendent, Government Printing, 1954.

Naim, C. M., ed. *Iqbal, Jinnah, and Pakistan: The Vision and the Reality.* Syracuse, N.Y.: Syracuse University Press, 1979.

Pakistan: An Official Handbook. Islamabad: Ministry of Information and Broadcasting, 1985.

Pirzada, Syed Sharifuddin, ed. *Foundations of Pakistan: All India Muslim League Documents—1906-1947,* Vol. II. Karachi: National Publishing House Ltd., 1970.

Quaid-i-Azam Muhammad Ali Jinnah: Speeches as Governor General. Karachi: Pakistan Publications, 1963.

Rahman, Fazlur. "Implementation of the Islamic Concept of State in the Pakistani Milieu." *Islamic Studies* 6, No. 3 (September 1967).

Rosenthal, Erwin J. *Islam in the Modern State.* Cambridge: Cambridge University Press, 1965.

Sayeed, Khalid B. *The Political System of Pakistan.* Boston: Houghton Mifflin Co., 1967.

Schofield, Victoria. *Bhutto—Trial and Execution.* London: Cassell, 1981.

Smith, Donald Eugene, ed. *South Asian Politics and Religion.* Princeton, N.J.: Princeton University Press, 1966.

Smith, Wilfred Cantwell. *Pakistan as an Islamic State.* Lahore: Shaikh Muhammad Ashraf, 1951.

Speeches and Statements by Field Marshal Mohammad Ayub Khan. Vol. III, July 1960-June 1961.

Vahid, Syed Abdul, ed. *Thoughts and Reflections of Iqbal.* Lahore: Sh. Muhammad Ashraf, 1964.

Weiss, Anita M., ed. *Islamic Reassertion in Pakistan.* Syracuse, N.Y.: Syracuse University Press, 1986.

EGYPT

Adams, Charles C. *Islam and Modernism in Egypt.* New York: Russell and Russell, 1968.

Amin, Osman. *Muhammad Abduh.* Washington, D.C.: American Council of Learned Societies, 1953. Translated by Charles Wendell.

Badeau, John S. "A Role in Search of a Hero: A Brief Study of the Egyptian Revolution." *The Middle East Journal* 9, No. 4 (Autumn 1955).

Berger, Morroe. *Islam in Egypt Today.* Cambridge: Cambridge University Press, 1970.

Borthwick, Bruce M. "Religion and Politics in Israel and Egypt." *The Middle East Journal* 33, No. 2 (Spring 1979).

Burns, William J. *Economic Aid and American Policy Toward Egypt, 1955-1981.* Albany: State University of New York Press, 1985.

Cooper, Mark N. *The Transformation of Egypt.* London: Croom Helm, 1982.

Crecelius, Daniel. "Al-Azhar in the Revolution." *The Middle East Journal* 20, No. 1 (Winter 1966).

Curtis, Michael, ed. *Religion and Politics in the Middle East.* Boulder, Colo.: Westview Press, 1981.

Esposito, John L., ed. *Islam and Development: Religion and Socio-political Chance.* Syracuse, N.Y.: Syracuse University Press, 1980.

Frye, Richard N. *Islam and the West: Proceedings of the Harvard Summer School Conference on the Middle East.* The Hague: Mouton, 1957.

Gershoni, Israel. "Egyptian Intellectual History and Egyptian Intellectuals in the Interwar Period." *Asian and African Studies* 19, No. 3 (November 1985).

Gilsenan, Michael. *Saint and Sufi in Modern Egypt.* New York: Oxford University Press, 1973.

Heyworth-Dunne, J. *An Introduction to the History of Education in Modern Egypt.* London: Frank Crass and Co., 1968. First published in 1939.

Hofstadter, Dan., ed. *Egypt and Nasser: Volume I. 1952-52.* New York: Facts on File, 1973.

Hopwood, Derek. *Egypt: Politics and Society: 1945-1984.* Boston: Allen and Unwin, 1985.

Hourani, Albert. *Arabic Thought in the Liberal Age: 1798-1939.* London: Oxford University Press, 1962.

Ibrahim, I., ed. *Arab Resources: The Transformation of a Society.* London: Croom Helm, 1983.

Ikram, Khalid. *Egypt: Economic Management in a Period of Transition.* Baltimore: Johns Hopkins University Press, 1980.

Kelley, Alan C., et al. *Population and Development in Rural Egypt.* Durham, N.C.: Duke University Press, 1982.

Kepel, Gilles. *Muslim Extremism in Egypt: The Prophet and Pharaoh.* Berkeley: University of California Press, 1985.

Kerr, Malcolm H., ed. *Islamic Studies: A Tradition and its Problems.* Malibu, Calif.: Udena Publications, 1980.

Khalid, Khalid M.   *From Here We Start.* Translated by Ismail R. el- Faruqi. Washington, D.C.:   American Council of Learned Societies, 1953.

Khoury, Nabil A.   "Islam and Modernization in the Middle East: Muhammad Abduh, An Ideology of Development."   Ph.D. dissertation, State University of New York at Albany, 1976.

Kraemer, Jörg.   "Tradition and Reform at Al-Azhar University."   *Middle Eastern Affairs.*   7, No. 1 (1956).

Lazarus-Yafeh, Hava.   "Contemporary Religious Thought Among the Ulama of Al-Azhar."   *Asian and African Studies* 7, Special Number (1971).

Massialas, Byron G., and Jarrar, Samir Ahmed.   *Education in the Arab World.*   New York: Praeger, 1983.

Milson, Menahem.   "Taha Husayn's 'The Tree of Misery':   A Literary Expression of Cultural Change."   *Asian and African Studies* 19, No. 3 (November 1985).

Mitchell, Richard P.   *The Society of Muslim Brothers.*   London: Oxford University Press, 1969.

Nasser, Gamal Abdel.   *The Philosophy of the Revolution.*   Buffalo, N.Y.: Smith, Keynes and Marshall, 1959.

Nyrop, Richard F., ed.   *Egypt: A Country Study.*   4th ed.   Washington, D.C.:   American University, 1983.

O'Kane, Joseph P.   "Islam in the New Constitution: Some Discussions in al-Ahram."   *The Middle East Journal* 26, No. 2 (Spring 1972).

Pullapilly, Cyriac K., ed.   *Islam in the Contemporary World.*   Notre Dame, Ind.:   Cross Roads Books, 1980.

Sadat, Anwar el.   *Revolt on the Nile.*   New York: John Day, 1957.

Safran, Nadav.   *Egypt in Search of Political Community.*   Cambridge, Mass.:   Harvard University Press, 1961.

Sharabi, H. B.   *Government and Politics of the Middle East in the Twentieth Century.*   Princeton, N.J.:   Princeton University Press, 1963.

Szyliowicz, Joseph S.   *Education and Modernization in the Middle East.*   Ithaca, N.Y.:   Cornell University Press, 1973.

Thompson, Jack H., and Reischauer, Robert D., eds.   *Modernization of the Arab World.*   Princeton,N.J.:   D. Van Nostrand, 1966.

Tibawi, A.L.   *Islamic Education.*   New York: Crane, Russak and Company, 1972.

Tütsch, Hans E.   *From Ankara to Marakesh: Turks and Arabs in a Changing World.*   London: Allen and Unwin, 1964.

Vatikiotis, P. J.   *The Modern History of Egypt.*   New York: Praeger, 1969.

————.   *The Egyptian Army in Politics.*   Bloomington: Indiana University Press, 1961.

————, ed.   *Egypt Since the Revolution.*   New York: Praeger, 1968.

Warburg, Gabriel R.   "Islam and Politics in Egypt: 1952-80."   *The Middle East Journal* 18, No. 2 (April 1982).

Warburg, Gabriel R., and Kupferschmidt, eds.   *Islam, Nationalism and Radicalism in Egypt and the Sudan.*   New York: Praeger, 1983.

Waterbury, John.   *The Egypt of Nasser and Sadat: The Political Economy of Two Regimes.*   Princeton, N.J.:   Princeton University Press, 1983.

Wheelock, Keith.   *Nasser's New Egypt.*   New York: Praeger, 1960.

Wikan, Unni. *Life Among the Poor in Cairo.* London: Tavistock Publications, 1980.
Youssef, Michael. *Revolt Against Modernity: Muslim Zealots and the West.* Leiden: E. J. Brill, 1985.

TURKEY

Abadan-Unat, Nermin, and Yücekök, Ahmet N. "Religious Pluralism in Turkey." *Turkish Yearbook of International Relations* 10, 1969-1970.
Aktan, Resat. "Problems of Land Reform in Turkey." *The Middle East Journal* 20, No. 3 (Summer 1966).
Ayres, Ron, and Thompson, T.C. *Turkey: A New Era.* London: Euromoney Publications, 1984.
Barnes, Robert John. *An Introduction to Religious Foundations in the Ottoman Empire.* Leiden: E. J. Brill, 1987.
Berkes, Niyazi. "Ziya Gökalp: His Contribution to Turkish Nationalism." *The Middle East Journal* 8, No. 4 (Autumn 1954).
————, trans. and ed. *Turkish Nationalism and Western Civilization: Selected Essays of Ziya Gökalp.* London: Allen and Unwin, 1959.
Bisbee, Elanor. *The New Turks: Pioneers of the Republic—1920-1950.* Philadelphia: University of Pennsylvania Press, 1956.
Ergil, Dogu. "Secularization as Class Conflict: The Turkish Example." *Asian and African Affairs* 62, Part I (February 1975).
Frye, Richard N., ed. *Islam and the West.* The Hague: Mouton, 1957.
Grant, John. *Through the Garden of Allah.* London: John Gifford Ltd., 1938.
Güclü, Meral. *Turkey.* Oxford: Clio Press, 1981.
Heper, Metin. "Islam, Polity and Society in Turkey: A Middle Eastern Perspective." *The Middle East Journal* 35, No. 2 (Summer 1981).
Heyd, Uriel. *Foundations of Turkish Nationalism: The Life and Teachings of Ziya Gökalp.* London: Luzac and Co., 1950.
Kazamias, Andres M. *Education and the Quest for Modernity in Turkey.* London: Allen and Unwin, 1966.
Kramer, Martin. *Islam Assembled: The Advent of the Muslim Congresses.* New York: Columbia University Press, 1986.
Landau, Jacob M., ed. *Atatürk and the Modernization of Turkey.* Boulder, Colo.: Westview Press, 1984.
Lewis, Bernard. *The Emergence of Modern Turkey.* London: Oxford University Press, 1961.
Linke, Lilo. *Allah Dethroned: A Journey Through Modern Turkey.* London: Constable and Co., 1937.
MacEoin, Denis, and Al-Shahi, Ahmed., eds. *Islam in the Modern World.* London: Croom Helm, 1983.
Morris, James A. "Recent Problems of Economic Development in Turkey." *The Middle East Journal* 14, No. 1 (Winter 1960).
OECD Economic Surveys. *Turkey.* Paris: OECD, 1987.
Özbudun, Ergun, and Ulusan, Aydin., eds. *The Political Economy of Income*

Distribution in Turkey. New York: Holmes and Meier, 1980.

Parla, Taha. *The Social and Political Thought of Ziya Gökalp: 1876-1924*. Leiden: E. J. Brill, 1985.

Roos, Leslie L., and Roos, Noralou, P. *Managers of Modernization: Organizations and Elites in Turkey (1950-1969)*. Cambridge, Mass.: Harvard University Press, 1971.

Saqib, Ghulam Nabi. *Modernization of Muslim Education in Egypt, Pakistan, and Turkey: A Comparative Study*. Lahore: Islamic Book Service, 1983.

Sayari, Binnaz. "Religion and Political Development in Turkey." Ph.D. dissertation, City University of New York, 1976.

Sharabi, H. B. *A Handbook of the Contemporary Middle East*. Washington, D.C.: Georgetown University, 1956.

A Speech Delivered by Ghazi Mustapha Kemal, President of the Turkish Republic, October 1927. Leipzig: K. F. Koehler, 1929.

Tikku, Girdhari, ed. *Islam and its Cultural Divergence*. Urbana: University of Illinois Press, 1971.

Tomlin, E.W.F. *Turkey: The Modern Miracle*. London: Watts and Co., 1940.

————. *Life in Modern Turkey*. London: Thomas Nelson and Sons, 1946.

Ulman, A. Haluk, and Tachau, Frank. "Turkish Politics: The Attempt to Reconcile Rapid Modernization with Democracy." *The Middle East Journal* 19, No. 1 (Winter 1965).

Webster, Donald Everett. *The Turkey of Atatürk: Social Process in the Turkish Reformation*. Philadelphia: American Academy of Political and Social Science, 1939.

Weiker, Walker F. *The Modernization of Turkey: From Atatürk to the Present Day*. New York: Holmes and Meier, 1981.

INDEX

About the Author

JAVAID SAEED, a political scientist and native of Pakistan, holds degrees from the Pakistan Military Academy, Indiana State University, and the University of South Carolina. He has taught at Columbia College, South Carolina, and at the University of South Carolina.